WOMEN AND AGRIBUSINESS

WOMEN'S STUDIES AT YORK SERIES

General Editors: Haleh Afshar and Mary Maynard

Haleh Afshar
ISLAM AND FEMINISMS: An Iranian Case-Study

WOMEN AND EMPOWERMENT: Illustrations from the Third World
(*editor*)

WOMEN IN THE MIDDLE EAST: Perceptions, Realities and Struggles
for Liberation (*editor*)

Haleh Afshar and Stephanie Barrientos (*editors*)
WOMEN, GLOBALIZATION AND FRAGMENTATION IN THE
DEVELOPING WORLD

Haleh Afshar and Carolyne Dennis (*editors*)
WOMEN AND ADJUSTMENT POLICIES IN THE THIRD WORLD

Judy Giles
WOMEN, IDENTITY AND PRIVATE LIFE IN BRITAIN, 1900–50

Mary Maynard and Joanna de Groot (*editors*)
WOMEN'S STUDIES IN THE 1990s: Doing Things Differently?

Haideh Moghissi
POPULISM AND FEMINISM IN IRAN: Women's Struggle in a
Male-Defined Revolutionary Movement

Women's Studies at York
Series Standing Order ISBN 0–333–71512–8
(*outside North America only*)

You can receive future titles in this series as they are published by placing a standing order.
Please contact your bookseller or, in case of difficulty, write to us at the address below with
your name and address, the title of the series and the ISBN quoted above.

Customer Services Department, Macmillan Distribution Ltd
Houndmills, Basingstoke, Hampshire RG21 6XS, England

Women and Agribusiness

Working Miracles in the Chilean Fruit Export Sector

Stephanie Barrientos
Senior Lecturer in Economic Development
University of Hertfordshire

Anna Bee
Lecturer in Geography
University of Leicester

Ann Matear
Lecturer in Iberian and Latin American Politics
University of Portsmouth

and

Isabel Vogel
Research Administrator
Birkbeck College
University of London

First published in Great Britain 1999 by
MACMILLAN PRESS LTD
Houndmills, Basingstoke, Hampshire RG21 6XS and London
Companies and representatives throughout the world

A catalogue record for this book is available from the British Library.

ISBN 0–333–68292–0 hardcover
ISBN 0–333–68293–9 paperback

First published in the United States of America 1999 by
ST. MARTIN'S PRESS, INC.,
Scholarly and Reference Division,
175 Fifth Avenue, New York, N.Y. 10010

ISBN 0–312–21998–9

Library of Congress Cataloging-in-Publication Data
Women and agribusiness : working miracles in the Chilean fruit export
sector / Stephanie Barrientos ... [et al.].
p.   cm. — (Women's studies at York series)
Includes bibliographical references and index.
ISBN 0–312–21998–9
1. Women agricultural laborers—Chile.   2. Fruit trade—Chile–
–Employees.   3. Seasonal labor—Chile.   I. Barrientos, Stephanie.
II. Series.
HD6073.A292C585   1999
331.4'83'0983—dc21   98–30662
                                                                      CIP

This book is printed on paper suitable for recycling and made from fully managed and
sustained forest sources.

10   9   8   7   6   5   4   3   2   1
08   07   06   05   04   03   02   01   00   99

Printed and bound in Great Britain by
Antony Rowe Ltd, Chippenham, Wiltshire

Contents

List of Tables, Figures and Maps		vii
Acknowledgements		ix
List of Acronyms and Spanish Terms		xi
Preface		xvii
1.	Introduction	1
2.	Women and Agribusiness – an Overview	13
3.	Gender, State and Rural Transformation – Background to the 'Fruit Explosion'	36
4.	The Fruit Export Sector and Global Supply Chain	62
5.	Female Fruit Employment – *Las Temporeras*	86
6.	Case Study: Rural Fruit Workers in the North	109
7.	Case Study: Urban Fruit Workers in the South	134
8.	State Policy and the *Temporeras* in the Transition to Democracy	167
9.	Global Policies for Temporary Workers in Agribusiness – Conclusion	185
Notes		205
Bibliography		213
Index		227

List of Tables, Figures and Maps

TABLES

Table 3.1   Changes in women's temporary employment in
             agriculture   41

Table 4.1   Production and export of principal fruit
             commodities, 1994–5   66

Table 4.2   Fruit exports by region, 1994–5   67

Table 4.3   Principal export companies, 1993–4   69

Table 4.4   Principal regions of destination for all
             horticultural exports   76

Table 4.5   Main southern hemisphere exports of fresh
             fruit   77

Table 5.1   Fruit production and estimated employment by
             region, 1992–3   88

Table 5.2   Marital status and age of temporary fruit
             workers   92

Table 5.3   Distribution of the fruit labour force by sex   98

Table 5.4   The percentages of women and men with
             specific jobs in the grape economy, 1993–4   98

Table 5.5   Fruit workers and health problems related to
             agro-chemicals   101

Table 5.6   Wages earned for selected tasks in a packing
             plant, summer 1993/4   103

Table 5.7   Examples of wages earned for numbers of
             boxes packed, summer 1993/4   103

Table 6.1   Seasonality of female employment in the grape
             economy of Norte Chico   117

List of Tables, Figures and Maps

Table 6.2	Female employment in the grape economy in Norte Chico	117
Table 6.3	Household responsibility for domestic chores	120
Table 7.1	Demographic characteristics of the interviewees	139
Table 7.2	Average monthly earnings of the *temporeras* and their male partners, 1993/4 season	141
Table 8.1	Coverage of pre-school education by income quintile	175
Table 8.2	Regional childcare centres	178
Table 8.3	Employer contributions by region	179

FIGURES

Figure 4.1	Total fruit exports, 1982–94	64
Figure 4.2	Structure of fruit export chain within Chile	72
Figure 4.3	Global production and distribution chain of Chilean fruit, 1993–4	80
Figure 4.4	Estimate of price structure of seedless grapes from Chile	82
Figure 5.1	Division of tasks of the temporary workers	97

MAPS

Map 1.1	Map of Chile	4
Map 4.1	World Map – Fruit and horticultural exports from Chile, 1993–4	75
Map 6.1	Map of case study area in the North	110
Map 7.1	Map of case study area in the South	136

Acknowledgements

First and foremost, we wish to thank all those in Chile who provided unstinting help in carrying out the research for this book. Most importantly we thank the many *temporeras* who gave up precious time for long interviews, and the many other professionals, academics and friends who assisted us with our work; many others also provided important support in a number of ways. To all of them we are indebted. Our hope is that this book will provide a greater knowledge and understanding of all temporary fruit workers, which will help to improve their lives.

This book would never have come about without the help and inspiration of Robert Gwynne, Cristóbal Kay and Haleh Afshar. We had been working independently on different aspects of the *temporeras* in Chile for a number of years. Bob Gwynne first brought us all together to present papers as part of a session he organised on agrarian reform in Chile at the annual conference of the Society for Latin American Studies in Swansea in 1995. We each attended the session with some trepidation that our research was being replicated by another, but found on the contrary that our work was complementary in interesting ways. At the end of the session Cris Kay planted the seed for the book by suggesting we collaborate in writing on the *temporeras*, and Haleh Afshar later sealed our fate when she encouraged us to produce our collaborative effort as a book. All three have remained an important source of encouragement through the long process of writing and have provided helpful comments on earlier drafts. We are forever grateful to them. Many others also helped through discussion and by providing comments on draft chapters. We would like to thank especially Armando Barrientos, Duncan Green, Liz Orton and Georgina Waylen. None is responsible for the outcome, but we thank all for their time and help.

We would also like to thank Cathy Bennett for her help in the library, Andy Sherman for providing computer support, Mel Rist for helping to draw the figures and Ruth Pollington for drawing the maps.

The book was written in part through a series of weekend meetings, which we all enjoyed and will greatly miss. However, as is often the case, these involved juggling multiple roles. We would like to thank Liam (who often played while we talked), Kym and Ricardo for their patience and endurance through the many meetings, and hope that this small contribution will help to improve their futures.

List of Acronyms and Spanish Terms

a trato	piece rate
al día	daily rate
andan en los treinta	'they are around thirty' (phrase used to describe the average age of *temporeras*)
Area Mujer	Women's Unit
asentamiento	co-operative land-holding settlement
aseo	daily set of cleaning tasks in the home
Asociación de Exportadores	Association of Exporters (organisation representing fruit exporters' interests)
BIH	basic irrigated hectare
botillería	liquor store
campesina/o	traditional peasant engaged mainly in traditional agriculture
casetas	small, plastic-covered plots used in the cultivation of tomatoes
CEMA-Chile	reorganised CEMAS under military regime
CEMAs *Centros de Madres*	Mothers Centres (national network of neighbourhood women's handicrafts centres)
CERAs *Centros de Reforma Agraria*	Centres of Agrarian Reform (collective landholdings established under Allende's government)

CIDEM Centros de Información de los Derechos de la Mujer	Centres for the Information of Women's Rights, run by SERNAM
CNC *Comisión Nacional Campesina*	National Peasants' Commission
comuna	borough
comuneros	term used specifically to describe the members of the common land-holding communities in the *Norte Chico* region
Concertación de Mujeres por la Democracia	movement of working and middle-class feminists and political activists incorporated into the opposition movement of the *Concertación,* bringing gender-based demands for democracy
Concertación, Concertación de Partidos por la Democracia	coalition of parties which first formed the opposition to the military regime and subsequently won the elections to form the first civilian government in 1990 and continue to hold power.
conviviente	unmarried, cohabiting partner
CORA *Corporación de Reforma Agraria*	Agrarian Reform Council
CORFO *Corporación de Fomento*	National Development Council (national body for promotion of trade and industry)
cruzando los brazos	literally, 'crossing arms' as a refusal to work, *temporeras'* most effective method of affecting output
CUT *Central Unica de Trabajadores*	National Federation of Trades Unions
Demanda de la Mujer Rural	Rural Women's Demands
Departamento Femenino	Women's Department

desmochadura	task of cutting off stem and roots of onion
Dirección de Trabajo	Labour Directorate, part of the Ministry of Employment
double shift	two-fold burden of paid and domestic work faced by women
el boom *frutícola*	the fruit 'explosion'
FEDEFRUT *Federación de Fruticultores*	Fruit Producers' Federation
FOB	Free on Board
Fundación Chile	Chile Foundation
GIA *Grupo de Investigaciones Agrarias*	Agrarian Research Group – NGO
hacendado	owner of *hacienda*
hacienda	large-scale estate, with resident tenant-farmer population, established in colonial period
huerto	family plot, also common usage for orchard
ILO	International Labour Organisation
IMF	International Monetary Fund
INDAP *Instituto de Desarollo Agropecuario*	Institute for Agrarian Development
INE *Instituto Nacional de Estadísticas*	National Statistics Institute
inquilino	resident tenant farmer on *hacienda*
ISI	Import Substitution Industrialisation
jardines infantiles	nursery schools for children aged 3–5
JUNDEP	NGO in Ovalle

JUNJI *Junta Nacional de Jardines Infantiles*	National Association for Nursery Schools
La Mujer en el Gobierno de la Unidad Popular	Women's Role in the Popular Unity Government
latifundio	large-scale estate (similar to *hacienda*)
machismo	ideology of masculinity based on patriarchal, male-dominated gender relations
marianismo	ideology of femininity based on the cult of the Virgin Mary
minifundio	small to medium-sized family-run farm
minifundista	owner of *minifundio*
Ministerio de Bienes Nacionales	Heritage Ministry
NAFTA	North American Free Trade Agreement
NGOs	Non-Governmental Organisations
Norte Chico	'Little North' (commonly used to describe the mid-northern region which is semi-arid rather than the full desert of the extreme northern region)
NTAEs	non-traditional agricultural exports
OEPs *Organizaciones Económicas Populares*	Popular Economic Organisations (umbrella term for urban grassroots organisations)
parcela	family-sized land-holding from agrarian counter-reform
parronales	vineyards
patrón	boss

PET *Programa de Empleo y Trabajo*	Programme of Labour and Employment – NGO
Plan Laboral	Labour Plan (labour legislation implemented in 1979 which established flexible labour market conditions)
El Poder Femenino	Feminine Power (movement of right-wing women in opposition to Allende Government)
PRODEMU *Programa de Promoción y Desarrollo de la Mujer*	Women's Development Programme (national women's skills and handicrafts network, set up during civilian government as state-sponsored alternative to the now privately-run CEMA-CHILE)
salas cunas	nurseries for children aged 0–2
Señora	older, married woman
SERNAM *Servicio Nacional de la Mujer*	National Women's Service (Women's Ministry)
temporada	fruit season
temporera/o	seasonal agricultural wage-worker
Unidad Popular	Popular Unity (coalition government, headed by Salvador Allende and the Socialist Party, in power 1970–3)
WTO	World Trade Organisation

Preface

This book reflects a new reality in the Chilean countryside – the remarkable increase of women in the labour market and among waged workers. This feminisation of the agricultural and agro-industrial labour force is the outcome of the worldwide process of globalisation and Chile's dramatic shift to a neo-liberal model of development since the mid-1970s. The change from an inward-directed development to an outward-oriented development process was largely built on the spectacular growth of fruit exports. Chile's agriculture, which for decades had been stagnant and backward, suddenly became one of the country's most dynamic sectors. The transformations brought about by this modernisation process have been profound, especially with regards to gender relations.

This engaging book is the outcome of the authors' individual research on various aspects of this process. By combining their expertise in this collaborative effort they have produced an unusual book, characterised by its originality, wide coverage and depth. Although the authors have all undertaken postgraduate studies in the UK, their varied national and cultural backgrounds (not immediately discernible from their names) are an added advantage for enhancing their understanding of Chile, and Chilean women in particular. Perhaps because of my own background, I am particularly pleased at this cross-fertilisation of Latin American and European intellectual traditions.

This study is, to my knowledge, the first book published in English to focus on women's central role in these major transformations in the Chilean economy and society. Given the depth and complexity of these changes, it is to be hoped that this study will encourage further research. In particular, men should also be interviewed in order to gain a fuller understanding of the changes in gender relations. The relevance of this fine book goes beyond Chile and will be of interest to all those engaged in understanding the impact of globalisation on women, especially in those countries where similar processes of feminisation and greater flexibility of the labour market have occurred.

Cristóbal Kay
Institute of Social Studies, The Hague

1 Introduction

Chile is now a major Southern Hemisphere exporter of fresh fruit, and the seasonal employment of women is an important factor underlying its fruit export production. This book examines the process of change which has taken place in Chile, leading to the integration of a significant female labour force into the fruit export sector. Chile is a good example of a country that has successfully integrated itself into non-traditional agricultural exports, which is regarded as contributing to the Chilean economic 'miracle' (Murray 1996). For a short period at the beginning of each year, Chilean fruit can be found in shops and markets throughout the developed and even developing world. Behind these fruit exports lies the seasonal employment of a large number of seasonal temporary workers (*los temporeros*), over 50 per cent of whom are women (*las temporeras*) (Venegas 1993). The expansion of agribusiness in Chile has involved a radical transformation of the rural sector over the past three decades (Hojman 1990 and 1993b; Kay and Silva 1992). The effects of this process on women working in this sector have been complex and contradictory. A consequence of the transformation, however, is that the *temporeras* have become central to the production of high quality fruit for export. They have been integrated into modern global agribusiness and form a vital element in the success of Chilean fruit exports.

Chile is not alone in following this path. The past two decades have seen an expansion of global agribusiness as a number of developing countries have become important exporters of fresh horticultural produce – fruit, vegetables and flowers – to the developed world. This global trade has both stimulated and responded to changing consumption patterns, as consumers have become increasingly accustomed to buying a wide range of fresh fruit and vegetables at lower prices, all year round independent of season or location of production (Cook 1994; Friedland 1994b). In many developing countries, the expansion of agribusiness in areas supplying the world market with these types of exports has led to a radical transformation of the rural sector. A significant aspect of this transformation in many countries has been the rise in female employment generated by the production of non-traditional agricultural exports (Sachs 1996; Thrupp 1995). This employment is usually seasonal, insecure and poorly paid, but it has

1

led to the integration of large numbers of women into the rural wage labour force, many of whom may have taken up paid work for the first time.

In this book we take an interdisciplinary approach, drawing on geography, economics, politics, history and feminist studies, to provide an in-depth exploration of this process in Chile. We examine how the expansion of female employment in Chilean agribusiness has shaped, and been shaped by, gender relations within the rural sector, as 'traditional' gender relations have been transformed and adapted through the extension of 'modern' agribusiness. The reasons underlying this new form of female employment are discussed, as well as the nature of gender segregation within the sector in the context of sustaining rapid output to meet export demand. We consider the partial and fragmented form of this work, focusing on the interaction between 'traditional' and 'modern' gender roles as an essential element underpinning the functioning of agribusiness. We explore the impact of this employment on rural women themselves, as they mediate the tensions between their multiple roles, while simultaneously negotiating the dichotomy between new forms of subordination and new opportunities for empowerment brought about by the expansion of global agribusiness. Finally, we consider the global dimension to their integration into the fruit export sector, and whether codes of conduct being developed by northern supermarkets might improve their position at the heart of this modern export sector.

BACKGROUND TO THE CHILEAN FRUIT EXPORT EXPANSION

The 'explosion' of Chilean fruit exports, which took place during the 1980s, was the result of a combination of factors. Its beginnings can be traced back to the early 1960s, when the Christian Democratic government of Eduardo Frei first introduced agrarian reform into the rural sector and launched the 'Fruit Plan', aimed at developing Chile as a fruit exporter (Echeñique 1990). During this period, the state played an important role in transforming agriculture and providing the technology and infrastructure for the expansion of fruit production (Jarvis 1994). The military coup of 1973 led by General Pinochet precipitated a policy of agrarian 'counter-reform', which forced large numbers of peasants to leave the land and stimulated the expansion of a private commercial farming sector in the central regions of the country. Fruit exports now became a central tenet of the military government's neo-liberal, free market model of export-led growth, which took off in the mid-1980s. Between 1982 and 1992, the period of greatest expansion, the volume of fruit exports increased by 256 per cent (Asociación de Exportadores 1992), with Chile's main exports being vine and temperate fruit, especially grapes, nectarines, peaches and apples. Since the return to democracy in 1990, fruit exports and the free market, export-led model have remained central to government policy.

Natural conditions have particularly favoured Chilean fruit production. It is a relatively small country, forming a narrow wedge between the Andes to the east and the Pacific to the west. Its climatic conditions range from desert in the north to freezing Antarctic conditions in the extreme south. The central regions (where the majority of the population is concentrated) enjoy a Mediterranean-type climate, which is ideal for the production of temperate or deciduous fruit. In addition, the Andes and the desert both act as a natural form of protection against possible infestation of crops from neighbouring countries, and the melting snow from the mountain range is an important source of water throughout the year. Fruit production tends to be concentrated between the III Region to the north and VII Region to the south; these are shown on Map 1.1. The regional variations in climate enable Chile to export fruit for an extended season of up to six months during the year. The expansion of fruit exports has involved a high degree of export specialisation and monocultivation in the temperate central regions. Production starts in November each year in the arid north, using advanced computerised drip irrigation systems, facilitating exports principally of grapes to the lucrative Christmas markets of the Northern Hemisphere. Production then moves southwards as the season progresses, bringing in peaches, nectarines and apples among other species, with the main volume of exports being concentrated between January and April.

A number of other factors also contributed to the early expansion of Chile's fruit export sector, facilitating its 'comparative advantage'. Infrastructure is relatively well developed within the central region, with a road network connecting the fruit-growing areas to the main container ports (the largest of which is at Valparaiso) and the airport of Santiago (for airfreighted produce). The capital, Santiago, lies at the heart of the fruit-growing area, and contains the nerve centre of commercial and financial activity which services the export sector. Technological expertise and innovation were adopted from the outset by Chilean producers and exporters, often emulating the Californian

Map 1.1   Map of Chile

model, with early assistance from the government (Jarvis 1994). Transnational firms, which entered Chile after the sector had been established by national entrepreneurs, also imported highly sophisticated methods of production and packing. The types of systems used include: computer-controlled drip irrigation systems in production, the intensive use of fertilisers, pesticides and hormones; sophisticated packing plants resembling large modern factories; and temperature and atmospherically controlled storage and transport systems. All these contribute to a 'cool chain' supply system, which allows the fresh produce to be exported over long distances during extended time periods without perishing (Fundación Chile 1990/1). In addition, Chile has had the 'advantage' of a cheap labour force, which forms the subject of this book. These 'comparative advantages' have combined to favour the export of high quality, low cost fruit, during a period when there is no competition from Northern Hemisphere producers.

Another factor in the expansion of fruit production in Chile has been changing consumption patterns in the developed countries (Cook 1994; Goldfrank 1994). The growing availability of low priced fruit in northern markets has helped to stimulate changing consumption patterns, as northern consumers have become increasingly accustomed to buying a wide range of fresh fruit all year round. By the early 1990s, Chile had established itself as a major off-season supplier of temperate fruit to the Northern Hemisphere, along with South Africa and New Zealand. As such, Chilean production forms part of the generalised growth in non-traditional agricultural exports, which have been a marked feature of 'globalisation' over the past decade.

LAS TEMPORERAS

The process of commercialisation of the agricultural sector has effectively eliminated peasant-based agriculture in the main fruit-growing regions of the country. Large numbers of rural households have lost access to land and now live in rural or urban shantytowns where they depend solely on wage labour for survival (Hojman 1990; Kay and Silva 1992). This has generated a large rural labour force which is the basis of the army of temporary seasonal workers (*los temporeros*) employed in fruit export production every year. These seasonal workers are employed for 3–6 months a year, particularly during December to March. There are no precise figures for the numbers employed, but estimates put the figure at around 287,500 workers in 1993, of whom just over half, or approximately 150,000, are women (Barrientos 1996). This employment is not only temporary, but is precarious and highly flexible. Pay, conditions and duration of employment vary from one employer to another, and at different times of the season. At the peak of the season, when the demand for labour is at its height, women, who tend to be concentrated in the packing houses, can work anything up to 16 hours a day, six days a week (Díaz 1991; Venegas 1992a). As the fruit regions rely on monocultivation, many rural households depend on temporary work in fruit by all able adult members (male and female) during the season as a main source of income for the year.

The effect of integration into global agribusiness on gender relations in the rural sector has been both complex and contradictory. On the one hand, the women are drawn into a modern wage labour force which has a transformative effect on traditional gender relations. On the other hand, they are employed on a seasonal basis only, which constrains this transformation. During the season, the women have to negotiate insertion into the labour force with their multiple roles as wife, mother and carer, in charge of the domestic responsibilities, mediating the tensions which arise from these conflicting roles. Out of season, however, their situation often reverts to a more traditional role as they return to their homes as isolated 'housewives'. Moreover, this group of workers is very heterogeneous in terms of age, marital status, domestic situation, residence and alternative forms of income or livelihood. It is, therefore, difficult to give a general characterisation, particularly as this heterogeneity means that there is a great diversity in their personal and social experience of fruit work. As a group of workers they are also atomised, with high job insecurity and minimal organisation. All these factors combine to make an analysis of the *temporeras* as a group a complex undertaking.

To understand their situation, however, it is not sufficient to focus solely on the interaction between the women's employment and household relations. Their formation as a social group is a result of a process of historical change in the rural sector, the transformation of agricultural production and the insertion of Chile into global export markets. These factors have shaped and formed the expansion of the temporary fruit labour force in important and contradictory ways. Therefore, to analyse the *temporeras,* we need to examine the changes that have taken place in rural Chile, facilitating its insertion into the world fruit market. We also need to examine how production and export distribution are organised in order to understand the structure of temporary employment and women's insertion into it. Throughout the process of change, the state has played an important role, either directly or indirectly, in shaping the agricultural sector and women's position within it. In turn, all these factors have influenced and been affected by the global context within which women's role in the temporary wage labour force has evolved.

To summarise, therefore, we have four main aims in this book. First, to provide an overview of women's participation in the fruit labour force in the context of rural transformation, new 'flexible' employment patterns and Chile's integration into the global division of labour. Second, to provide a study of the impact of this employment on women's role in the household and community, both in a traditional peasant and more urbanised context, considering the extent to which the *temporeras* have been empowered by their changing role. Third, to examine the attitudes and policies of the state towards the *temporeras* in the context of the transition to democracy. Fourth, to explore how the *temporeras* are integrated through agribusiness into a global market, considering the significance of this for international policies to improve their position. Throughout the book, we have aimed to look at these four as interrelated aspects, in order to provide an integrated overview of the *temporeras*. We examine them in the context of analysing gendered employment as an aspect of the 'industrialisation' of agriculture under agribusiness, and the extent to which employment of women within the sector contributes to their empowerment.

OVERVIEW

Chapter 2 analyses the nature of gender and agribusiness, providing a framework which draws together the different dimensions of the empirical material. It explores the insertion of women into non-traditional agricultural production globally, and the partial and contradictory nature of this process. It examines the way in which agribusiness has involved the integration of industrial processes into agriculture, arguing that despite immense advances, agricultural production is still subject to constraints by nature, risk and consumption patterns which are specific to the sector. Industrial transformation has stimulated new forms of non-traditional production in countries such as Chile, and has generated a large seasonal workforce, incorporating

women into new forms of employment in rural areas. However, risk
and seasonality are reflected in both the fragmented structure of the
sector and in the instability, insecurity and heterogeneity of the seasonal employment it generates. In this chapter we argue that women's
employment forms a nexus between the industrial and agricultural
production processes, and that the gendered characteristics of that
employment are not coincidental. Female employment reflects the
commercialisation of tasks traditionally undertaken by women in the
home, and that, as seasonal workers, they are only partially integrated
into the labour force. Women have had to mediate the boundaries
between their 'traditional' work and 'modern' employment in complex
ways, returning to their role within the household when the season is
over. They must also negotiate the changing boundaries within the
household which allow them to take up seasonal employment, but
which nevertheless add to their burdens, often leading to tensions and
conflict. Despite this, the insertion of women into agribusiness contains elements of an empowering and unifying nature, at a local and
global level. These themes are explored in order to frame our analysis
of the *temporeras* in Chile.

Chapter 3 traces the processes that generated the expansion of the
fruit export sector in Chile. From an historical perspective it explores
some of the relationships between state and agrarian transformations,
and the ways in which these processes have led to the incorporation of
large numbers of women into waged agricultural employment. The
structural changes that took place in Chilean agriculture throughout
the latter half of this century are examined, as well as the shifting role
of the state in initiating and shaping the direction of agrarian transformation, leading to the establishment of a highly successful fruit export
industry. Such changes have dramatically altered social relations, patterns of landholding and productive relations in the countryside.
Changes in gender relations are an integral part of these processes of
rural change. We examine how the persistence of traditional, patriarchal relations obscured rural women's productive roles on the
hacienda and *minifundio,* while state policies, both directly and indirectly, perpetuated the subordination and marginalisation of rural
women through the subsequent periods of agrarian reform and socialism in the late 1960s and early 1970s. After 1973, the military regime
with its neo-liberal agenda set out explicitly to reinforce the traditional role of women. However, the counter-reform policy instigated
by the military regime often produced paradoxical results. Rural
women were forced to abandon their traditional roles (at least in part)

in order to take on paid work, as rural households became dependent on multiple-wage incomes in order to survive. In this way, hitherto marginalised rural women became a key element to the success of the Chilean fruit 'miracle'.

Chapter 4 examines the structure of production and the export sector. It examines the specific relations between producers and exporters, depicting the internal supply chain which swings into operation each season to facilitate the surge in export output. It explores the way in which industrial processes have been integrated into agriculture, leading to the dominance of agribusiness. It examines the global supply chain, and how Chile is integrated into northern consumer markets based on rotating sources of supply throughout the year. It thus gives an overview of the context in which female employment in fruit export production takes place, providing the framework for examining the specific nature of this employment and women's insertion into the fruit export sector.

Chapter 5 explores how flexible female labour meets the needs of agribusiness, generating new forms of work with a clear pattern of gender segregation. Women are particularly employed in tasks that meet the stringent requirements for exported fruit to meet high standards of quality, facilitating the high value added of exported produce, maximising profitability of output. In this context, the pay and conditions of temporary workers are examined, and issues are raised regarding the effect of this work on women's health. It is argued that female employment in particular helps to provide a buffer for producers and exporters in the face of risk and fluctuations in production and sales, an important factor underlying the instability and insecurity of their work. Women, who return to the home in the counter-seasons, provide a dependable and pliable labour force, whose cycle of future employment meets the rhythm of production.

Chapter 6 moves on to explore a specific case study from the IV Region, where peasant, or *campesina,* women are employed. This region has experienced a dramatic increase in the export production of table grapes. Here traditional small-scale production also continues alongside modern export production and the rural population combines employment in both the traditional and modern agricultural sectors. This chapter explores the experiences of *campesinas*, who juggle work on the family plots and large-scale export farms. It also examines patterns of landholdings which underlie the coexistence of the two forms of agriculture, and how production for the domestic market is able to coexist with that for export. To some extent, this phenomenon is specific to the IV Region, but it reflects the diversity and heterogeneity which persist through the fragmented insertion of industrial production processes into agriculture. In this context we examine women's specific experiences, their perceptions of their work and the ways in which they are able to mediate between their traditional and modern roles, which are the result of their partial insertion into the fruit labour market.

Chapter 7 explores the other extreme of the urbanised *temporeras*. It examines case studies from the VI and VII Regions, where agribusiness has become well established. In these regions, a wide range of fruit species are cultivated for export, from grapes to apples, nectarines, peaches, cherries and plums. This has led to differences in the nature of the *temporeras'* insertion into agribusiness, both in terms of working conditions and employment opportunities, as well as their household backgrounds. This chapter explores the specific experiences and perceptions of some of the *temporeras* from these regions, their motives for working, the impact of their paid work on gender relations at the household level, and the ways in which they negotiate the demands of the 'double day'. The implications of ensuring the survival of households in an urban setting through the precarious dependence on agricultural wage-labour is drawn out, given the inherent seasonality of work in agribusiness. This chapter also explores the ways in which the women mediate old and new forms of gender relations, both inside and outside the workplace. It examines how the potential for the empowerment of women is, on the one hand, fostered by the experience of working in modern agribusiness, while on the other, this potential becomes constrained by the nature of the *temporeras'* partial insertion into this process.

Chapter 8 takes the analysis on to a different plane, by moving from the household and the specific localities to the level of the state in the period of the transition to democracy in the 1990s. Following the end of dictatorship, the newly elected democratic government combined a continuation of the export-led growth model with a greater commitment to more equitable social development. The chapter explores the tensions and contradictions that are inherent in actions to advance the gender interests of the *temporeras* through legislation and other initiatives such as the provision of childcare facilities during the peak season. These measures are problematic in so far as they represent an attempt to increase employment opportunities for women and pursue development with equity, while at the same time continuing the neoliberal economic policies that exacerbate inequality. We examine how the state, in conjunction with employers and social organisations, has intervened directly to meet some of the *temporeras'* most urgent demands at a practical level. Yet the government's room for manoeuvre is tied by the economy's reliance on fruit exports and agribusiness's dependence on the availability of a temporary labour force, which prevents such measures taking on a truly transformative dimension.

Chapter 9 concludes, and explores some of the issues raised at a global level. We draw together the different dimensions of our study of the *temporeras*. We summarise the contradictory nature of female employment within agribusiness, which is mediated by global capital as it interacts with and transforms traditional forms of subordination of women. On the one hand, this can lead to certain improvements for women, but on the other, the cycle of oppression and poverty continues. The global supply chains on which this consumerism is built have a gender dimension which underpins the links between women as employees and consumers in developed and developing countries. It discusses the way pressure from northern NGOs and consumer campaigns have spurred northern supermarkets into adopting a more ethical stance, introducing codes of conduct to be implemented along their supply chains in developing countries. This chapter asks whether these provide new forms of regulation of global agribusiness in the absence of state regulation, and whether they are able genuinely to address the needs of women workers employed seasonally within a heterogeneous and fragmented production process. It concludes by summarising the main themes of the book and considering whether insertion into agribusiness has an empowering effect for women.

Compared to manufacturing, research into female employment in agribusiness and especially non-traditional agricultural exports has been relatively limited to date. Through this in-depth case study on Chile we aim to contribute to the development of research in this field, and hope to stimulate further debate and analysis in this important area. This book is based on research initially done separately by each of the authors on different aspects of the *temporeras*, with most of the fieldwork being undertaken independently in Chile between 1992 and 1995. All four of us came to the topic from different academic disciplines: economics, geography, politics and feminist studies. When we first discussed pooling our work to write a book, we could have decided on producing an edited volume. We felt, however, that this would reinforce the disciplinary boundaries in our work and lack the multidimensional insights which a more interdisciplinary approach might provide. We thus set out on the harder path of jointly writing a book which would integrate our different perspectives in examining the *temporeras* at all levels, from the local and national through to the global, analysing the interconnections between each. We certainly do not think we have eliminated the boundaries between our different disciplinary approaches. But hopefully, through interaction and discussion in the process of writing, we have coalesced our ideas sufficiently to provide a unity of approach, which simultaneously captures the diversity of the subject without undue disjunction. We hope that our examination of the *temporeras* in Chile will contribute to further research and help to advance understanding of this important area.

2 Women and Agribusiness – an Overview

Agribusiness, over the past decade or more, has stimulated an increase in female employment in many countries, not only Chile. In order to analyse the integration of women into Chilean fruit exports, we need to explore some of the broader analytical issues connected with the insertion of female labour into agribusiness. This enables us to draw together the various dimensions relevant to understanding the issues. There are a number of important case studies on women and agribusiness (for example Arizpe and Aranda 1981 and 1986; Barrón 1994; Collins 1993; Kritzinger and Vorster 1996; Macintosh 1989; Marcus 1989), and some comparative studies (Barrientos and Perrons 1996 and 1998; Jarosz 1996). However, the development of a broader analytical framework, which links gender and agribusiness in developing countries, remains an area that needs further research (Raynolds 1991), and often the literature on agribusiness itself tends to ignore the gender dimension (Bernstein et al. 1990). While this chapter considers some of the broader analytical issues, our purpose is to obtain further insights into our particular case study rather than develop a generalised perspective, although we hope the issues we raise will help contribute to the latter.

In this chapter we ask: what are the specific features of female employment in agribusiness, how do these compare with female employment in the industrial sector and what are the effects of this type of employment on gender relations? We start by considering the role of women in agriculture in Latin America and then examine ways in which gender and social relations have been transformed by the expansion of agribusiness. To approach this theme from an analytical perspective we consider agribusiness as a more 'advanced' form of internationally integrated commercial agricultural production, within which industrial processes have reshaped the agricultural sector. We analyse how non-traditional agricultural exports fit into this process. We then examine the role of female labour within this labour-intensive branch of agribusiness and ask why large numbers of women are being employed in this form of export production, not only in Chile but in many other countries as well. Next we examine some of the effects this type of employment has had at a household level, and pursue its contradictory implications by exploring issues of empowerment arising from women taking up paid work in the sector. The focus of our analysis throughout is on the heterogeneity and fragmentation of the female labour force drawn into non-traditional agricultural work, but aware of the highly contradictory nature of the process, we also consider the unifying effects of the global integration of non-traditional agricultural production for women.

GENDER AND AGRICULTURE IN LATIN AMERICA

The extent of female involvement in agriculture has been the subject of some debate within feminist literature on Latin America. The role of women within agricultural production has long been identified as being conditioned by the nature of production, existing social relations and the interconnected patriarchal relations that prevail. Boserup (1970) attributed the differences in sexual divisions of labour between Africa, Latin America and Asia to differences in population density and cultivation patterns. She described Latin America as having a 'male' farming system, and argued that through mechanisation, women would be driven out of waged employment into the subsistence sector. This view was questioned on further investigation by a number of writers (see Deere and León 1987). Boserup was criticised for focusing on the more technically determined production relations, depending too heavily on formal statistical evidence and failing to draw out the importance of the relationship between production and reproduction (Benería and Sen 1981 and 1986; Deere and León 1987). Feminist literature has emphasised the need to examine the relation between the 'productive' and 'reproductive' roles of women. The subordination of women needs to be analysed from the standpoint of employment as well as household relations within their social and historical context, and it is the interaction of these which shape the specificities of gender relations at different times and in different locations.

It is difficult to generalise about the specific nature of women's participation in farming, as there is significant variation between countries across Latin America. In contrast to Boserup, Deere and León (1987) define Latin American agriculture as based on family farming systems. In many countries, female labour has constituted an important element in family farming, and women have long worked as unremunerated family labour on their husband's land or under their husband's contract on that of a landowner, often providing extra labour at seasonal peaks (Wilson 1985). In addition, outside the family farms and *haciendas*, there were women seasonal workers among the landless wage labour force, who were often forced to migrate to find work. These women represented one of the most marginalised and impoverished groups in Latin American rural society. In more 'traditional' agricultural systems, where subsistence production and commercial production originating from family farms or peasant holdings still prevail, the division between productive and reproductive activity remains blurred.[1] Much production is of use values which are consumed within the household (Benería and Sen 1981) and much production for exchange is the product of unpaid family labour, often that of women and children (Goodman and Redclift 1991; Redclift 1985). Unpaid female labour has thus helped to produce both goods for farm and household consumption, as well as contributing to production for exchange. As capitalist agriculture has developed, women have indirectly provided a means for keeping the wages of male agricultural labour down through their unpaid contribution to subsistence, as well as directly contributing to the generation of surplus through their unpaid work in production.

The socio-legal framework facilitating these gendered production relations often denied women effective ownership or control of land and women had little control over their own labour, except in the case of landless peasants forced to work as seasonal workers (Wilson 1985). Patriarchal relations played an important social role in maintaining the subordinate position of women both at an ideological and a practical level, reinforcing the notion of the inferiority of women, while maintaining their position both as domestic and reproductive labour within the household, and as unremunerated family labour in production.

The presentation of women as subservient, meek and vulnerable reinforced the ideological domination of men in an overtly *macho* society and helped to play down the effective significance of women's economic contribution. Within Latin America, traditional patriarchal gender relations are often referred to as *machismo*, an ideology of overt male dominance (Gissi 1976). *Machismo* forms the basis for an idealised masculine identity, incorporating stereotypical traits of physical strength, aggression and the sexual domination of women. Inherent in this ideology is the notion that masculine traits are superior to feminine ones, providing a cultural basis for the subordination of women within existing gender relations, and allowing men to exercise control over women's activities. Some authors identify the existence of a counterpart to *machismo*, which forms the basis for an idealised feminine identity, incorporating stereotypical traits of docility, passivity and submission, legitimising women's gender role within the household. This is often referred to as *marianismo*, and has its origins in the times of the conquest of Latin America (Montecino, Dussuel and Wilson 1988; Montecino 1990).

State policies have often reinforced cultural norms and how much control women and men had over their lives. The lack of recognition of women's role is reflected in the well-documented statistical underestimation of female labour in agriculture, both in paid and unpaid work, within the traditional and modern sectors (Anker 1983; Deere and León 1987; Dixon 1982; Nash and Safa 1986). The marginalisation of women in agriculture has been reinforced through social and legal processes which have denied women formal legitimisation of their role, both with regard to traditional agrarian systems and also with the advance of industrialisation.

The effects of agrarian reform and agricultural modernisation on women have been variable from place to place, depending on the type of production and the specific socio-cultural context. During the early phase of import-substitution industrialisation, agriculture was either largely ignored or discriminated against through the implementation of a range of pro-industrial policies (Deere and León 1987). Hence 'backward' forms of rural organisation continued into the phase of industrial expansion, perpetuating the traditional role of women in the rural sector. Although agricultural neglect stimulated the introduction of land reform policies, there was little concern for the need to address the position of rural women specifically. During the 1960s and 1970s state policies in agriculture tended to be interventionist with important implications for women's access to resources and control over the economic benefits of resources (including land and labour). Women were either subjected to outright discrimination in the law by being excluded from holding property and land, or were not explicitly included in the distribution of lands and thereby remained marginalised by cultural practices and norms. Land in many countries was redistributed primarily to male heads of household, and the subordination of women continued under the guise of new forms of male land tenure (Deere 1986 and 1987).

Since the 1980s, however, there has been a shift away from state-led policies to a more liberal free market approach, with greater emphasis on export agriculture. In this context there has been an expansion of commercialised agriculture and a growth in agribusiness. The expansion of agribusiness has transformed social relations in those rural sectors drawn into its ambit, with important implications for gender relations. In many countries commercialised farming has displaced peasant farming, and it has become increasingly difficult for smaller farms to compete (Carter et al. 1996). Rural labour has been displaced from the land, there has been a growing dependence on wage labour in the rural sector as a result of commercialisation (Goodman and Redclift 1991), and much of the labour employed in the growing agribusiness sector is female (Thrupp 1995; Wilson 1985). To this extent, agricultural production is being drawn into processes more commonly associated with urbanisation and industrial production, with important implications for gender relations. As access to land becomes restricted and the agrarian labour force becomes increasingly 'proletarianised', the exclusive male peasant ownership and control of property is reduced, thereby undermining an important material element of the traditional subordination of women in rural societies.

The greater commercialisation of agriculture and new forms of production increase the separation between productive and reproductive activities. With less access to land there is a reduction in women's role in subsistence production and unremunerated labour, except in terms of more limited domestic functions within the household. Simultaneously, the process of capitalist development increases the availability of cheap commercial consumer goods. Households become increasingly dependent on purchasing goods on the market to meet their needs, and female labour becomes a potential source of income to acquire these goods. This process can be very uneven, but is more pronounced in areas where agribusiness predominates (Wilson 1985). As agribusiness expands its dependence on wage-labour bought in each season to work on commercial farms, paid female temporary employment has increased, and women working as unpaid household labour has declined. On both counts, therefore, the *unpaid* contribution of women to the generation of an agricultural surplus is reduced. Although women have long been part of the marginalised seasonal workforce in Latin America, agribusiness has shifted to and indeed expanded the use of this type of wage-labour, and women have been 'released' to become part of this labour force.

The effect of this on more traditional forms of agricultural production has been uneven and diverse, and the implications for women have often been contradictory. We shall first explore the effect of agribusiness with specific reference to non-traditional agricultural exports, and then consider the gender implications of this form of agricultural production in more depth.

AGRIBUSINESS AND NON-TRADITIONAL AGRICULTURAL EXPORTS

Agribusiness is at the other end of the spectrum from traditional forms of subsistence farming, where production and consumption are largely contained within the household or farm unit. It denotes an expanded system of production, processing, distribution and retailing in which commercial relations are dominant, and on-farm agricultural production is only one phase. Agribusiness has been succinctly defined as 'the sum total of all operations involved in the manufacture and distribution of farm supplies; the production operations of the farm; storage, processing and distribution of farm commodities and items made from them' (Davis and Goldberg 1957, cited by Whatmore 1995: 38). The growth of agribusiness, in the postwar period has led to its increasingly 'global' character, as supply chains have expanded internationally, linking developing and developed countries throughout the world. It has been dated back to what has been labelled the 'second food regime', which prevailed during the postwar period from 1947 to 1972 (Friedmann 1993; Friedmann and McMichael 1989).[2] This was a period of US dominance, in which large transnational corporations integrated upstream and downstream input supplies, production, processing and distribution across countries, increasing their domination of the global food chain. However, it has been argued that, in the 1970s, a crisis in the international food system emerged as a result of oversupply and transnational domination coming into conflict with national forms of regulation (Friedmann 1993). As a result, a 'new political economy' of food has emerged in the context of an increasingly liberalised global economic order, in which transnational domination has intensified and food production is increasingly for the global market (Friedland et al. 1991). This global integration of the food system has led to its being characterised by 'agro-food "chains", "complexes" and "regimes"' (Whatmore 1995: 39); and a growing body of literature has emphasised the need to analyse agricultural production in the context of the broader global food system (Fine et al. 1996; Friedland et al. 1991; Goodman and Redclift 1991; Jaffee 1993; Le Heron 1993; McMichael 1994).

There is some debate over the extent to which agribusiness generally is synonymous with the process of industrial accumulation on a global scale. There are those who equate the development of agribusiness over the postwar period with categories of industrial development, such as Fordism and post-Fordism. According to this approach, the second food regime from the end of the Second World War until the 1970s took the form of intensive accumulation, dominated by the US, in which agricultural production was based on the use of industrial inputs, and agricultural output was increasingly destined as an industrial input. The period since the 1970s, in which agribusiness has expanded through the use of contract farming, is seen as comparable to industrial development and the increased use by transnationals of outsourcing and subcontracting, defined from an industrial perspective as 'flexible specialisation' (McMichael 1994). Criticism of this approach has been developed by Goodman and Watts, who argue that the parallels between industry and agriculture have been overdrawn, forcing analysis of the agricultural sector into a 'straitjacket', and that the analysis is better informed through recognition of the differences between industry and land-based production and consumption (Goodman and Watts 1994: 5). Much of this debate, however, has taken place at a broad level, categorising all sectors of agribusiness as a totality. The focus of our study is specifically non-traditional agricultural export production in developing countries, and we shall explore these issues solely from this perspective.

Non-traditional agricultural exports have formed part of a transformation in agricultural trade from developing countries since the 1980s. There are different definitions of this type of export agriculture, but it is often termed 'non-traditional' agricultural export to distinguish it from more traditional forms of export production. According to Barham, Clark, Katz and Schurman:

> The term *non-traditional exports* is used in the literature to describe three distinct phenomena. First, an export can be non-traditional because it involves a product that has not been produced in a particular country before, such as snow peas in Guatemala. A second type of non-traditional export is a product that was traditionally produced for domestic consumption but is now being exported, like various tropical fruits. Finally, the term can refer to the development of a new market for a traditional product such as exporting bananas to the Soviet Union. (Barham et al. 1992: 43)

This is one of the more succinct definitions of the term non-traditional agricultural exports (NTAEs), but some blurring of the concept remains. First, there is a temporal problem as to what point a product switches from being non-traditional to traditional; and second, as Thrupp (1995) points out, it is a relative concept in which the same products are traditional exports from one country and non-traditional exports from another. To overcome this problem, the other definition used by Jaffee is based on the production for export of 'high-value food commodities':

> Compared with traditional staple foods (such as foodgrains, legumes, roots and tubers), these horticultural, livestock, fisheries, oilseed and prepared foods have considerably higher unit values and face much higher income elasticities of demand ... World and developing country trade in high-value food products – defined here to include meats, dairy products, fish products, edible horticultural products, spices, oilseeds, animal/vegetable oils, and animal feeds stuffs – is now considerable. In 1988/9, world exports in such products totalled approximately $144 billion. (Jaffee 1993: 1)

The advantage of this definition is that it avoids the issue of when the switch from non-traditional to traditional takes place. But it still raises the question of where we place the boundary between low unit value and high unit value, which is particularly blurred in the case of prepared foods, when staple ingredients are used to produce higher value products. Both the above definitions can include processed as well as non-processed products, and are not necessarily confined to fresh horticultural produce, although it is in this area that much of the expansion has taken place over recent years. Latin America in particular has seen a rapid growth in non-traditional or high-value exports since the 1980s, as part of the switch towards an export-oriented policy based on primary produce (Thrupp 1995; Jaffee 1993; Barham et al. 1992; Carter et al. 1996). Between 1985 and 1992 the value of non-traditional agricultural exports from Central America increased by an annual average of 17.2 per cent, and from South America (excluding Brazil) by an annual average of 48 per cent (Thrupp 1995: 3). This expansion has seen the transformation of the agricultural sector in many countries, not only through the growth of agribusiness, but also through integration into the global system of food production, processing and retailing, broadly defined as the agro-food system or complexes.

While non-traditional agricultural exports can cover a range of products, the focus of our study is more specific in that we are analysing only the production and export of fresh horticultural produce. This includes fresh fruit, vegetables and flowers, although in the specific case of Chile we focus mainly on fruit. The export of fresh produce from developing countries is not a new phenomenon, but previously it tended to be restricted to certain more durable produce such as bananas and citrus fruit, or expensive airfreighted produce for very select, niche markets. Since the 1980s, this trade has rapidly expanded, and a broad range of fresh produce, including exotic varieties, is widely available all year round at affordable prices in northern markets. To define trade in this produce we use a combination of the above definitions, but employ the term 'non-traditional agricultural exports' (NTAE), which is more commonly used in relation to Latin America. Given the specific focus of our book, this covers mainly fresh horticultural produce (fruit, vegetables and flowers), which were (1) not traditionally exported in any significant quantity by the supplier country; and/or (2) were not previously easily available at that time of the year in the markets of destination; and (3) have a higher unit value and income elasticity of demand than staple produce.[3] NTAEs are part of an expanding world trade in edible horticultural products, whose total value in 1988/9 was US\$40.3 billion, exceeding trade in cereals which was US\$38.6 billion (Jaffee 1993: 1).

The expansion in this trade has taken place in the context of the changing economic and political strategies of developing countries since the early 1980s and the global expansion of the agro-food system. Following the onset of the debt crisis in the early 1980s, most developing countries, especially in Latin America, switched away from protectionist policies aimed at developing domestic industry to a policy of greater economic liberalisation, with the emphasis on export-led growth. This strategy was promoted by the International Monetary Fund and World Bank through their stabilisation and structural adjustment programmes, stimulating the expansion in non-traditional agricultural exports (Barham et al. 1992). Behind the neo-liberal approach lies the theory of 'comparative advantage', which in the case of many developing countries was seen to be in primary produce and agricultural products. Economic liberalisation and globalisation also witnessed rapid technological innovation, the expansion of global communication systems, a transformation in consumption patterns and the increasing dominance of transnational companies. In this environment, large agro-food exporters have been able to expand their year-round sourcing of fresh produce from new locations in developing countries. They have been able to produce high quality horticultural products at the right point in the season to meet demand on the world market. Those developing countries able to lock into this trade[4] have thus been able to generate a new form of 'comparative advantage' through the expansion of non-traditional agricultural exports. Economic liberalisation provided the environment for the expansion of agribusiness in this area, which in certain locations has transformed production in agriculture, with complex effects on the developing countries themselves.

An important factor which distinguishes fresh horticultural trade from that of more durable or processed foods is the higher degree of fragility and perishability of the produce. Unlike production for local and regional markets, the produce often has to withstand export over long distances and periods of time, and is produced according to strict production schedules. Fresh horticultural trade has grown to meet changing consumption patterns in the north and the produce has to arrive in pristine condition to meet the increasingly stringent quality demands of northern purchasers, notably large supermarkets (Cook 1994). The expansion of this trade has therefore necessitated a high degree of technological innovation in the production process (through the development of bio-technology, the intensive use of pesticides and fertilisers, and in many cases the application of computer-controlled drip irrigation systems). But it has also required sophisticated investment in the packing, storage, transport and distribution systems which are integrated into a 'cool chain' in which the produce is kept in precisely controlled temperature and atmospheric conditions to delay maturation and maintain freshness and quality through to the point of retail (Friedland 1994b). Non-traditional agricultural trade thus requires a well-integrated and co-ordinated global supply chain, in which industrial processes are used to channel the fresh horticultural produce. This has led some commentators to remark on the increasing 'industrialisation' of the agricultural sector, as it has been integrated into the broader agro-food complex (Friedland 1994a; Teubal 1987).

From this perspective, Friedland (1994a) has analysed the fresh fruit and vegetable sector using an industrial organisation approach. He defines the sector as an industry and divides it into three key segments: production, distribution and marketing. He argues that the production and marketing segments tend to be located in specific countries, and are national or regional in character. They are also the more labour-intensive, employing larger numbers of people. In contrast, the distribution segment is 'very capital and energy intensive, requiring trucks, aeroplanes, and ships, all with refrigeration capacity.

It is also the system that deals with physically distant spaces, transporting fresh fruits and vegetables between continents over thousands of miles' (Friedland 1994a: 179). The industry is described as a dumbbell, in which national production and marketing are 'two large weights on each end connected by the narrow channel of distribution' (ibid.). It is the distribution segment, he argues, which has the highest degree of transnational domination. Despite clear differences between fresh fruit and vegetables and other industries, it provides an example of the process of transnationalisation, and the integration of industrial processes into agricultural production and trade. The result has been a greater homogeneity of production, using the same techniques and plant varieties, so that standardised produce, sourced at different times from different locations, can be fed into a globally integrated supply chain. Consumers in most developed countries can now buy standardised produce (same variety, colour, shape and size) at any time of the year, independent of the season.

Friedland's analysis provides important insights into the application of industrial methods to horticultural export production, particularly at the point of distribution, facilitating the expansion of this trade. However, in the production and distribution segments, the 'dumbbells' at each end, the industrial transnationalisation analogy becomes less appropriate. Our primary interest is in gender and employment at the more labour-intensive production end, and when we focus on this segment, the analysis in our view becomes more complex in that we are examining the interaction between industrial processes and more diverse forms of agricultural production. Non-traditional agricultural exports from developing countries are largely based on heterogeneous and diversified producers feeding a standard homogeneous product into the globalised supply chain dominated by transnationals. For example grapes, imported into northern markets by the same export/import companies throughout the winter, are practically identical in terms of colour, size, shape and taste, but they could originate from co-operatives of peasant producers in India, medium-sized commercial farms in Chile, large commercial farms in South Africa or plantations in Brazil. It is possible that these supply structures are synonymous with the development of industrial subcontracting by large companies, but we must also consider the constraints on industrial accumulation specific to the horticultural sector.

Goodman and Redclift argue that farming systems have long facilitated a degree of organisation of the production process, but 'the biological production–consumption cycle underpinning this system has

imposed distinctive constraints on the technical and social organization of production' (Goodman and Redclift 1991: 91). In consequence, the extent to which the industrial accumulation process has
been able to extend into agriculture has been constrained and fragmented, which may account for the 'atomistic structure of agriculture,
centred on family labour forms of production' (Goodman and Redclift
1991: 91). Relating this to fresh horticultural produce, there are a
number of constraints on the extension of industrial processes.
Production by its nature is seasonal in any specific location, and is still
subject to risk from natural hazard, pest and disease. Monocultivation
increases control of agricultural processes at one level, but it can also
generate new risks. While consumption has been increasingly standardised, there are still risks to profitability from volatility of price and
supply. Furthermore, although agribusiness has been able to integrate
deeper into Latin American agriculture, stimulating its 'modernisation' and further export orientation, spatially this has remained
limited to pockets suitable to the types of export production required.
At the same time, in many countries, more traditional forms of
subsistence production persist to a greater or lesser extent, often even
in the same region. In many locations, production is done through
subcontracting or informal supply agreements with smaller producers,
reinforcing the coexistence with more traditional production. The
degree of integration of agriculture into the global accumulation
process has thus remained fragmented and variable.

This debate about the degree of industrial integration into the agricultural process is important, we believe, in helping to analyse gender
and non-traditional agricultural export production. However, much of
the literature in this area tends to ignore the significant role played by
female employment in the sector. We shall examine the role of
women in NTAE production, and then further explore these issues
from the gender dimension.

GENDER AND NON-TRADITIONAL AGRICULTURAL
EXPORTS

The effects of structural adjustment, economic liberalisation and
export promotion on women generally has been well documented
(see, for example, Afshar and Dennis 1992; Elson 1991). Research
into gender and non-traditional agricultural exports is still relatively
limited, but the evidence that is emerging from different case studies

suggests significant female participation in this sector in a number of different countries, including Chile. In Colombia 80,000 workers are employed in flower production, 80 per cent of them women (Thrupp 1995: 87); in Mexico early studies showed a high level of participation of women in strawberry export production for the North American market (Arizpe and Aranda 1981), and a more recent estimate is that 25 per cent of the active rural population is now absorbed in fruit and vegetable production, 50 per cent of them women (Barrón 1994: 139). In Brazil, there is extensive female employment in grape production in the São Francisco Valley (Collins 1993) and one estimate gives women as 70 per cent of the grape labour force (Christian Aid 1996: 37). In Ecuador, approximately 69 per cent of non-traditional agricultural employment is female, and in Guatemala, Costa Rica and Honduras evidence shows that women occupy more than half the jobs associated with post-harvest handling and greenhouse cultivation of non-traditional agricultural exports (Thrupp 1995: 88).[5] We need to consider why, in all these cases, 50 per cent or more of the employment is female. Does this reflect a general tendency towards 'feminisation' of the labour force, also seen in the industrial sector, as a result of globalisation, or are there specific features inherent to agriculture that increase the probability of female employment in this sector? As our in-depth research is on Chile alone, we are not in a position to provide generalised answers to these questions, but we shall explore the issues in order to enhance our understanding of Chile and to raise questions for further research.

We start by exploring the links between globalisation and the feminisation of the labour force in both industry and agriculture (particularly NTAE). Economic liberalisation and the commercialisation of agriculture have undermined peasant farms and stimulated the expansion of a rural *wage*-labour force increasingly dependent on paid employment (Goodman and Redclift 1991). As peasant farming declines relative to commercial production, and peasant labour loses access to the land, the disparity between rural and urban forms of employment is reduced. This is particularly pronounced in areas dominated by agribusiness where monocultivation reduces the availability of alternative work. As we have seen, in more traditional forms of agriculture in Latin America and other developing countries, women have often played an important role as unpaid family labour in peasant production or as marginalised seasonal workers. Commercialisation of agriculture and expansion of a rural wage labour force has increased the relative importance of the latter, with the survival of poor rural households increasingly depending on both men and women finding paid employment. In many rural areas, the transformation of production through the expansion of agribusiness has thus helped to generate a rural wage-labour force in which there is significant participation of women, and has created the conditions for employment closer to the urban industrial sector.

Globalisation has also had effects on the forms of employment in NTAE similar to other sectors of export industry. The growth of transnationals during the postwar period led to a relocation of parts of industrial production away from the main industrialised to developing countries. This generated a 'new international division of labour', in which fragmentation of the production process allowed the separation of production between countries, but also facilitated outsourcing and subcontracting of production within countries (Frobel et al. 1981). The employment so created was increasingly insecure, flexible and low paid, and in many developing countries women were integrated into this type of work (Mitter 1986; Standing 1989).

A slightly different process, but with similar results has taken place through the growth of NTAE production. Non-traditional agricultural exports were not previously available to developed countries in any quantity throughout the year. This is, therefore, generally a new form of export production, rather than a relocation of production, and involves the entire product being produced in different locations as seasons rotate globally (unlike the assembly of manufactured products in a permanent location from parts originating in different countries). But the year-round sourcing of fresh produce has led to the dispersal of production across different countries as the seasons rotate around the globe, all of which have to be integrated into the supply chain at different times. Within many of the producer countries large exporters and transnationals use forms of contract arrangements and informal agreements to source their supplies (Barrett et al. 1997). Local producers connected to agribusiness are constantly seeking ways to reduce labour costs to remain competitive, particularly in NTAE production, which is relatively labour-intensive. This has helped to generate insecure, flexible, low-paid employment, much of which is female. To this extent, there are similarities with the growth of flexible female employment in subcontracted industrial employment.

Intensification of the division of labour through the expansion of agribusiness into NTAEs has also helped to generate forms of female employment analogous to export industry. In export industry, global fragmentation has meant the subdivision of production between countries, and a greater division of tasks within any production location. The separation of tasks has intensified the specific skilling of those tasks and facilitated a gendered division of those tasks between male and female labour. As technology has developed, women have increasingly been employed for their supposed 'feminine' skills and 'nimble fingers' to undertake delicate work. But as Elson and Pearson (1981) have clearly shown, these are not 'natural' or 'innate' skills, but are based on social skilling embedded during the upbringing of girls to undertake household duties as part of their socially defined, subordinate position within society.

Similarly to export industry, NTAE production has both increased the division of labour within production and generated new skills. Traditional production for the internal market meant that fresh produce would usually be picked and packed into boxes *in situ* with little preparation for immediate distribution, requiring a very basic division of labour, if any. Production of NTAEs, on the other hand, requires sophisticated preparation and packing processes generating new skills and a much greater diversity of tasks. The study of Chile, and evidence from other countries, suggests that a gendered division of these tasks has taken place. Women in particular have been employed to undertake delicate tasks, essential to maintaining the quality of the produce, for which women's supposedly 'feminine skills' have been deemed appropriate. Similar to sectors of export industry, therefore, the socially acquired skills of women have been appropriated to undertake delicate tasks relating to high quality export output.

There are clear analogies, therefore, between female employment in NTAE production and export industry. But we also need to ask whether this sector of agribusiness has specific traits, beyond those of export industry, which also underlie the gendered nature of employment. Are there differences between the industrial and agricultural sectors which differentiate the forms of employment in the two, and help to explain further the level of female employment in the NTAE sector? Goodman and Redclift (1991) point to the natural and organic constraints on the integration of industrial processes into agriculture, which we believe are relevant in analysing the gender dimension of NTAE employment, and which the industrial analogy alone does not explain. We have examined these constraints above – seasonality of production, perishability of the produce, risk of pest, disease and natural disaster, volatility of prices and demand – and now consider their implications in terms of the nature of employment.

Employment in the NTAE sector is often characterised by a lack of contracts, pay by piece rate, insecure employment within the season and the ignoring of any labour rights such as collective negotiation (Thrupp 1995). This precariousness partly reflects the drive by smaller producers to minimise labour costs through the payment of low wages and minimal labour standards and conditions. To this extent the analogy between smaller agricultural and industrial producers supplying larger export companies and transnationals pertains. But the precarious nature of employment is also endemic to NTAE production because of constraints and risks inherent to the sector. The most obvious of these is that production is seasonal, as determined by nature and over which there is little or no control. This generates the temporary pattern of employment and lack of continuity and insecurity underpinning the work. However, even within the season temporary agricultural workers are a highly marginalised group whose employment is unprotected, insecure and low paid. This not only keeps labour costs down, but also helps to protect employers against natural variations in output, risk of infestation by pest or disease and fluctuations in price and demand. In other words, we would argue there are natural factors reinforcing the precarious nature of employment in the NTAE sector beyond those which affect the industrial export sector. Women have always been part of a seasonal agricultural labour force, but whereas previously this operated at the margins of agricultural production, under NTAE production it is central. Women are an essential part of a cheap seasonal labour force, which is at the base of the profitability of a competitive global NTAE sector, and their labour helps to buffer the risks to producers of this type of production.

In many areas where monocultivation predominates, the seasonal nature of production also generates such intense labour demand at the peak, that all available experienced labour, both male and female, will be drawn on. As workers become skilled through repetitive seasonal work, they become in effect a 'permanent' seasonal rural labour force, available year after year. Women have become fully integrated into this 'permanent' workforce, and it is this seemingly contradictory situation of 'permanent' temporary seasonal employment which also provides a key to understanding the gender relations within agribusiness. This is clearly not 'permanent' employment in the traditional sense, where *formally* there was a sexual division of labour between men's full-time, 'productive' economic activity and women's 'reproductive' activities within the household, and women were dependent on the income generated by their male partner. For landless rural households, employment is often so insecure, and wages so low, that families can no longer depend solely on male income generation, and have to organise their survival strategies around all working adult members, including women. If the dominant local employment is in agribusiness, this ensures the permanent availability of a labour force, even if the work itself is for the most part only temporary. In the industrial sector seasonal constraints on production exist, but are generally are less overt; in the NTAE sector however seasonality is a central factor, and female employment plays an important role for employers in overcoming this constraint.

The fragmented nature of agricultural production and the constraints on its insertion into industrial processes mean that while gender relations can be reworked at one level, traditional patterns are reinforced at another. This contradiction lies at the heart of the complex impact of agribusiness onto gender relations in the rural sector, and the heterogeneity of women drawn into employment in the sector. First, given that employment is only seasonal and there is a lack of alternative work in areas dominated by monocultivation, women can only be economically active within the labour force for limited periods each year, reverting to their more traditional role within the household when no employment is available. This leads to a disjointed transformation in gender relations as women take on increasing employment opportunities during the season, while traditional social and ideological pressures reinforce their subordinate position in a patriarchal household structure out of season. Second, given that agribusiness continues to interact with more traditional forms of production in order to source its supplies, much employment is not necessarily by large transnational companies, but through informal supply agreements with smaller local producers and sometimes even family farms. Thus, employment relations can differ between type of employer, and these are intertwined with patriarchal attitudes which continue to prevail, especially among smaller producers. In this way, a contradictory mediation between old and new forms of gender segregation persists. Agribusiness feeds off this contradiction, transforming gender relations through the integration of women into the modern wage labour process at one level (where male and female labour are formally equal), but relying on women returning to their 'reproductive role' and unequal position within the household, to retain a source of labour that can be tapped according to the needs of production. Agribusiness thus depends on the traditional subordination of women to maintain a permanent supply of 'docile' female labour.

GENDER RELATIONS AND THE HOUSEHOLD

In the light of this, it is important to consider how the contradictory transformation of gender relations through NTAE employment is mediated at the household level. The household not only represents a unit of economic activity, but also a set of socially constructed relationships. These relationships help shape the freedom that individuals have in managing their own actions. This holds true across geographic and cultural boundaries, although the actual form and degree of household/family influence vary. The dynamics of the relations between individuals within the household are mediated by social constructions of gender roles, a gender division of labour and generational hierarchies, and how these are interpreted by individuals. These relations are significant in shaping the extent of the control and allocation of household resources, as well as employment patterns of households. In turn, these relations are shaped by the ideologies and cultural expectations of the local community, present in the workplace and also in 'the more immediate social world within which the household is located' (Morris 1991: 166; Young 1992). Women's participation in waged employment, therefore, is conditioned at various levels by economic and political factors, with influences operating at the ideological level, such as patriarchal principles which order both household and employment relations.

While 'third world' women should not be viewed as a homogeneous and uniformly oppressed group, certain patterns of subordination can be discerned and the household is frequently presented as the primary site for this subordination (see Bruce and Dwyer 1988; Redclift and Mingione 1985; Sokoloff 1981; Young, Wolkowitz and McCullagh 1981). The social construction of households, therefore, needs to be considered in any examination of female employment and economic change, especially if we accept that households are not characterised by the virtues of pooling, sharing and generosity (Bruce and Dwyer 1988; Folbre 1988; Harris 1981). Avoiding the rather simplistic assumption that households are coherent units with an agreed coping strategy, we see, on closer inspection, that individuals within the household usually have their own aspirations, based on their family status, gender and age.

Within individual households, traditional gender relations come into conflict with new forms of social relations driven by agribusiness and the expansion of female employment in the NTAE sector. This has led to tensions as old and new relations are mediated in different and contradictory ways, often with paradoxical consequences. In Latin America, traditional cultural norms tend to allocate the major source of familiar control to the male head of household through the 'bread-winner' role. When women go to work in NTAE production, they become independent wage earners, making an often vital contribution to household income. This appears likely to alter the dynamics of gender and power relations as women gain direct control over their wage, potentially improving their bargaining position within the household, and challenging the authority of the male head of household.

However, in NTAE employment women only hold this wage-earning role for part of the year, which constrains the possibilities for gaining greater independence. Moreover, most evidence suggests that women retain the bulk of the domestic responsibilities even during this period, resulting in a double burden of paid and domestic work. However, as the 'disruption' of the domestic role need only be managed for part of the year, the potential for renegotiating the division of labour within the household is also constrained. These contradictions are mediated in different ways within households, leading to a great variety of experiences as women negotiate these multiple, and often conflicting, roles.

The relation between production and reproduction and the subordination of women both in employment and outside needs to be analysed and understood in the context of the driving force of globalisation. The consequences are contradictory in that the traditional and modern continue to interact. We have discussed the ways in which gender relations undergo a disjointed transformation through integration into agribusiness, a process which may also help to explain the heterogeneity of the women seasonal workers themselves. They have to mediate not only the different roles demanded of them socially, as worker, mother, wife, community worker, etc., they also have to mediate the interaction between modern and traditional social relations, which further complicates an analysis of their experiences. Instead of any linear effect, only a refracted picture can be obtained, as each woman's experience is different, depending not only on her personal circumstances, but the extent to which she has been drawn into this partial employment role. Heterogeneity is thus an essential element of female integration into NTAE employment, not only because the women happen to come from diverse backgrounds and situations, but because of the fragmentation of the process itself. This is not accidental, but has to be understood as an essential element in the accumulation process of transnational agribusiness, which we have explored to some extent.

EMPOWERMENT

Women's incorporation into employment in agribusiness raises the question of the potential empowerment this process may offer. Despite the continued subordination of women through segregation in employment and more traditional relations within the household, work in agribusiness can potentially empower women. The opportu-nity to take on paid employment draws women out of isolated household production into socialised production, offering them new roles and collective experiences which can form the basis for organisation and unity. This in turn can engender self-confidence, allowing women to improve their bargaining position within the household. However, again, the seasonality of agribusiness and the fragmented labour process mean that women usually return to the isolation of their homes and the domestic role once the season is over, which results in a partial transformation of gender relations at the household level. Nevertheless, as many rural women have been integrated into the seasonal labour force on a 'permanent' basis, the impact of agribusiness on gender relations within the household is lasting.

The question of women's 'empowerment', together with the concept of power, has formed a central debate in development theory (Afshar 1998; Hartsock 1990; Kabeer 1994; Rowlands 1997). In day-to-day experience, the ways in which individuals stand in relation to each other requires a negotiation of relationships of power. In any given interaction, these relations are personalised, but they are nevertheless imbued with ideology and embedded in wider social, political, economic or cultural relations of power. As such, the question of empowerment should be addressed from 'an examination of how power is present in multiple and heterogeneous social relations' (Nelson and Wright 1995: 8). Through these multiple relations, power relationships are reproduced, negotiated and challenged (Hartsock 1990).

With regard to women, empowerment is connected to how power differentials inherent in gender relations might be transformed. Within this context there are three dimensions to empowerment: personal, relational and collective (Rowlands 1997). The process begins on a personal level, where an event or a new experience may prompt a questioning of hitherto accepted realities. Through this, isolated personal experience could become connected to a wider system of social relations, allowing new interpretations and understanding to arise from the experience (Nelson and Wright 1995). In terms of our analysis, women's experience of moving out of isolated household production into collective relations of production through agribusiness often means an expansion of social horizons, offering a potential opportunity to develop self-confidence and skills, and perhaps share with other women a new collective experience. Despite the partial nature of this process, because of the seasonality of NTAE employment, the experience could provide a basis for changing attitudes on a personal level, and may also change individuals' understanding of wider social and gender relations.

From this, changes in attitudes and behaviour, as well as increasing confidence may allow individuals to influence and alter surrounding power relationships (Nelson and Wright 1995). Women's incorporation into the wage-labour force means that they receive a money income which is paid directly to them. This is likely to alter their bargaining position within relations at a household level, enabling them to increase their control and negotiate power relations within the family more effectively (Kabeer 1994). As the women are incorporated into a new set of employment relations, a commonality of experience is created, providing a potential nexus for collective activity, perhaps allowing a group of individuals to expand their influence over wider aspects of their lives. Incorporation into the larger social and economic relations that agribusiness represents may offer women the possibility to voice their views as a group, and discover areas where organisation within the workplace could improve their power position within employment relations. Moreover, as women are drawn into a unified labour process on a global scale the possibility of collaboration through the supply chain is raised.

However, agribusiness presents a fragmented and uneven terrain, in which contradictions are rife in terms of its effects on gender relations. The circumstances which form the unifying basis for collective organisation are present only when women are working during the season, disappearing when they return to their homes. Out of season, the heterogeneity of the women drawn into employment in this sector makes sustaining organisations through this period a difficult task, limiting any potential empowerment. Paradoxically, then, despite the apparent fragmentation and marginalisation of women seasonal workers in NTAE, the expansion of agribusiness does create a nexus of unifying relations between a heterogeneous group of women, allowing for their potential empowerment in ways that did not previously exist. At the same time, the partial nature of this incorporation means that any empowerment is likely to be uneven and constrained.

CONCLUDING REMARKS

The insertion of women into agribusiness has not been an even process. Agribusiness has seized on those locations and those countries that facilitate the expansion of the year-round global supply chain of fresh agricultural products. In those areas drawn into the process, a transformation has taken place in traditional social and economic relations with significant consequences for women. Many areas which have not been drawn in are marginalised, and more traditional relations both in agricultural production and household relations continue to persist. Even in regions where agribusiness has spread its net, the consequences have been complex and contradictory. The organisation of global production based on modern technology and high levels of capital investment has stimulated the 'industrialisation' of agriculture in many important respects. Yet despite the advances of biotechnology and new production methods, agriculture continues to remain subject to natural constraints and risks beyond those of industry. The latter underlies the specific context of female employment in the sector.

The expanding employment of women in agribusiness has many parallels with female employment in global industry. In both sectors women are often preferred for their so-called 'nimble fingers', their work is insecure, low paid and 'flexible'. However, we have argued that these traits are reinforced in agribusiness by the specific characteristics of the sector. The natural constraint of seasons, combined with intensive monocultivation in some areas, generates the demand for a large temporary labour force at particular times of the year. Women are drawn out of their more traditional role in the household to meet this demand, forming a 'reliable' temporary workforce with the requisite 'social' training to produce high quality produce for export. Agriculture involves additional risks of infestation or unexpected climatic variation, along with market volatility, which reduce the certainty of supply. As a highly 'flexible' labour force within the season, the employment of temporary female labour can be rapidly adjusted to meet the ebbs and flows of output. In the NTAE sector of agribusiness, women thus act as a buffer between the vagaries of production and the more concentrated export sector which feeds the global market. The employment of female labour is an essential element in sustaining and expanding agricultural export production, and agribusiness feeds off traditional gender relations to sustain an experienced workforce.

The effects on gender relations, however, have been complex and contradictory. At one level, traditional gender relations have been transformed as women have been drawn out of unpaid household production into paid employment, often for the first time. At another level, that employment is usually at best temporary, and out of season women revert to a more traditional role within the household. Seasonal employment can provide the basis for greater socialisation and more independence, enhancing the bargaining power of women within the household. But many women have to juggle their multiple roles, and confront tensions, which are mediated in different ways according to personal circumstances. In the main, women working in agribusiness are a heterogeneous, marginalised group. Yet their insertion into a global production sector has at the same time raised the potential for their empowerment both at a personal level and in terms of the possibility of their social organisation. In consequence, agribusiness can work both for and against women, and its effects can have paradoxical results.

The above analysis is based on assessing our in-depth knowledge of women in Chilean agribusiness complemented by similar case studies elsewhere, in the context of the broader literature on global agro-food systems and the expansion of the NTAE sector. As we have seen, Chilean exports are only one moment in a global supply chain which links producers from many parts of Latin America as well as Africa and Asia. Growing research on this sector suggests widespread female employment in NTAE production in many if not most of these countries, but further research is required to understand fully the processes underlying NTAE production. As work progresses, we hope more comparative studies will explore further the common elements of this employment, helping to inform better the analysis of gender and non-traditional agriculture. Ours is only an initial exploration of the analytical framework, which we have felt necessary to understand the Chilean case and contribute to further work in the area. We now examine in depth the specific form of integration of women into the fruit export sector in Chile from its evolution to its global implications.

Historical Context

3 Gender, State and Rural Transformation – Background to the 'Fruit Explosion'

An important aspect of women's integration into agribusiness is its mediation of the traditional and the modern. At one level, the commercialisation of agriculture has transformed social and gender relations in the agrarian sector, but at another level it has perpetuated traditional relations as an essential element of its functioning. In the Chilean case, therefore, we must explore the historical context in which agribusiness evolved, before examining women's employment in NTAE production and the specific effects this has had on gender relations. We need to consider the role of women in more traditional agrarian relations, and the process of change that preceded and was surpassed by the expansion of Chilean fruit export production. This will allow us to assess better the extent to which traditional relations have been transformed and the extent to which they have been reinforced and embedded through the expansion of agribusiness. We shall explore three aspects in particular: the role of women under the traditional agrarian system in Chile; the outcome of state policies in the reform of agriculture and the marginalising effects of these policies on gender relations; and, finally, how the boom in the fruit export sector led to the employment of a large female temporary labour force.

We contextualise this by exploring the background to the agrarian structures in rural Chile, how government policy towards agriculture evolved during the period of ISI, and the subsequent process of agrarian reform and counter-reform. The emergence of the fruit sector in particular will be traced from the formulation of the Fruit Plan, which put in place the initial infrastructure and investment necessary for the later expansion of the fruit export sector. We then examine the subsequent shift to a neo-liberal export-oriented policy, which finally enabled agriculture to take off as a major export sector in 1982. We explore women's roles in the context of these agrarian transformations, tracing the contradictory processes of inclusion and exclusion that led

36

them to enter the *temporera* workforce. Finally, we examine the growth of the fruit export sector under the military. Here, we concentrate on the period prior to the 'fruit explosion' in 1982, leaving the deeper examination of how the sector itself functions to the following chapter.

GENDER RELATIONS UNDER THE *HACIENDA* SYSTEM

Underlying changing gender relations within the processes of agrarian transformation in Chile were the traditional systems of landholding, originating with the institution of the *hacienda*. These were large estates, established during the colonial period, which formed the power base of the handful of families, who made up the oligarchy through to the period of the Republic. Outside the *hacienda* system were the *minifundia*, small and medium-sized family farms, while a further rural sector were *campesinos*, peasants engaged in subsistence-oriented production (Campaña, 1985; Campaña and Lago 1982; Furtado 1976, Kay and Silva 1992). As the dominant form of land-holding, the *haciendas* concentrated vast tracts of arable land, together with large resident populations of tenants and their families. The *haciendas* produced a variety of agricultural products, including cattle, grain and horticultural produce, for the domestic and international markets. Tenants, *inquilinos,* and their families usually lived their whole lives on the *hacienda*, under a system of semi-feudal and patriarchal relations with the landowner. The *inquilino* and his family worked on the estate in return for a remuneration which consisted partly of money wages, a residence, food, as well as the right to a small portion of land, pasture and a family plot. Thus, subsistence products were also cultivated in order to feed this permanent resident labour force. An important aspect of this system of landholding was its highly gendered structure, in which only the male *inquilino*, the head of the family, enjoyed the rights of tenancy. This meant that women who became widowed often were obliged to leave their homes to make way for younger tenant families. Widows then became dependent on other family members or the charity of the *hacendado,* or else were forced off the estate altogether (Valdés, Rebolledo and Willson 1995).

Agricultural production on the *hacienda* required extra labour on a seasonal basis. This was usually drawn from the family members of the *inquilinos,* who were resident on the estate, and who were hired as day and wage labourers. Wives and daughters from *inquilino* house-holds also worked as seasonal wage labourers (Bradshaw 1990; Valdés

1988, 1992 and 1993). Alongside the resident population of the *hacienda*, there was a substantial migratory population of landless poor who moved from estate to estate seeking waged work. These were known as *peones*, and both women and men found seasonal employment on the *haciendas* (Valdés, Rebolledo and Willson 1995). It is possible that members of both *minifundista* and *campesino* households also sought seasonal work on the *haciendas* in order to supplement subsistence production and household income. Although there is little direct evidence available from this period, studies suggest that seasonal work on the *hacienda* by members of *minifundista* and *campesino* households depended on local conditions such as landholding relations, the size and productivity of family farms and social relations in the area (Bradshaw 1990; Campaña 1985; Campaña and Lago 1982). The picture that emerges is of a limited seasonal labour market, drawing together men and women from different backgrounds: landless *peones*, *minifundista* and *campesino* family members from outside the *hacienda*, as well as the relatives of the *inquilinos* from within. This early heterogeneity is, in many respects, analogous to the heterogeneity of the modern seasonal wage labour force that will be explored in later chapters.

In terms of women's roles within traditional agriculture, we saw in the previous chapter that, historically, women's involvement in productive work in Latin America has been severely underestimated, and much feminist research on gender in rural areas has worked to end women's invisibility. In particular, their productive roles and contributions to the rural household as unpaid family labour or petty commodity traders had been virtually ignored (Barría et al. 1985). Within Chile, the prevailing gender ideology on the *hacienda* meant that women's role as a permanent resident worker was dependent on the husband's position as *inquilino*, making their contribution to the labour of the *hacienda* merely part of the total labour contributed by the *inquilino*. In *minifundista* and *campesino* households, similar gender divisions of labour operated, obscuring the important productive contributions made by women through their 'unpaid family labour' on the family farm. This gendered structure of labour and the invisibility of women's work made it all but impossible for women to gain access to land in their own right, a discrimination that persisted into the period of agrarian reform (Bradshaw 1990; Valdés 1988; Venegas 1995).

Nevertheless, within this division of labour a few permanent posts on the *hacienda* existed for women in activities that were regarded as 'feminine'. These activities revolved around the milking and the care of small livestock, namely chickens and hens. The vast kitchens of the *hacienda* prepared the food for the whole labour force of the estate and the majority of posts for women were to be found here. In addition, women were responsible for maintaining the *huerto* (family plot) as part of their household and domestic duties (Valdés, Rebolledo and Willson 1995). This was also the case in the *minifundio*, where the cultivation of the *huerto* and the care of yard livestock were exclusively female responsibilities (Bradshaw 1990; Campaña 1985; Campaña and Lago 1982). Women made further contributions to household income through domestic-based income-generating activities such as knitting and textile production and cheese-making, either for family consumption or for sale (Bradshaw 1990: 118). In addition, women held significant community roles within the estates as healers and midwives, with specialised knowledge of the medicinal use of herbs (Valdés et al. 1995). Given that traditional agricultural activities were highly gendered, it seems that the identification of work in the *huerto* cultivating vegetables and fruit as 'women's work' may have been carried through to modern agribusiness as rural women's subsistence production became commercialised. This may form the basis for the gendering of individual tasks within the production process.

The *hacienda* remained the dominant form of landholding until late into the twentieth century, while agricultural production also remained relatively unaltered. Much of the land was used for fodder for livestock or lay fallow. Indeed it is estimated that in the 1930s only one thirteenth of the land area was cultivated and no more than a quarter of this was farmed intensively (Collier and Sater 1996: 265). With agricultural stagnation it is unsurprising that rural living standards fell. Unlike urban workers, rural labourers were largely unprotected by unions and were forced to accept wages that were barely sufficient to sustain life.

The implementation of the import-substitution economic model from the 1930s onwards instigated a process of modernisation within the agricultural sector, introducing mechanisation and the industrialisation of agricultural production, increasing regional specialisation in agriculture (Valdés 1988). This had the result of deepening capitalistic relations of production in the countryside. As the *hacienda* modernised and became more efficient, the resident labour force was reduced, and remuneration in food and land rights was replaced with a monetary wage. The overall number of permanent workers on the *haciendas* decreased, as many tasks became mechanised. The number of women permanently employed fell as their specific jobs on the *hacienda* disappeared, most notably in the milking process, which became a 'masculine' occupation with mechanisation (Bradshaw 1990: 112). Up to 1935, women still appeared in census data as *inquilinos,* but their presence had diminished by the 1960s.

As agricultural production expanded, and the payments in land and food made to *inquilinos* were cut back, there was a subsequent expulsion of the population from the interior of the *hacienda.* As a result, the huge estate kitchens closed down, and with them disappeared the other principal sector of 'feminine' jobs on the *hacienda* (Valdés 1988; Valdés et al. 1995). The previously resident population joined the growing ranks of the landless, and often homeless, rural population. As a result, the levels of poverty in the countryside increased dramatically as access to land became restricted and dependence on wage labour increased, while the rural wage labour market itself had yet to fully develop. With the closure of women's permanent posts within the estates, women's productive work in the countryside became practically invisible, as women's participation in agricultural activities became simply characterised as 'unpaid family labour' on family farms, while their household income-generating activities became hidden within the domestic sphere.

By the 1940s, the state was beginning to adopt a more favourable position towards rural labourers. Family allowances and a minimum wage were introduced for *inquilinos*, although landowners were able to undermine the state's efforts by abusing their powers over the largely illiterate *inquilino* population. The power of the landowner remained virtually unchallenged until the electoral reforms of the late 1950s, which freed up the vote of rural workers, including women who been enfranchised in 1949. It was the political parties' desire to capture the emerging rural vote which provided the impetus for the radical alterations in the balance of power in the countryside, initiated in this period (Collier and Sater 1996). The decline of the permanent remunerated activities for women within the *hacienda,* coupled with the difficulties in obtaining land in their own right, meant that women were effectively excluded from reforms within the agricultural sector. While labour legislation gave minimal employment rights to permanent male agricultural workers, women were only able to find work as temporary and seasonal labourers. Increasing numbers of women from the remaining *inquilino* households joined the growing pool of landless labour, establishing an important seasonal wage labour force. Table 3.1 shows how the shift of female labour from permanent posts within agriculture into the category of 'unpaid family labour' led to a

Table 3.1   Changes in Women's Temporary Employment in Agriculture

Year	Total Women Workers in Agriculture	Temporary Women Wage Workers in Agriculture	Temporary Women Wage Workers as a Percentage of Total of Women in Agriculture
1955	133,656	9,992	7.48
1965	143,213	13,720	9.58
1976	128,101	17,840	13.92

Source: Valdés 1988: 396.

decline in the numbers of women recorded in agricultural production, with an accompanying increase in the proportion of women working as temporary agricultural workers.

The existence of female temporary agricultural workers during this early period is significant when analysing the transformation of women's roles within the agricultural sector. Their early participation as seasonal labour can be viewed as an incipient form of the *temporera* workforce and it also provides evidence of women's productive activities as paid seasonal labour outside the family farms. However, the agricultural labour market did not become fully established until the institution of the *hacienda* was largely dismantled, freeing the previously captive pool of labour from the interior of the *haciendas*. This occurred in the mid-1960s with the extensive transformations that were brought about by agrarian reform under the government of Eduardo Frei.[1] It was in this period that state policy towards the agrarian sector became increasingly pro-active, with important implications for women. The next section examines this process of reform: the far-reaching changes in land tenure, which laid the basis for the emergence of a dynamic fruit export sector, as well as the specific effect of these changes on gender relations in the countryside.

AGRARIAN REFORM AND THE GENDER IMPACT OF STATE POLICIES

As we have seen, productive and social relations in the Chilean rural sector were already undergoing transformations before the commencement of the reform process proper.

Economically there was a need to improve agricultural output to meet the demands of industrialisation and urbanisation under ISI. But such reforms were also often the state's response to waves of peasant protest and revolts which threatened to destabilise the political system. The reforms aimed to redistribute wealth and resources by increasing peasants' access to land and thus their control over the means of production. A further aim of agrarian reform was to break the political and economic power of the rural elites and to spur on the processes of modernisation, reinforcing the dominance of new, emergent, commercial, financial and industrial elites. These were based on shifts in class power and, as such, were simply not concerned with the issue of the subordination of women within a society in which the culture of *machismo* continued to prevail. Therefore, few, if any, state policies on agrarian reform included any suggestion of a transformative gender perspective.

In the 1960s agrarian reform was introduced in many Latin American countries with the support of the US Alliance for Progress. In the wake of the Cuban Revolution, the US perceived that the alleviation of poverty and inequality was necessary to avoid the radical social upheaval occurring elsewhere in Latin America. In contrast to the Cuban experience (and later the reforms implemented in Nicaragua), agrarian reform programmes supported by the Alliance for Progress generally emphasised the individual ownership of the redistributed lands, rather than a co-operative or collectivised system of production. These reform programmes aimed to defuse the revolutionary potential of the peasantry and to increase agricultural production for domestic consumption, thereby stimulating the expansion of an internal market (Deere 1987). Aside from the obvious benefits of acquiring land, the reform also heralded the beginning of a process of political democratisation in rural areas which had previously seen the landowners control the peasant vote and deny the rural poor a voice in national affairs.

Within Latin America, the role of the state in agricultural development has assumed diverse forms in different countries and at different historical periods. This has ranged from direct intervention through the restructuring of land tenure (agrarian reform), to the diversification of the sector through the promotion of non-traditional agricultural produce (investment incentives, tax benefits, preferential credit and access to markets), to outright neglect (by favouring the development of the urban, industrial sector at the expense of the rural sector). This diversity of approach can partly be attributed to material factors such as the limitations imposed by climate, local geography, the availability of a labour force, social and cultural context, and access to national or international markets. But it has clearly also been moulded by political ideologies and economic strategies, which have resulted in a wide range of systems of land tenure and land use between countries and even within countries. The latter has often resulted in tensions between rural areas and between the rural and urban populations, with diverse effects on women and men.[2]

In Chile the process of agrarian reform initially began in a very limited form under the Alessandri government in 1962 but, rather than directly tackle the concentrated ownership of lands, legislation was passed that permitted the expropriation of arable land which had been left idle, with government compensation. Although limited, the creation of this law was an important step towards reforming the agrarian system because it established the principle of redistribution of wealth (in this case land) which was to be reaffirmed later under the Frei and Allende governments. During the Frei government (1964–70), the process of agrarian reform moved forward more rapidly, although again not as rapidly as the government or the peasantry would have liked.

During the 1960s, the role of the state expanded, both within the national economy and in many other areas of society. Yet, it would be misleading to present state policies as being somehow homogeneous – on the contrary, they more often than not produced tensions and contradictions. Such tensions were particularly evident in the differential benefits that accrued to competing social groups, as well as the differential impacts on urban and rural populations, with related implications for gender relations. Although there was an economic rationale for agrarian reform, the aims of social redistribution implicit in Frei's agrarian reform were not evident in other sectors of the economy. As Castillo and Lehmann (1982) point out, there was no attempt to collectivise production in the urban and industrial sectors, nor to introduce structural economic reforms. In fact, the state was promoting individual consumption and competition within the urban sectors. In this manner, the promotion of collectivisation and solidarity in rural areas was in direct opposition to the revolution of aspirations in consumption which government policies were awakening throughout other sectors of society.

Within Frei's agrarian reform programme, there was intense government intervention in order to effect a radical transformation of both agrarian structures and agrarian production. This was done through high levels of capitalisation and an acceleration of the process of regional specialisation which was encouraged by specific policies such as the Cattle Plan (1961–70) and policies to encourage poultry rearing and corn production (ODEPA 1970). Several state institutions were established to implement these policies. The Development Corporation (*Corporación de Fomento* or CORFO) was charged with directing economic planning and national development. The Agrarian Reform Council (*Corporación de Reforma Agraria or* CORA) oversaw the process of expropriation, while the Institute of Agrarian Development (*Instituto de Desarollo Agropecuario* or INDAP) provided technical assistance and credit to the peasantry and the re-organized rural sector (Castillo and Lehmann 1981; Collier and Sater 1996).

Frei's government made a commitment to restructure land tenure by creating a system of co-operatives complemented by individually owned plots, by means of the Agrarian Reform Bill which came before Congress in November 1965. This was finally passed two years later, in 1967 and it aimed to extend intermediate sized family holdings and created the *asentamientos* – the co-operatively farmed agricultural communities. These were conceived as a transitional form of landholding which could subsequently be transferred to individual peasant ownership or continue to be farmed collectively (Castillo and Lehmann, 1981).[3] The reform bill established limits on the size of property and holdings in excess of 80 basic irrigated hectares would be expropriated. There was, however, provision for 'reserve lands': these could be retained if the landowner could demonstrate that the lands were worked efficiently, workers were paid at twice the minimum wage and shared in the profits (Sigmund 1977). In practice, the landowners could select the lands which they wished to retain (invariably they retained the most productive) and they concentrated their resources, labour and machinery on them.

Within this reform process, however, the issue of women was not addressed – a common failure of agrarian policy in Latin America at this time (Deere 1987). Bourque (1989) states that policy reform cannot incorporate a transformative gender dimension if the state does not recognise the existence of women's labour and acknowledge its economic importance. Staudt (1990) reminds us that it is crucial that policy-makers differentiate between women's contributions within the household, as treating women as analytically indistinct from the family or from men perpetuates their invisibility to planners and policy-makers. In the case of Chilean agrarian reform, while it is clear that women made an important contribution to peasant agricultural production and were employed as temporary workers on the *hacienda*, the agrarian reform largely excluded women as beneficiaries whether through direct or indirect means. This stems from the fact that the state failed to acknowledge the existence of peasant women's interests as separate and distinct from men's. Instead, policy-makers continued to assume that the peasant household as a whole would benefit from the reforms, although this ignored the existence of hierarchical gender relations operating within the household and disregarded the reality that not all members would benefit equally. Women's indirect participation through the head of household was not equivalent to their direct participation as beneficiaries in their own right.

Consequently, only the head of the household was designated the beneficiary and, according to the prevailing gender norms, the head of the household was assumed to be male, unless there was no male present. Support services such as credit and technical assistance were also targeted to the head of household, thereby effectively excluding women (Deere 1986 and 1987). This unequal and unjust situation was compounded by the fact that the benefits of reform were extended only to the permanent agricultural workers on the *hacienda,* who were predominantly male, and did not apply to temporary or seasonal workers, thereby excluding a significant number of women.

It can be argued that the state's failure to incorporate a transformative gender perspective into the process of agrarian reform is a reflection of the conceptualisation of social relations of the period and the inherent patriarchal nature of the state itself, given the influence of *machismo* in shaping gender relations. However, although rural women had been effectively marginalised from the benefits of agrarian reform by the state's failure to recognise their needs as distinct from rural men's, there is evidence that by this time women were beginning to be conceptualised as a distinct social group, at least by the political parties. These were seeking to expand their electoral bases and had become aware of the importance of gaining the support of groups such as women, students, workers and the peasantry now that the franchise had been fully extended.

Thus, the Christian Democrats' restructuring of agrarian structures was also driven by their political objective of increasing their electoral support in rural areas in order to compete with the more urban-based Socialist and Communist Parties. They aimed to mobilise sectors of the population which had until then been politically, economically and socially excluded. They targeted the peasantry, workers, students and, significantly, women, in their 'Revolution in Liberty'. Within this broad programme of popular participation, they encouraged the unionisation of the peasantry and the organisation of women (in both rural and urban areas). However, the ways in which rural women and men were drawn into the process of social and economic modernisation were clearly differentiated according to the state's perception of gender roles in the rural household. Men were viewed as productive while women's roles were severely circumscribed and reduced to the reproductive sphere, according to traditional gender relations. Thus, men's participation was encouraged through the peasant unions, while women were incorporated through Neighbourhood Associations and the *Centros de Madres* (CEMAs) (Valdés 1993).[4] These 'Mothers' Centres', as they were officially known, encapsulated in their name the state's perception of women and gender roles

For the first time, the CEMAs were co-ordinated nationally by the Christian Democratic government from 1964 to support women's needs as perceived by the government (Valdés and Weinstein 1993). They did not pursue an agenda that aimed to alter the gender hierarchy within the household. Instead, they continued to provide women with training in manual skills and were more concerned with women as housewives and mothers than as producers. State policies, combined with the orientation of the CEMAs, imposed on rural and urban women alike a homogeneous notion of 'housewife'. This idealised stereotype was based on the urban woman who was located firmly in the home, caring for her children and dependent on a male wage; an image that was wholly inappropriate to peasant women who were actively involved in productive activities (often unpaid) or who worked as seasonal waged labour (Valdés 1993; Garrett 1992).

As the CEMAs grew in size and number they created mechanisms of representation at the national level and as a result, they became increasingly politicised as legitimate instances of representation (Valdés and Weinstein 1993). However, women's exclusion from membership of the *asentamientos* meant that the social problems that arose were not addressed by CEMAs, and the CEMAs were never actually integrated into the *asentamiento* structure. Female membership of the peasant unions remained low, and even at times of great mobilisation in the countryside, by 1972 women's membership had not risen above 10 per cent of the total (Valdés 1993). Despite this, and even though women were being co-opted by a *machista* state through their traditional domestic gender roles and encouraged to participate through the CEMAs rather than the mainstream national political channels, at least they were now firmly established in the political consciousness of the nation as a distinct social group and potential political base.

Given the ambitious scale of the reforms, few of the expectations that had been generated by Frei's Revolution in Liberty could be met. In the agrarian sector only 30 per cent of the land had been reformed by 1969 and the demands of the urban and rural poor, the landless, young people, indigenous peoples and women were placing tremendous pressure on the political system. This was the situation that Allende inherited in 1970.[5] As part of its socialist aims, the Allende government deepened the process of agrarian reform, aiming to extend its benefits to those sectors of the rural population that had been marginalised under previous reforms. The new government sought to address the central imbalance between permanent and temporary workers on the *asentamientos* by incorporating the latter. Thus, the general assemblies of the *Centros de Reforma Agraria* (CERAs, as the *asentamientos* were renamed) were opened to all individuals over 18 years of age, whether male or female, temporary or permanent workers, single or married household heads (Hojman 1993a). In theory, these changes removed many of the barriers to women's participation in agrarian reform. However, as Garrett (1982) makes clear, other obstacles of a cultural and ideological nature remained, with the persistence of traditional expectations that women would carry out 'female' tasks such as cooking, sewing and taking care of children, and keep out of 'male' jobs.

This was largely due to the lack of clarity in state policy regarding the roles which women might play in the new socialist Chile. While the Popular Unity government (1970–3) viewed women as supporters of the class struggle, they were not perceived to be engaged in the struggle in their own right and much less *for* their own rights. It was widely assumed among the Left that socialism would lead to gender equality, without addressing the fact that the government's programme contained considerable confusion regarding women's position in society. Although government rhetoric was explicitly addressing women as a distinct social group, the possibility that gender subordination and patriarchy could exist independently of capitalism and class subordination was not explored, nor was the idea that capitalism could be potentially liberating for women, as entry into the labour force subverted traditional gender power structures in the home. In fact, in the publication *La Mujer en el Gobierno de la Unidad Popular,* which appeared in 1970, the government blamed capitalism for women's oppression by forcing them to work outside the home while simultaneously retaining their traditional roles within the family. Yet, it pledged itself to liberating women from the oppression of the home by increasing services in the community, rather than addressing the fundamental nature of gender relations (McGee Deutsch 1991).

Aside from the ideological battles to be waged, it was a matter of primary urgency for the *Unidad Popular* government to increase agricultural production to feed the urban population. Food imports were making inroads into already scarce foreign exchange reserves, shortages were becoming increasingly frequent and economic chaos soon ensued from the restructuring of the economy along socialist lines. Although under Allende the expropriation of lands was accelerated, the number of expectant beneficiaries continued to outstrip the supply, adding increasing internal social and political pressure on the government. This inevitable dislocation was compounded by external opposition and the subsequent blockade of the Chilean economy by the US, together with the drop in investment and capital flight, prompted by internal opposition to Allende from the elite. The Popular Unity coalition itself was divided in its aims for the rural sector: the Socialists called for the collectivisation of agriculture, while the Communists proposed a continuation of the *asentamiento* system. Inflation rose to unmanageable levels and the Chilean peso was overvalued on the money markets. The prospect of impending political crisis and the economic uncertainty which hung over the Allende government gave no incentive for private investment. The government had insufficient reserves to invest in the expropriated lands, while labour costs rose as rural wage labourers went on strike (Jarvis 1994).

Few of the political, economic or social reforms, which had been initiated in the 1960s and 1970s, came to fruition, as events in Chile took a radical turn in September 1973. Continued internal and external opposition erupted in a military coup that overthrew the Allende government and instigated 17 years of military dictatorship.

Having reviewed the broader context of the agrarian transformations taking place in this period, we shall now examine the origins of the fruit sector itself. While it is clear that the economic conditions and the political uncertainty surrounding the Allende government were not favourable to the growth of the fruit export sector, the early roots were nevertheless put down under the reforming governments of

Frei and Allende. We then discuss the period of military rule, which was when fruit export production finally took off as a dynamic sector.

THE FRUIT PLAN – LAYING THE BASIS FOR FRUIT EXPORTS

Although Chile has natural advantages which favour the cultivation of fruit, there were only sporadic exports of fresh fruit to the US and Latin America in the period prior to the 1960s (Jarvis 1994). The process of agrarian reform began to stimulate agricultural production, co-ordinated and implemented through CORFO. Between 1962 and 1965, CORFO laid the groundwork for the Fruit Plan which was intended to operate parallel to the agrarian reform programme. The Plan was initiated in 1965, but because of a severe drought it did not become truly operational until 1969. It was intended to run until 1980, but was cut short by the upheaval of the Allende period and by the counter-reforms initiated under the dictatorship.

The Fruit Plan was envisaged as a means of rapidly increasing production in the agricultural sector, with the aim of making it one of the most dynamic sectors of the economy. The Frei and Allende governments aimed to combine modernisation and high productivity with social development and a reduction in rural poverty and inequality. To this end, the Fruit Plan incorporated many elements, which were aimed at developing a modern, highly productive export sector. Studies to ascertain the percentage of land already under fruit cultivation were carried out under the Plan and future output estimated; the potential demand for produce in foreign markets was analysed in order to establish production targets; new varieties of produce imported mainly from California were introduced; and some large refrigeration plants were constructed in strategic locations to facilitate the transportation of the harvested produce. Health controls for export produce were also established and semi-subsidised credit facilities were offered for orchard investment (Jarvis 1994; Murray 1997).

CORFO employed highly skilled and innovative agronomists, who had been trained at the University of California, to design and implement the Plan. In order to sustain and improve training and technical co-operation, a ten-year co-operative plan between the Universidad de Chile and the University of California was established. From this, a high calibre faculty of fruit-related sciences emerged at the Universidad de Chile, providing highly qualified personnel to the government agencies and other universities.

The Fruit Plan sought to incorporate the peasantry as active participants in this process of rural change, both as beneficiaries of the redistribution of lands and through the expansion of membership in the newly created peasant unions and organisations. Such organisations were to be supported by training programmes to prepare small farmers for taking on leadership positions and for business management. The Plan outlined the government's expectations on the future collaboration between the state and the private sector on questions such as the provision of technical assistance and credit, the construction and administration of the necessary infrastructure for commercialisation, sanitation and irrigation (Jarvis 1994; ODEPA 1970). However, these expectations of co-operation were not realised, and during the 1960s and early 1970s, it fell to the state sector alone to develop the scientific and technological know-how in the fruit export sector (Jarvis 1994).

The public sector research and development carried out as part of the Fruit Plan established the groundwork for a dynamic fruit sector. However, while the productive potential of the fruit sector was considerably increased by the Fruit Plan, production did not rise to fulfil this expectation during the 1960s, although fruit exports rose from US$10 million to just over US$25 million between 1962 and 1970 (Murray 1997: 136). Government policy in this period was marked by protectionism, while the instability generated by agrarian reform also prevented fruit exports from taking off fully. These conditions worsened under Allende's government: the imposition of foreign exchange controls with an unfavourable rate for fruit exports, increased economic instability with rising inflation, currency overvaluation, as well as the increasing political disruption as land reform was extended all exacerbated the situation (Jarvis 1994: 248). Consequently, the volume of fruit exports actually fell between 1972 and 1973.

Despite these problems, it is important to note that during this earlier phase, the state provided the vital initial investment and planning, which could be built upon later. Most importantly, the Fruit Plan initiated the development of the technical expertise, and provided research and direction for future development of the sector, establishing the foundations from which fruit export production was later able to take off. It took the establishment of neo-liberal economic policies to provide the final impetus for the establishment of a highly successful fruit export sector.

THE NEO-LIBERAL MODEL AND AGRARIAN 'COUNTER-REFORM'

The Allende government was brought to an end by the military intervention of 11 September 1973. Although the military had previously intervened in political life for brief periods during the 1920s and 1930s, the 1973 coup d'état represented a dramatic break with traditional political practice, and the repression that followed was brutal and extensive. The military embarked on a total restructuring of the Chilean state and economy. Political, economic and social relations were radically transformed (Remmer 1989). The *junta* engaged in a political counter-revolution by eradicating the political system and mechanisms for popular participation, and by converting the state into a militarised authoritarian bureaucracy. The regime repressed all means of protest and dissent, the pluralist democratic system was dismantled and the military (supported by right-wing civilian groups) assumed the administrative and legislative functions of the state. The economic role of the state was greatly reduced and the power of the technocrats over government policy increased. This permitted the introduction of neo-liberal economic policies that favoured the rise of the 'New Right'. State-oriented industrialisation (ISI) was rapidly abandoned, and a 'shock' programme was introduced based on free market policies: privatisation of state companies, deregulation of factor markets, financial liberalisation and an end to protectionist trade policies (Foxley 1983; Meller 1992). The main strategy was now one of 'export-led growth'.

The military's strategy reversed previous redistributive policies, exacerbating the socio-economic inequality in Chilean society.[6] In the 1960s and early 1970s, agrarian reform had been an important redistributive tool that broke the political and economic power of the traditional land-owning class and empowered the peasantry for the first time. The military takeover heralded the end of this period of government intervention and agrarian reform, as the regime sought to reverse the process as part of its application of free market, open economy policies, embarking on a process of agrarian 'counter-reform'.

The partially transformed agrarian social structure was radically altered by the introduction of neo-liberal policies. Rural unions and peasant organisations were banned, workers' employment rights were removed and real wages dropped. The military government embarked on an extreme policy of agrarian counter-reform, dividing the lands held in the reformed sector into *parcelas*, plots of land large enough to support a family, and sold to be worked as private family farms (Kay and Silva 1992; Yotopoulous 1989). The lands in the reformed sector were allocated as follows: 28 per cent of the lands expropriated under the Allende government were judged to have been seized illegally and returned to their original owners; 56 per cent of the lands were retained by the reformed sector for parcelisation; of the remaining 16 per cent, some were auctioned to the private sector, and the rest went to private forestry interests (Yotopoulous 1989: 689–90).

Although peasants were initially targeted as beneficiaries in the counter-reform, this was not done with the aim of gaining the political support of the peasants, the landowners or the agricultural entrepreneurs. Rather, the restructuring was implemented primarily with the express purpose of eradicating the achievements of the agrarian reform and the political support for the Centre and the Left associated with it. Moreover, as the *parcelas* were to be privately held, there were no restrictions on their resale, allowing the establishment of a dynamic land market (Kay and Silva 1992). Owing to rising poverty, many of the new owners were forced to sell their land, permitting entrepreneurs and non-peasants access to land and attractive new agricultural investment opportunities (Bradshaw 1990; Campaña 1985; Murray 1997). This led to the consolidation of landholdings geared towards commercial rather than traditional subsistence production, freeing up the agrarian sector to competition and modernisation (Jarvis 1994; Murray 1997). Thus, although under the military rural poverty increased and development was uneven, the traditional structures of semi-feudal backwardness were finally replaced by modern, capitalist agriculture (Kay 1993).

A new agrarian professional elite was created who owned medium-to-large capitalist farms of between 20 and 80 basic irrigated hectares (BIH) which were often restored 'reserve' lands or lands auctioned by the government. (Kay 1993). The *parcelas* were farms comprising between 5 and 20 basic irrigated hectares. The number of the *parcelas* created was far outstripped by the number of families from the reformed sector, causing competition and division among the peasantry (Bradshaw 1990; Silva 1991). Those peasants who were excluded from the 'parcelisation' process in fact constituted over half the applicants from the reformed sector, and many were rejected for political reasons or because they did not possess the business acumen required by the selection process (Silva 1991). Those peasants who were rejected formed a new rural marginal class, and were only dissuaded from migrating to urban areas by record levels of open unemployment and the general deterioration of living standards in the towns and cities. Many of those peasants who were landless were also made homeless, as the majority had previously lived on the *hacienda* or in co-operatives. This displacement of peasants led to the construction of rural shantytowns (Díaz 1990). Here semi-urbanised landless peasants congregated, often in conditions of extreme poverty, forming the basis for a wage labour force which was ready to be drawn into seasonal employment in the emerging fruit sector.

In the new commercial regime of free enterprise many peasants who had been beneficiaries were unable to sustain their *parcelas*. By 1979, an estimated 50 per cent of the beneficiaries of the *parcela* process had lost their lands because they were unable to repay the loans they had contracted to purchase lands and machinery (Yotopoulous 1989).[7] As in the industrial sector, the repossessed lands and physical assets were auctioned at low prices to larger entre- preneurs who had preferential access to finance and who benefited from economies of scale. Increasing numbers of *parcela* owners were professionals, often from urban areas such as Santiago, with a strong commercial orientation. This practice led to a greater concentration of lands than was originally provided for in the reforms, although it never approximated the levels of the *hacienda* system. The parcelisa- tion of lands was very much in keeping with the neo-liberal objectives of freeing up the rural land and labour markets, while simultaneously achieving the ideological objectives of breaking down class solidarity.

GENDER AND THE NEO-LIBERAL RIGHT

The supremacy of the family in the military's ideology had important implications for gender relations. An analysis of gender and right-wing ideology is facilitated and yet complicated by the way in which conser- vative discourse has accommodated normative gender roles – male breadwinner, wife responsible for the home and the children or, at most, a secondary earner who 'helps out' with the family budget – and has integrated them into its ideology virtually intact. Yet, this does not mean that the Right was somehow neutral on gender, for its political discourse was highly manipulative of identities and roles. The New Right of the 1970s and 1980s gave particular emphasis to 'moral' issues which were perceived as essentially beyond politics, and one of the key issues within this framework was the family. State policies on the family can function as a means of social control by defining the

gender roles and boundaries that are deemed acceptable. These ideological constructs can, in turn, influence and be reinforced by economic policies which shape family structures and the roles of individual
members within the household (Tusscher 1986; Waylen 1986).

The strength of traditional gender ideology was demonstrated
during the period leading up to the coup, when upper- and middle-
class women organised themselves in a right-wing movement across
party lines, known as *El Poder Femenino*. This movement organised
successful protest marches of women ostensibly against food shortages. The first successful protest was the 'March of the Empty Pots',
employing a powerful discourse of 'private' women reluctantly driven
into the 'public' streets in defence of their families, morality and the
social order. In reality, this movement represented a much deeper
class mobilisation of the opposition groups and parties in defence of a
social order that the Popular Unity threatened to overturn. This
mobilisation of women around a seemingly apolitical discourse of
defence of the family and morality played a crucial role in bringing
about the downfall of the Allende government (Boyle 1991; Mattelart
1976).

Following this mobilisation, patriarchal gender ideology became
central to the new conservative doctrine of the military regime. After
the coup in September 1973, women became a strategic sector for the
military regime's discourses on order. The home became the symbol
of the nation, and the apparently 'natural' hierarchy of the home, with
everything and everyone in their place, was extended to the nation.
The *de facto* leader of the military junta, General Pinochet, proposed
that the head of state should assume the role of the patriarch, who
leads through knowledge and experience. The family was perceived as
the 'first link in the conception of the *Patria*', or fatherland, and
women were assigned the roles of 'educators and formers of con-
sciences' – if women could bring up the next generation according to
the military's plans, then the future of Chile was assured (Munizaga
and Letelier 1988). This emphasis on women's responsibility for the
moral values of the family, particularly the male members', comes
from Marianist ideology, as does the stereotype of a female who was
semi-divine, morally superior, spiritual, self-sacrificing and submissive
to men's demands (Montecino 1991). However, the military junta was
carefully selective in its manipulation of women's roles and the ideology of the family. Although some large families were singled out for
special praise for service to the *Patria*, the regime did not actively
encourage women to increase the birth rate. The links between

poverty and large families alerted them against disproportionately increasing the numbers of the working class, and hence the number of potential subversives (Mattelart 1977).

The military organised women through the restructured CEMA-Chile[8] centres. These provided poor women and their families with access to many of the social resources of which the state's stringent political and economic restructuring had deprived them: health care, education and training, welfare provision, a means of earning a living and a space to meet in the community. These benefits were often sufficient reason for women to become members, whether they agreed with the regime or not. The CEMA-Chile centres reinforced women's traditional roles by switching their traditional dependence on the patriarchal head of the household to the patriarchal state. Women's access to goods and services, traditionally provided either through the male breadwinner's income or the welfare system, had disappeared in the face of massive male unemployment and the contraction of the state. The subsequent increase in poverty meant that CEMA-Chile provided a viable avenue to access these welfare services for the whole household. However, the trade-off was that beneficiaries had to comply with the regime's ideological portrayal of women firmly in their traditional roles, as reproducers rather than producers, in order to access these benefits. CEMA-Chile, and through it the military regime, had considerable power over those women who attended the centres – even at the end of the dictatorship in 1989, they could boast 200,000 members in 9814 centres (Valdés and Weinstein 1993: 100). Despite these figures, many women did not support the dictatorship, and the benefits that membership of CEMA-Chile provided were not always sufficient to secure that support, as women would often join up and then leave, preferring to employ alternative survival strategies (Valdés and Weinstein 1993).

Perhaps the most forceful paradox emerges in the contradiction between the military's discourse and the reality of the economic crisis brought about by the effects of its neo-liberal policies on female employment. During the early 1980s, male unemployment had become a critical problem, with men's paid employment declining by 10.9 per cent over the 1980–2 period (Waylen 1992: 161). The problem of unemployment became even more acute following the collapse of the economy in 1982. Although the rhetoric of the military regime encouraged women's traditional roles within the home and family, women began to seek paid work in an attempt to compensate for falling family incomes. The female workforce grew by 4.5 per cent between 1970 and 1985, with a high increase in the numbers of women seeking work for the first time (Waylen 1992: 161; Valenzuela 1991: 168). The depth of the crisis meant that women were willing to take any paid employment that was available, notably domestic service.

This sharp increase in female employment undermined the ideological stance that women's place was in the home. The impact of the ensuing reversal of gender roles had considerable effects on households. The number of female heads of households within the workforce increased by 4 per cent between 1970 and 1972 (Valenzuela 1991), and by 1990 40 per cent of female heads of household were in employment.[9] This increase points to various factors such as the migration of male partners seeking work further afield, but more importantly, to the conflicts created within relationships as women became principal breadwinners, and unemployed male partners failed to adjust (Valenzuela 1991; Chukryck 1989; Boyle 1987). The increase in female-headed households was a trend that showed up in many parts of Latin America, following economic liberalisation and structural adjustment (Chant 1997). As a result, the discourse of the military, centred as it was on traditional gender roles and the defence of the family, was in direct opposition to the real effects of its economic strategy.

In contrast to the coercive mobilisation of women through CEMA-Chile, a grassroots movement of women in opposition to the regime was emerging in the same period. As a response to the economic crisis, women from low-income sectors began to organise in order to satisfy basic needs. These popular organisations were a collective response to the crisis, and, as they expanded in number and range of activities, they became known as *Organizaciones Económicas Populares* (OEPs), an umbrella term that covered a whole range of groups and activities. These activities included all-women knitting and embroidery groups aimed at income-generation, neighbourhood soup kitchens, collective shopping and primary health care groups. As well as fulfilling economic needs, these female-dominated OEPs provided women with a whole new experience of communal organisation and activity that led to the emergence of a strong gender and political consciousness. This grassroots mobilisation broke with the pattern of state-propelled attempts to organise women around their traditional female role, and led to the emergence of discussion groups around a whole range of gender issues which questioned the dominant gender ideology (Chukryck 1989; Serrano 1987; Valdés and Weinstein 1993; Valenzuela 1991; Vogel 1995; Waylen 1992 and 1995).

These diverse collectives formed the basis for an autonomous women's movement, which also included participation of middle-class feminists. The broad-based 'movement of women' perceived the clear links between women's subordination and the political, economic and social conditions in Chile, making specific proposals for the essential participation of women in national democratisation and development (Matear 1996). Although the majority of those women who mobilised in opposition to the dictatorship were from urban areas, rural women also organised and linked their demands to the pro-democracy movement through the length and breadth of Chile. Throughout its activities in the 1980s, the women's movement drew out the links between women's oppression and the broader issues of social and economic inequality and political democratisation (Valdés and Weinstein 1993). As will be discussed further in chapter 8, the most significant advance made by the women's movement was to move beyond immediate protest action to identify gender demands. Moreover, it was able to link up to the national project for democratisation, tenuously developing a strategy for political and social change for women within it. Towards the end of the 1980s, the various organisations became grouped under the *Concertación Nacional de Mujeres por la Democracia,* a highly important part of the opposition movement. This brought gender-based issues and demands into the movement for democracy, as a grassroots and autonomous social movement of women, incorporating women into the political process in a way which had not been witnessed before in Chilean society. The aims of the *Concertación de Mujeres* were two-fold and succinctly expressed in the slogan: *'Democracia en el país y en la casa'* ('Democracy in the country and in the home') (Boyle 1991; Matear 1995 and 1996; Valenzuela 1991). This 'movement of women' played an important role in bringing about the end to the regime.

The changes in women's roles in society during the Pinochet dictatorship reveal a stark contrast between the rhetoric of social conservatism and the harsh realities of economic liberalism. The state had targeted women through their traditional gender roles of wives and mothers, yet the regime's rhetoric was at variance with the changes that were perforce taking place in women's lives. The economic crises of the late 1970s and throughout the 1980s forced an unprecedented number of women to enter the labour force. It was in this context that employment of the *temporeras* expanded as an essential element in the fruit export sector, and their employment has become a notable element of the female rural labour force in Chile. We now turn to a closer examination of the factors leading to the expansion of the agro-export sector, in order to understand how the broad changes in Chilean agriculture have shaped the processes by which women have become incorporated into seasonal waged agricultural employment.

EXPANSION OF FRUIT EXPORTS AND TEMPORARY EMPLOYMENT

As we have discussed, it was not until after the military coup of 1973 that the fruit export sector began to reach its full potential. The military's strategy of export-led growth focused on the expansion of primary exports, especially 'non-traditional' products such as fruit, fish and timber, although the emphasis was on free market incentives to encourage this.[10] With the advent of neo-liberal policies, there was an initial sharp devaluation of the peso in 1974, which brought down the cost of fruit exports on the international markets, and import tariffs were dramatically reduced, lowering the cost of inputs. Much of the bureaucracy surrounding export procedures was cut, as the economy opened up to the workings of the market. The expansion in fruit exports was initially slow to take off, however. Some larger, well-capitalised producers were able to expand their exports and take advantage of the economic environment, such as David del Curto, a long-established Chilean producer who was to grow into one of the country's leading fruit exporters (Gómez and Echeñique 1988). However, much of the agricultural sector suffered during the early phase of the neo-liberal model as the exchange rate became less favourable to exports, and farmers faced competition from cheap US imports. Many peasant beneficiaries of the agrarian counter reform did not have the technical expertise or financial backing to enter the export sector, and there was a lag between the counter-reform and takeoff in the export sector (Murray 1996).

The counter-reform, however, created a dynamic land market that allowed investors easy access to land. As *parcelas* were increasingly bought by professional, entrepreneurial farmers with greater access to technology and investment, export production grew. Where previously agricultural production had been more diversified and geared towards supplying the large urban centres with foodstuffs, it now became a sector in which Chile's 'comparative advantage' was allowed to work freely, with increasing concentration on fruit production for exports. The volume of fruit exports grew steadily, from approximately

50,000 tonnes in 1971 (Murray 1996: 143), to reach 340,000 tons in 1982 (Asociación Exportadores 1992: 4). However, following the economic crash of 1982 the government was prompted to make changes in exchange rate policy, and to provide financial and credit support, which greatly benefited the export sector. This helped to stimulate the fruit explosion of the 1980s, when fruit exports expanded at a phenomenal rate. The trajectory and structure of fruit exports will be explored in greater depth in chapter 4, where we will focus on the period after 1982, once the fruit export sector had become firmly established as one of the most productive and dynamic within the Chilean economy.

Although emphasis was on the free market stimulating expansion, the benefits of previous public sector research and investment in infrastructure and technology, which we examined above, were now reaped by the private sector. In line with the military's agenda, there was a shift away from public sector to private sector research, with the larger companies employing agronomists and other technical expertise to facilitate further development. However some limited cross-fertilisation from the public sector remained. Although the university sector was cut back as part of the reduction of the public expenditure, agricultural research at the Universidad de Chile continued along with co-operation between academic research and the private sector (Jarvis 1994). In addition, in 1977 a joint initiative between the government and the private sector (specifically the ITT Corporation) led to the establishment of *Fundación Chile*, whose aim was to identify and promote new business ventures in Chile (Jarvis 1994; Goldfrank and Gómez 1991). Although this organisation had a broad remit, it employed a small number of fruit experts who contributed to developments within the sector, and provided research information. Hence despite the shift of emphasis to private sector innovation, the contribution of public sector research, especially in the early phase, was not insignificant.

As we saw, the agrarian counter-reform also laid the basis for the creation of a landless wage labour force, which could be employed as seasonal labour in the expanding fruit export sector. Military policy also helped the export sector to minimise labour costs. Initially, this took place as political repression effectively outlawed most unions, and with them the ability of the newly emerging seasonal labour force to defend labour conditions. The implementation of labour market reform through the *Plan Laboral* in 1979, and further legislative reform during the 1980s, codified restrictions on labour rights and the deregulation of labour markets. The legislation in particular restricted the rights of temporary workers relative to permanent workers, limited legal trade union activity and shifted away from collective bargaining to individual bargaining between employer and employee (Ruíz-Tagle 1991; Jarvis 1992; Barrientos and Barrientos 1996). The restriction of labour rights helped the establishment of a rural labour market based on flexible and cheap labour, with a large pool of landless labour now 'free' to take up employment in the expanded agro-export sectors, reinforcing Chile's 'comparative advantage' in the world market.

The demand for cheap, flexible labour led to the emergence of a demand for specifically female labour. We shall examine the gendering of fruit employment in some depth in the next chapter, but from the beginning some employers demonstrated a preference for women, at least in some tasks, and even in periods of high unemployment women would be employed in preference to men (Barrientos 1996). The reasons for this partly relate to the 'feminisation' of some tasks, which we shall explore later, but they also relate to the context of transformation. As we have seen, women were largely hidden under previous agrarian systems, with much of their labour being unpaid. One sector in which they did have a significant presence was among the most marginalised temporary workers (Lago 1987). Effectively, agrarian counter-reform and export agriculture greatly increased the significance of temporary work, and with it the level of seasonal female employment. Another factor was that women had no history of unionisation because of their marginalisation under the traditional agrarian structure, which, together with socialised attitudes of obedience and acceptance of authority, meant that they were seen by employers to be less likely to oppose the new forms of flexible employment being imposed in fruit (Díaz 1991). Hence, in direct contrast to previous agrarian systems, commercial modernisation of export agriculture was for the first time leading to the employment of women in their own right.

Agrarian transformation also stimulated an increase in supply of female labour. Under previous agrarian systems, rural households had been able to subsist on household production, unpaid female labour and the income generated by the male head of household. Agrarian counter-reform greatly reduced peasants' access to the land, and increased household dependence on wage earnings for survival. In the context of the neo-liberal model, male earnings were insufficient for many households to subsist. Increasing levels of poverty caused by the structural changes of the 1970s and early 1980s, forced many rural women out of their homes and into the *temporera* workforce. As a result, many rural areas households have come to depend on multiple earnings by both men and women, ending a gender division of labour in which most female labour was unpaid. The net result of agrarian transformation under Pinochet, therefore, was the emergence of the *temporeras* as an essential element in the fruit labour force, reversing the previous marginalisation of women's productive activities. However, the ultimate irony in this was the fact that the integration of women into the paid seasonal labour force came about as a result of the imposition of the neo-liberal model by a dictatorship with extremely conservative views on the role of women in the family. For part of the year at least, women were leaving the home to find employment at the cutting edge of one of Chile's most important export sectors, undermining both their traditional subordination within the agrarian system, and Pinochet's overt discourses on the position of women in society.

In this chapter we have seen how the historical and structural changes in agrarian structures since the 1960s, although at times contradictory and uneven, combined to favour the expansion of a booming export sector. The inevitable process of modernisation began to slowly dismantle the grip of the inefficient *hacienda* system, while the programmes of agrarian reform, counter-reform and agricultural development speeded up this process. The resulting changes in land tenure, accompanied by the expansion of urbanisation in rural areas, increasingly displaced peasants from the land. This led to the release of a growing workforce of both men and women whose households were dependent on wage labour. The fact that this labour is seasonal, and is only required for part of the year creates anomalies, which we will explore. But as we can see, the transformation which took place in rural Chile between the 1960s and 1980s was dramatic, with important gender implications, leading to the creation of the *temporeras* as a central clement in the labour force sustaining fruit export production, helping to underpin its success.

4 The Fruit Export Sector and Global Supply Chain

We have seen how the fruit sector evolved as a result of a combination of factors, but coalesced during the late 1970s in the context of the neo-liberal economic and political reforms. These reforms not only created a commercialised farming sector which could lock into the export market, but also created a large, landless, rural labour force which could be drawn in as seasonal workers to meet the labour requirements of the producers and exporters. This chapter provides an overview of the structure of the emergent fruit export sector, in order to provide the context in which fruit employment takes place. The chapter concentrates on the period of the 1980s and early 1990s, once fruit exports had become established. It explores the structure of fruit production and exports, which has formed the basis of Chile's integration into the world fruit market, describing the internal supply chain from producer to the point of export. We then examine Chile's position within the world fruit export market, and how it connects to the global supply chain for fruit. We explore how the relatively fragmented production process is linked to a more concentrated high tech export 'funnel' facilitated by international accumulation and dominated by large multinational firms. These interconnected levels are considered in the context of the constraints inherent within agricultural production, as discussed in chapter 2, which limit the extension of the industrial processes within agriculture, despite monocultivation and the dominance of agribusiness. The fragmented production process, provides the context for employment of the *temporeras*, which we then examine in more detail in the next chapter.[1]

FRUIT SPECIALISATION AND THE EXPORT BOOM

While there was a gradual expansion of exports during the 1970s, the 'explosion' of fruit exports, or '*el boom frutícola*', did not take place until after 1982. This is depicted in Figure 4.1, which shows that between 1982 and 1994 fruit exports expanded by 258 per cent from approximately 340,000 tons to over 1.2 million tons in 1994. The highest rates of growth of exports were concentrated in the 1980s, and since 1990 there has been some levelling off of the rate of growth of exports. A number of factors contributed to Chile's takeoff in the 1980s. Internally, the combination of investment in infrastructure and technology plus the commercialisation of agriculture did not yield its effects until the late 1970s. Although government policy at this time was export-oriented, it was not until after the economic crash of 1982 that exchange rate policy really benefited the export sector. There was also a lag between the expansion of commercial fruit farming during the 1970s and export output in the 1980s, as vines and many varieties of fruit tree take a number of years to reach maturity. Externally, during the 1980s there was a rapid increase in the Northern Hemisphere winter consumption of fresh fruit from the South. During this period, Chile was able to enter this expanding market with little competition.

Since the early 1990s, however, this market has become much more competitive, and the rate of growth of Chilean fruit exports has slowed as can be seen in Figure 4.1.[2] There are a number of factors behind this, both external and internal. With concentration on export-led growth by many developing countries, exports of non-traditional agricultural produce from the Southern Hemisphere have expanded during the 1990s, increasing competition in the sector. The return to democracy and success of the Chilean economy during the 1990s has also led to falling unemployment and rising real wages, increasing the labour costs of production. An appreciation of the peso relative to the US dollar during this period has further undermined the competitiveness of fruit exports (Murray 1996). As a result of these combined factors, the profitability of Chilean producers has been reduced relative to the boom of the 1980s, and there has been a comparative levelling off of export growth. Despite this, Chile remains a dominant Southern Hemisphere exporter of fresh fruit, and has managed to sustain its successful export position throughout the mid-1990s.

The principal fruit exports from Chile are table grapes, apples, kiwis and peaches/nectarines. As shown in Table 4.1, the largest export are table grapes,[3] which accounted for approximately 38 per cent of exports in 1994/5, with apples and pears accounting for 29 per cent and 13 per cent respectively. Production for export is distinct from production for the internal market, often involving different (mainly larger) producers, specific fruit varieties and using more sophisticated production and post-harvest methods. Some of the fruit which is part of export production enters the internal market, either for processing

64

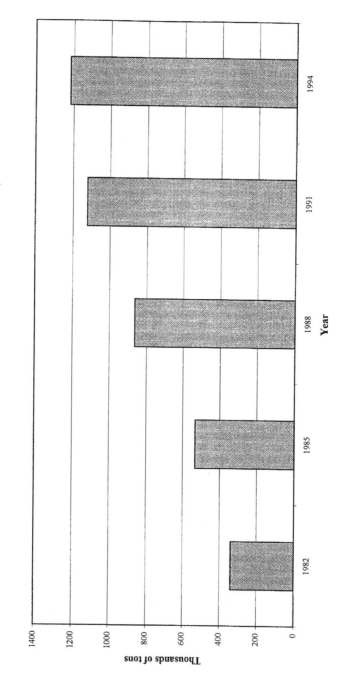

Figure 4.1 Total Fruit Exports, 1982–94 (thousands of tons)

Source: Asociación de Exportadores, 1993/4 and 1994/5.

(and possible later export), or because it is surplus, or not of the appropriate quality. Compared to many other exporting countries however, a relatively high per cent of Chile's fresh fruit is exported (Rabobank 1993). As Table 4.1 shows, 80 per cent or over of the requisite available grapes, apples and pears were exported in 1994/5, representing over 50 per cent of the country's total production of both grapes and pears and over 40 per cent of total apple production.

There are different levels of regional specialization in the production of fruit. As can be seen in Table 4.2, grapes are grown mainly in the III Region in the north and the central regions around Santiago; whereas apples, kiwis and pears are gown in the central regions and the VII Region in the south. The majority of all production is concentrated in the three central regions, V, VI and Metropolitan, which together account for 74 per cent of total exports (see Table 4.2). These regions are the most climatically suited to fruit growing, and were the earliest regions to develop an export sector. They have close access to the main container port of Valparaiso (and main airport at Santiago for airfreighted fruit), benefit from relatively good regional infrastructure, and are close to the main commercial and financial centre of Santiago. The later extension of fruit production to the north and south of these three regions has often involved the use of more modern and sophisticated technology in production and packing. The other main ports of embarkation are Coquimbo to the north and San Antonio to the south.

THE STRUCTURE OF EXPORT PRODUCTION

The early development of fruit exports in the 1960s–1970s had an important impact on the structure of the sector. Initially, most ownership was by domestic rather than foreign producers and exporters. As the sector has expanded, there has been an increase in transnational ownership among the export companies, but producers remain primarily Chilean. Many of the farms were bought up by professional producers during and after the period of counter-reform under Pinochet, and are run on the principles of capitalist production, specialising primarily in exports. The majority of production formally takes place on medium-sized farms. In the late 1980s it was estimated that the average size of fruit farms was 13–14 hectares (Gómez and Echeñique 1988; Codron 1990), but this includes those producing for domestic as well as export markets, and export producers tend to be

Table 4.1 Production and Export of Principal Fruit Commodities 1994-5 (thousands of tons)

Fruit	Total Commodity Produced	Total Available for Export	Total Commodity Exported	% of Total Commodity Production Exported	% of Available Commodity Exported	% of Total Fruit Exports(a)
Table grapes	826.3	551.1	480.7	58.2	87.2	37.7
Apples	978.9	502.2	406.7	41.5	81.0	28.5
Pears	320.9	215.0	170.9	53.3	79.5	12.9
Kiwis	242.1	169.5	47.3	19.5	27.9(b)	7.0

Notes: (a) Source: Asociación de Exportadores de Chile 1994/5.
(b) 100 per cent of kiwis were exported until 1991/2, see note 7.
Source: Pontificia Universidad Catolica de Chile, Facultad de Agronomia, 1993.

Table 4.2 Fruit Exports by Region, 1994–5 (thousands of boxes)

Fruit	III	IV	V	R.M.	VI	VII	Other	Total
Table grapes	4,279.4	11,485.0	14,527.0	16,244.9	15,392.2	482.4	456.1	62,867.0
Apples	0.0	25.4	481.0	1,111.9	10,271.5	9,691.5	989.3	22,570.6
Kiwis	0.0	0.0	5,576.9	11,327.6	8,258.8	8,206.2	216.4	33,585.9
Pears	4.6	8.8	385.2	1,848.0	4,393.0	1,869.1	156.2	8,664.9
Others	14.1	231.8	8,718.3	13,691.7	9,078.2	1,873.8	1,819.0	35,426.9
Total	4,298.1	11,751.1	29,688.5	44,224.2	47,393.6	22,122.9	3,636.9	163,115.3
% of Total	2.6	7.2	18.2	27.1	29.1	13.6	2.2	100.0

Source: Asociación de Exportadores de Chile, 1994–5: 125.

larger. It is likely that there is a higher concentration of ownership than indicated by formal land tenure, as many larger producers own separate farms, often across regions, which is not reflected in the data. It is estimated that in total there are over 8000 domestic producers who lock into the export sector (Gómez and Echeñique 1988; Gómez, 1994).

The producers feed into a smaller number of export companies, approximately 300 companies, with a much higher level of concentration in the export sector (Gómez 1994). Since the early period of predominantly Chilean ownership, there has been an increasing domination by transnationals, and only a minority of the largest companies are now Chilean owned. Table 4.3 gives a list of the main export companies in 1993/4. Dole-Chile was the largest single company, accounting for 11 per cent of exports. It is part of the Dole group, which is one of the largest transnational companies in fruit exports. It has a range of operations in over 71 countries (Gómez 1994), and a high degree of vertical integration including production, shipping, cold storage and distribution facilities (*Eurofruit*, December 1994, December 1995, March 1996). UNIFRUTTI, UTC and ZEUS are all foreign-owned companies (Italian, Arab and New Zealand respectively). David del Curto is the largest of the Chilean companies and the second largest exporter. It was founded in 1955 by a Chilean national of Italian decent, and has managed to maintain a leading position in a competitive global market through early innovation and investment (Jarvis 1994). The other Chilean firm in the top six exporters is COPEFRUT, a co-operative of Chilean producers founded in 1964 (Gómez 1994). In 1993/4, the top six export companies represented 46 per cent of total exports, and the top 20 export firms 72 per cent of total exports, reflecting the high level of concentration within the export sector (Asociación de Exportadores 1994).

On the whole there is a relatively clear division between producers and exporters.[4] Some larger producers are directly involved in exportation, especially where they have formed co-operative companies in order to export. Some larger farms are also directly owned by export companies, however anecdotal evidence from interviews suggests that normally this will only account for a maximum of 25 per cent of their exports, acting as a buffer if there is any short fall of supply from local producers. The main exception to this is the far north of the country, where production has been extended into semi-arid conditions in order to meet the high profit early demand of the Christmas market in the Northern Hemisphere (Gwynne and Meneses 1994). Here, high

Table 4.3   Principal Export Companies, 1993–4
(thousands of cases exported)

Exporter	Cases Exported	% Exports
Dole-Chile	15,725.6	11.2
David del Curto	14,293.2	10.2
UNIFRUTTI	12,902.0	9.2
UTC	9,931.0	7.1
COPEFRUT	6,086.3	4.3
ZEUS	5,422.4	3.9
Top 20 Exporters	100,918.9	71.9
Rest	39,516.8	28.1
Total	140,435.7	100.0

Source: Asociación de Exportadores, 1993/4, p. 157.

levels of investment in sophisticated technology and production methods, particularly the need for computer-controlled drip irrigation systems, raise the costs of production and investment, and smaller producers have been squeezed by larger producers and export companies (Murray 1996).

This relationship between a relatively concentrated export sector and a more fragmented production sector is partly a result of the national evolution of fruit exports, but also reflects constraints on the extension of international capital given the nature of agricultural production. Despite the use of biotechnology, computer-controlled production systems and cool chain storage and distribution facilities, fruit is still subject to risk from natural hazard as well as market conditions. Two problems which have confronted Chilean producers in recent years have been fruit fly infestation and drought. Any unpredicted variation in weather conditions can upset carefully planned production schedules (Echeñique 1990). International markets for fruit also contain an element of variability in price and profitability resulting from fluctuating supply conditions and exchange rate movements. Independent supply from local producers allows export companies to offset risk both in terms of variations of price and demand on international markets, and in terms of any natural hazard.

However, this formally 'independent' free market relationship between producers and exporters, is more complex in reality. Except for the few producers who are directly involved in exports, many producers are effectively in a dependent relationship with the exporters they supply. In the case of larger producers who have their own packing facilities, the export companies provide the boxes and other necessities for them to undertake their own packing, and once packed the export company oversees onward transportation and other arrangements. The vast majority of medium-sized and smaller producers forward their output directly to separate large packing plants owned by the export companies. The small and medium farms also receive technical support from the larger exporters, to whom they sell, reinforcing their dependence on them. The exporters provide the producers with the advice of professional agronomists relating to plant variety, use of pesticides, hormones and fertilisers, production methods and timing of output (Jarvis 1994).

The dependent relation between producers and exporters is further reinforced by the financial arrangements between the two groups concerning investment and payments. The exporters are an important source of financial assistance to the producers in the form of loans to purchase the necessary inputs at the beginning of the season and to cover any outstanding debts. Once a producer is indebted to a particular exporter, it becomes very difficult to break the link. The producers are not paid for their output when it reaches the packing plant. They receive their payment only after their fruit has been exported, and the time lag before receipt of payment can often take months. The price they receive for the fruit is formally determined by the prevailing price in the port of destination (Rotterdam or Philadelphia, for example), minus the percentage commission taken by the exporter (normally 8 per cent of FOB price) and transport costs (Jarvis 1994). However, as we shall see, fruit wholesale prices and exchange rates are variable, and producers are largely dependent on the price later reported to them by the exporter. Producers often complain about the payments they receive from the exporters (*La Epoca*, 26 August 1995). This situation is aggravated for producers who are indebted to exporters when their final payments fall short of the amount they owe, continuing their cycle of indebted dependency into the following season (Murray 1996). Since the early 1990s, with mounting problems of profitability, relations between the producers and exporters have at times become quite fraught (*El Mercurio*, various issues, August and September 1995), but despite this the dependent relation continues. In effect, therefore, the exporters have far greater control over production than their formally independent status indicates, but at the same time, they can offset risks which occur onto the producers.

The packing plants are dotted along the main roads throughout the fruit-growing regions. Many are highly sophisticated operations, similar to modern assembly-line factories. Producers send their fruit through to the packing plant of the export company with whom they are dealing. Once it enters the plant, fruit is fumigated and kept in cool storage facilities in which gases are emitted to repress the maturation process. During the packing process, the fruit is cleaned, selection of the best fruit takes place, some fruit is then individually wrapped (depending on requirements of the market of destination), and the fruit is packed into boxes or pallets according to fruit variety. Once ready, these are loaded into containers, which normally have computer-controlled cooling to maintain the fruit at the right temperature, and are driven to the main port of disembarkation (or airport in the case of a minority of fruit, which is airfreighted). Figure 4.2 depicts a simplified structure of the internal distribution chain from point of production to embarkation, also identifying the difference between the internal and external markets.

The export firms co-ordinate internal transportation and shipping, usually using specialist contracted haulage and shipping companies, and oversee export procedures. At the port, the fruit is subject to quality control and certification, which varies according to the port of destination, export registration and other formalities. The fruit is then loaded into container or reefer ships for transportation, where it is also kept in computer-controlled temperature and atmospheric conditions. Most export firms pre-book space on ships owned by independent shipping companies. Two of the main companies shipping fruit from Chile are CSAV (Companía Sudamericana de Vapores), which is Chilean-owned, and J. Lauritzen (Fundación Chile 1990/1). However, some of the largest transnational exporters, such as Dole, also have their own ships (*Eurofruit*, December 1994). Duration of the voyage varies according to port of destination. The two main ports receiving Chilean fruit are Philadelphia, which takes 12 days from Valparaiso, and Rotterdam, which takes 19 days from Valparaiso via the Panama Canal (Asociación de Exportadores, 1995; Fundación Chile, 1990/1).

The whole operation is subject to tight time constraints, given the perishability of the produce, and liaison between producers, exporters and shippers is crucial. The fruit has to pass rapidly through the chain linking production, packing and transportation as depicted in Figure 4.2. Much of the process of production and export is preplanned 6–9 months in advance to ensure co-ordination and efficient throughput from point of production to port of destination.[5] This

72

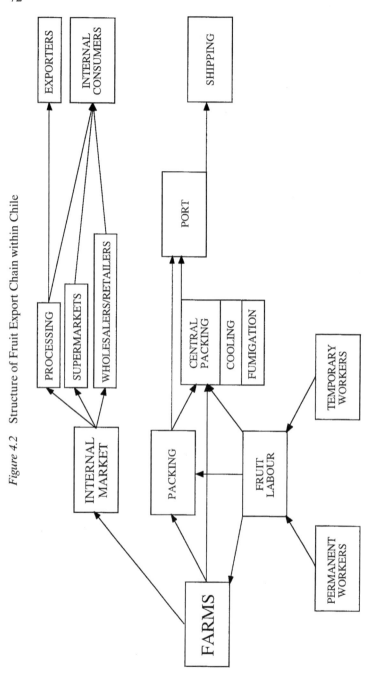

Figure 4.2   Structure of Fruit Export Chain within Chile

Source: Adopted from Fundacíon Chile 1990/1: 336–7.

pre-planning also involves importers and large retailers in the recipient countries, which we shall examine in the next section.

As can be seen from the above description of the internal supply chain, export production of fresh produce is a highly sophisticated operation, involving the use of advanced technology, communication and distribution methods. It is a far cry from the methods of traditional agriculture, or small-scale production aimed at the internal market. To a certain extent, agro-exports have thus involved the 'industrialisation' of the agricultural process. This is reflected in the application of a high level of capital investment, particularly in the export stage of the chain. Production itself is the relatively more labour intensive activity, although it is also subject to increasing control through the application of modern technology. But production remains subject to risk from natural hazard and market volatility, as well as being subject to natural seasonal cycles. Risk-minimisation limits the extent to which international capital and large export companies integrate into production, although in reality their control of production is far greater than the extent of their formal ownership. This helps to account for the persistence of a large number of domestic producers of varying sizes, the fragmentation of production relative to the export sector and the inherent tensions between producers and exporters.

CHILE'S POSITION IN THE GLOBAL FRUIT MARKET

Another important aspect in the growth of non-traditional agricultural exports has been the process of globalisation, and the shift towards export orientation by many developing countries. In pursuit of this aim there has been a search for new 'niche' markets, and off-season horticultural products have proved a successful growth area. This has been facilitated by the technological ability to export fresh products at much lower cost than previously due to changing production, transport and distribution systems. This has fed changing consumption patterns, especially the move towards the year-round consumption of a complete range of fruit and vegetables in the northern markets of the advanced countries. Chile, like other Southern Hemisphere countries, has been able to enter this expanding market as an 'off-season' supplier during the winter months in the Northern Hemisphere. It has also been increasing its exports within the Southern Hemisphere, including other developing countries, where social elites are emulating northern consumption patterns. Map 4.1 depicts exports of all Chilean horticultural products across the world in 1993/4. As can be seen, the main markets are in the North (the USA, Europe and Japan), but there are also markets throughout Latin America, parts of North Africa, the Middle East and Australasia. This shows the extent of Chile's integration into the global market, with its fruit exports supplying many parts of the world.

The majority of fruit exports go to the developed northern markets of the US and Europe. The main destination was initially the US, partly because of proximity to the North American market. It also resulted from high levels of consumption in the US, with Chile providing an alternative supplier during the winter months of Californian fruit production. Much of the technology, knowledge and production methods have been adopted directly from the Californian model with help from the US. In 1989, however, there was a slump in sales to the US when a small amount of cyanide was found in a consignment of Chilean fruit. The Chileans have always contested the origin of the cyanide, suspecting political sabotage, but the immediate effect had severe consequences for the sector at the time (Goldfrank and Gómez 1991). It was also a reminder of the dangers of a high level of dependency on a single market.

Following this, in the 1990s there was a diversification of exports to other markets, as can be seen in Table 4.4. Between 1989 and 1995, the total volume of exports going to most markets increased, but the percentage share going to the US fell from over 50 to under 40 per cent of the total. Chilean fruit exports to the European markets expanded in volume, but as a percentage of the total the European share has remained fairly stable at just under 35 per cent. Five per cent of Chile's total exports go directly to the UK, although the UK also receives Chilean fruit which has been re-exported through Holland and Belgium (Asociación de Exportadores 1995).[6] European imports have been facilitated by the development of more sophisticated, computerised container shipping, allowing a wider range of fruit to endure the longer sea journey. These exports were also stimulated by changing consumption patterns within Europe similar to those of the US, and the consumption of off-season fruit became more standard amongst consumers. The most significant expansion has been to Latin America, and other more diversified markets, especially Asia which is seen as an important area of further expansion. Despite these changes, as can be seen from Table 4.4, the US and Europe remain the primary points of destination.

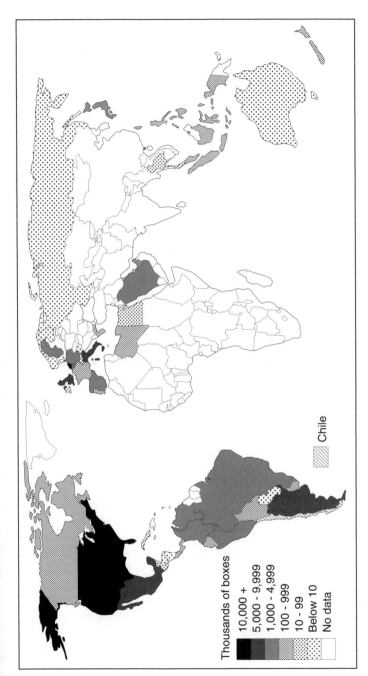

Map 4.1 World Map – Fruit and Horticultural Exports from Chile, 1993–4

Source: Asociacíon de Exportadores, 1993–4.

Women and Agribusiness

Table 4.4   Principal Regions of Destination for All Horticultural Exports
(thousands of boxes)

Region	1989–90		1994–5	
	Boxes	% of Total	Boxes	% of Total
US & Canada	58,255.0	50.1	63,626.0	39.0
Europe	40,485.3	34.8	53,775.2	33.0
Latin America	6,515.8	5.6	28,989.3	17.8
Middle East	8,025.3	6.9	7,034.3	4.3
Other	2,973.7	2.6	9,690.6	5.9
Total	116,255.2	100.0	163,115.3	100.0

Source: Asociación de Exportadores 1991/2 and 1994/5.

We have examined above the internal reasons for the comparative levelling off of export growth rates during the 1990s. The external reasons largely relate to the advantages Chile had enjoyed in being an early entrant into the newly emerging off-season non-traditional fruit export market. In the early phase of developing its fruit exports, the only other main competitors were South Africa and New Zealand. South Africa had political problems exporting because of consumer boycotts due to apartheid (a problem from which Chile was not immune due to its military dictatorship), and through the combination of new technology and a cheap labour force, Chile was able to compete favourably against New Zealand on cost grounds.[7]

In the 1990s the end of apartheid in South Africa gave it greater scope to expand its global exports. Table 4.5 shows the main exports of selected fruit from Chile's main competitors in the 1990s. As can be seen, Chile's main export is grapes, and in 1990 its exports accounted for 29 per cent of the total world exports of grapes.[8] However, as with all exporters of fresh produce, Chile only supplies the world market for a limited period (or 'window') each year, and its main competitors are other Southern Hemisphere countries. By 1994, other producers had begun to expand, particularly South Africa which had seen an 84 per cent expansion in its grape exports over the previous four years. As shown in Table 4.5, during the same period Chile's grape exports fell to 22 per cent of total world exports, despite the growing world market for grapes. With regards to apples, the volume of Chilean exports expanded between 1990 and 1994 by 10 per cent, but this was less than the expansion of 29 per cent in the world apple exports, and the Chilean share of world total fell from 9 to 7 per cent over the four years. It was only in pears that Chile managed to expand both its volume of exports and share of the world market. Overall, therefore, the picture is of an expanding but much more competitive world export market for fresh fruit, and in the early 1990s South Africa in particular proved a tight Southern Hemisphere competitor to Chile. With the global trend to export specialization, a number of Southern Hemisphere countries are now expanding their exports of temperate fruit and vegetables, including Brazil, Argentina and India (Jaffee 1993; *Eurofruit* various issues), which in the future could also pose a challenge.

Chile also had other advantages in the 1980s which diminished during the 1990s. Quality has always been an important factor in the newly emerging Northern markets for off-season fruit. In the early phase, when competition was not so tight and the demands of the supermarkets less stringent, Chile was able to sell fruit of variable quality. Increasingly, though, the dominance of supermarkets and expectations of consumers are necessitating greater rigour and consistency in quality of exports. In Chile there are many independent producers and exporters, and there is no export marketing board to oversee quality or quantity of exports. Poorer quality fruit slipping in is thus able to undermine the reputation and price of the majority of high standard exports. There has also been a tendency by Chilean exporters to oversupply the international market during their 'window', further undermining price. Unlike South Africa, Chile does

Table 4.5 Main Southern Hemisphere Exports of Fresh Fruit
(thousands of metric tons)

Country	Grapes		Apples		Pears	
	1990	1994	1990	1994	1990	1994
Chile	471.2	458.2	314.3	347.1	89.8	156.9
South Africa	54.2	99.9	202.3	245.4	79.4	98.6
New Zealand	0.2	0.1	201.2	201.1	2.8	4.7
World total	1,630.4	2,067.8	3,665.4	4,732.8	926.2	1,372.5
Chile as % of world	28.9	22.2	8.6	7.3	9.7	11.4

Sources: UN FAO Trade Yearbook 1992 and 1995.

not have a fruit export marketing board to monitor quality and quantity of exports.[9] Although there has been pressure to establish such a board in Chile during the 1990s (*El Mercurio* various issues), agreement between the producers, exporters and government as to how to achieve this had still not been reached at the time of writing. An anomaly in this is that continued adherence to the neo-liberal philosophy of unregulated markets, which helped to stimulate the growth of exports in the 1980s, is now hindering the competitive edge of Chilean fruit in the tougher market conditions of the 1990s.

Increased competition in the 1990s has been further aggravated in the Chilean case during the 1990s by a high exchange rate of the Chilean peso against the US$ (the currency in which most Chilean exports are sold). This has made Chilean exports less price-competitive and affected the export earnings of Chilean producers (Murray 1997; *El Mercurio* various issues). Chile has thus been facing difficulties maintaining its competitiveness on both the quality and price fronts. As a result, while Chile has remained a major off-season exporter of certain types of temperate fruit, and in the circumstances has succeeded in maintaining buoyant exports, it has faced greater problems sustaining that position in a competitive global market during the 1990s than during the 1980s.

THE GLOBAL FRUIT CHAIN AND THE INTEGRATION OF CHILEAN FRUIT

The transformation in consumption patterns over the past two decades has also played an important part in the growth of off-season fruit sales. Traditionally, the availability of fresh fruit was primarily based on local and regional seasons, with some fruit having a longer durability than others, and the year-round import of a few more durable varieties such as bananas and citrus. Fresh off-season soft and exotic fruit were confined to a small, expensive niche market. The combination of advances in the production of fruit, technological advances in preservation, storage and transport, plus advanced global communication chains, have all facilitated the rapid expansion of year round availability of lower priced fruit in the northern markets (Gómez and Echeñique 1988; Goldfrank 1994; Jarvis 1994). Consumption of most fruit is now largely independent of season (EIU 1991; Hinton 1991; Mintel 1994). This has been combined with changes in eating habits. On the one hand there has been an increase in the consumption of 'convenience' food, but at the same time greater health consciousness has helped to stimulate an increase in the per capita consumption of fresh fruit, which is also easy to eat without preparation (Arce and Marsden 1993; Barrientos and Perrons 1996; Bell and Valentine 1997).

The global fresh fruit and vegetable chain is defined as a consumer-driven commodity chain (Gereffi 1994; Goldfrank 1994). The chain is broadly divided into three sections: production, distribution (including export and transport) and marketing and retailing (Friedland 1994a). As we saw above, a large number of domestic producers (approximately 8000) lock into the export sector, and are mainly formally independent from the export firms. There is a much greater concentration at the point of export, and a higher level of ownership amongst the largest companies. Once we move through the export 'funnel', there is greater diversity in the distribution chain. The exporters tend to deal with a different set of importers in each country of designation (with the exception of some large transnational firms). The recipient import companies are then responsible for the onward supply of the shipped or airfreighted fruit. From the importers the fruit supply fans out through the wholesale markets to retailers, greengrocers and market traders, or directly to some of the larger retailers. Increasingly in some countries the fruit passes directly into large 'multiple' distribution centres with which the importers have established agreements (CEPAL 1990; Rabobank 1993).

The extent to which the fruit goes into the wholesale market or direct to the multiples varies between countries. In Europe the transformation in the retailing of fresh produce over the past two decades has been most pronounced in the UK. In 1980, 34 per cent of UK fresh produce was sold directly to multiples, the majority going through traditional wholesalers to outlets such as greengrocers and market stalls, but by 1994 this had increased to 64 per cent going direct to multiples, with predictions that the rise is set to continue rapidly (EIU 1991; *Fresh Produce Journal* 1994). This is leading to the displacement of the traditional wholesale markets. As a result of their more powerful market position, the larger UK multiples are able to play an increasingly dominant role along the supply chain. Supermarkets usually have established ties with a specified group of importers, exporters and producers. Through this they can exert direct influence right along the chain, and they have very specific quality specifications relating to size, shape, colour and pesticide residue which they implement and monitor.

An example of the supply chain linking Chile and the UK is shown in Figure 4.3. The upward arrows indicate the forward export of produce from Chile to the UK, and the downward dotted arrows indicate direct relations established by some UK supermarkets with their suppliers down to the producers. While UK multiples rely on the

Figure 4.3   Global Production and Distribution Chain of Chilean Fruit, 1993–4

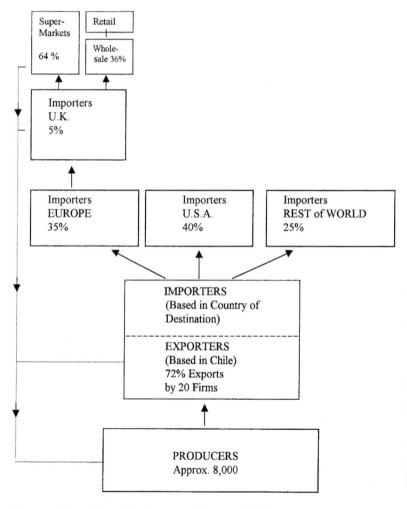

Source: Adapted from Barrientos and Perrons 1996.

import and export companies to oversee the supply chain, fresh produce buyers from the largest supermarkets also visit Chile to meet exporters and producers to ensure their standards and specifications are being met. Through their importers, the supermarkets pre-programme their supply up to six months in advance, from a rotating source of producer countries as the season shifts globally, maintaining a constant year round supply of a fairly homogeneous range of fruit. As multiple domination expands in European and North American countries, this trend is likely to be replicated in the main recipient markets. Thus, whilst heterogeneity in production and separation between the three sections of the fruit chain formally continues, changes in distribution and retailing are leading to greater integration in terms of co-ordination and control along the supply chain.

We have seen above that the producers are in a position of some dependency and vulnerability in relation to the larger exporters. An important factor within this is the way in which the pricing system works, with export prices not set until the fruit arrives at the port of disembarkation, and receipt of final payments taking up to a few months. Pricing is a very sensitive issue, on which it is difficult to obtain precise information, but Figure 4.4 gives an indication of both the potential volatility of external prices and how the final price is allocated along the chain. The volatility of both wholesale and retail prices is indicated in the first part of the figure, which compares prices of Chilean Flame seedless grapes on single days within the UK in January 1995, showing a £4 differential in wholesale price and a £0.40 differential in retail price between locations. In the second part of the figure we have taken the lower of the retail prices (£0.99) and made a rough estimate of the likely price structure of a 5 kg box of grapes with an equivalent retail price of US$17.4.[10] Assuming the retailer retains 35 per cent of the price, we estimate that the importer and exporter would receive approximately 26 and 28 per cent of the final price respectively (covering costs and commission), and that the final payment to the producer would be 11 per cent. Combined labour costs of the producer and exporter are estimated at approximately 9 per cent of final price. However, the total labour and input costs of the producer are estimated to be US$2.00, and if he only receives US$1.9 for the box he would be making a loss. In this case, he would be dependent on continued credit from the exporter or bank to remain in production, perpetuating the cycle of debt-related dependency on the exporters. Clearly, this example is based on the lowest of the retail prices, but it shows the problems that producers in particular face, given price volatility.

Figure 4.4   Estimate of Price Structure of Seedless Grapes from Chile

---

It is difficult to estimate precise price structure, partly because of the sensitivity of the information, and partly because of the variability of prices. An example of variability is shown by the latter:

Wholesale price of a 5 kg box of Chilean Flame seedless grapes on Tuesday 24 January 1995:

New Covent Garden	£8.00
Birmingham	£12.00

Retail price per pound of Chilean Flame seedless grapes for the week ending 28 January 1995:

Budgen	£0.99
William Jackson	£1.39

Source: *Fresh Produce Journal*, 27 January 1995 pp. 26–9.

The following is a rough estimate of the price structure of a 5 kg box of seedless grapes which retail in a UK supermarket at US$17.4 (most payments within Chile are calculated in US$) during the 1994/5 season. Chilean grapes are shipped to the UK in 5 kg boxes, and a box with an equivalent retail value of US$17.4 would sell in the supermarket at £0.99 per pound. (*Note*: The rate of exchange used is £1 = US$ 1.6.)

Rough Estimate of Price Structure of Chilean Seedless Grapes
Based on 5 kg box, January 1995

	US$	%
Producer	1.9	11
Exporter	4.9	28
Importer	4.5	26
Retailer	6.1	35
Retail Price	17.4	100

Source: authors' estimates.

Estimated labour costs in this are US$1.55 or 9 per cent of retail price (US$0.80 for the producer and US$0.75 for the exporter).

Chile is thus well integrated into the global fruit market, acting as a major exporter during its 'window' in the first few months of each year. The degree of control along the chain, both by large export companies and increasingly by multiples, also reflects growing concentration and domination by foreign firms, both at the distribution and, to a lesser extent, at the retailing ends of the chain. However, upstream at the point of production, the risks borne by the smaller, more fragmented producers are compounded by the form taken by the chain. Producers are not only exposed to immediate natural risks, such as fruit fly or drought, but the methods of payment and pricing structure also means they act as a buffer for volatile or low prices. Risks borne in the more concentrated segments of the chain by the larger retailers, importers and exporters can be partially offset along the chain onto the smaller weaker producers, who are locked into a relation of financial and technological dependency.

We can now summarise the key features of Chile's insertion into the global fruit market. Much of the initial investment in infrastructure and technology was stimulated by the Fruit Plan, and facilitated by the state. Under the neo-liberal export model introduced by the military government in the 1970s, the private sector became the main initiator of innovation and growth in the sector, and most production and exports were undertaken by national firms. The specific form of production, in which the sector is divided into a large number of medium-sized producers, resulted largely from the government strategy of dividing land into *parcelas* under its policy of agrarian counter-reform. As the sector integrated into the global market in the 1980s, the export segment became increasingly concentrated and transnational capital investment entered the export sector. However, this trend extends only very partially into production, and on the whole large exporters do not own production. By the 1990s, production is still largely nationally owned and relatively fragmented, whilst in the export funnel there is a high degree of concentration with transnationals playing an active role.

An important reason for this trend, we have argued, is the higher levels of risk and natural constraints which exist in agriculture. Given their formal independence, producers bear much of the natural risk arising from climatic variation, pest or disease. The specific nature of their contractual relations and the pricing system also means they act as a buffer along the supply chain for market volatility or price fluctuations. At the same time, production requires a high level of technical expertise, co-ordination and investment to meet export schedules and standards. This is provided largely by the export firms, with whom many producers are locked into a relation of dependence. The export firms are thus able to exert a significant degree of control over production without formal ownership. The export sector itself requires even higher levels of capital investment in modern technology, cool chain, packing and transport facilities. At this point the degree of 'industrial processing' involved means that the export of fruit appears increasingly similar to the processing of light manufactured goods. Hence we concur that the insertion of industrial processes into this sector of agriculture have facilitated its participation in the global agro-food system, but would argue this has also been a complex and contradictory process in which the inherent constraints prevalent in agriculture have been pushed back but not overcome. The heterogeneity of production relative to export is thus explained not only by the historical context in which the sector expanded, but also by features inherent to this type of agro-export production.

The context of globalisation has also provided another important dimension to the growth of Chilean fruit exports and the way the sector is structured. Changing consumption patterns mean that this type of produce is now consumed throughout the year, irrelevant of season or location. This has generated a global fruit market which is sourced around the year from different countries as the seasons rotate. The high degree of technological expertise means a homogeneous product can be produced in a wide range of locations, and many consumers will be unaware of the shifting origins of the identical seedless grapes they buy each week in their supermarket. This reflects the unifying effect the application of industrial processes and capital accumulation has had on agriculture and consumption across developed and developing countries. However, from the standpoint of any individual country, the season also imposes a natural constraint on their degree of insertion into this market, and, unlike manufacturing, the period of production is limited by nature. Transnational export firms in particular will shift their active operations from one country to another in line with the pattern set by the seasons to facilitate a constant global supply. All large export firms will seek to minimise their commitments and costs in any location out of season, whilst ensuring that their supply requirements will be met from that location in season. Chile links into this global market for approximately four months each year, and the structure of its production and export sector facilitates its role as a major Southern Hemisphere supplier of fruit. The more concentrated export firms limit their degree of commitment as they integrate into the production process, hence the relative fragmentation of the *parcelas* as they evolved under the military government's agrarian policy has not been substantially altered.[11] In sum, whilst industrial processes based on global capital accumulation have played an important role in the modernisation of the fruit export sector, natural constraints on their extension into the sector have also continued to be exerted. The way in which this sector is structured, and the timing of Chile's global exports, clearly have implications for the *temporeras/os*. The period of their employment, the type of tasks they are required to undertake, gender segregation and the form of their employment are all effected by the way the sector functions, which we shall now go on to examine.

5 Female Fruit Employment
– *Las Temporeras*

The transformation in the rural sector as a result of the expansion in agribusiness and the structure and operation of fruit export production together provide the context for temporary female fruit employment, and help us to understand the nature of women's insertion into the sector. Fragmentation in the production process is mirrored in fruit employment, and atomisation is most pronounced in the seasonal employment generated in both production and packing for export. This is reflected in a number of ways. Clearly, the cyclical nature of production determines the seasonality of employment itself, but employment is also very insecure within the season, and the temporary labour force itself very heterogeneous. The gender dimension is important in analysing the fragmentation and atomisation of seasonal employment, with women concentrated in some of the most insecure jobs whilst at the same time undertaking the most important tasks for attaining high quality fruit to meet export standards.

In this chapter we examine the specific form of employment in more depth and attempt to conceptualise the *temporeras*. We describe some of the characteristics of the *temporeras* and their employment patterns, highlighting the marked heterogeneity of the category of '*temporera/o*'. Finally, we consider the heterogeneity of the labour force as an essential component of the fruit export sector, and as a reflection of the tensions between global accumulation and a fragmented production process. We explore the argument that the seasonal labour force, and particularly its female component, acts as a buffer between meeting the requirements of capital accumulation in agriculture and offsetting the risks inherent in the naturally constrained and cyclically determined production process.[1]

EMPLOYMENT IN THE FRUIT EXPORT SECTOR

Any attempt at assessing the number of women working in the agro-export sector is hampered by the problem that national-level statistics frequently underestimate the rate of female agricultural employment, especially where much of this is seasonal. According to the official employment census, in January–March 1992 the male agricultural labour force was an estimated 807,450, while the female agricultural labour force was 88,860. If these estimates were correct, the fruit sector would not have had sufficient labour to maintain the level of export production. However, unofficial estimates of the number of temporary women fruit workers alone are far higher than the official figure for the total female agricultural labour force, and there is clear evidence of unreliability in the official estimates. In July–September 1993, the *Instituto Nacional de Estadísticas* (*INE*), in conjunction with the *Programa de Economía del Trabajo* (*PET*), added a supplement to the employment survey of women. In this, women who appeared to be economically inactive according to the national employment survey were asked whether they had worked at any time during the previous 12 months.[2] As a result, an additional 186,190 women were found to have worked in agriculture in the previous year, mainly as temporary workers between January and April (Henríque and Pérez 1994; Barrientos 1997). Unfortunately, this supplementary survey has not been repeated, but the result confirmed the gross inadequacy of official government estimates of the female agricultural labour force.

We therefore have to turn to unofficial estimates of the size of the temporary fruit labour force. These vary widely between 250,000 and 500,000 workers (Petras and Leiva 1994; Venegas 1992b and 1993). The reality is that it is difficult to get a precise estimate because of the heterogeneity of the workers and instability of employment. Some such as students work for short periods, and others form a semi-permanent seasonal workforce, migrating from one region to another as the season progresses. Venegas (1993) carried out one of the more conservative estimates of the size of the temporary workforce as part of a study for INDAP, a sub-section of the Ministry of Agriculture. She calculated that one permanent worker was employed per 3.7 hectares of land planted (whether or not fruit was in production), while two temporary workers were employed in harvesting and packing per 1 hectare of land in production. These can only be rough average estimates, as there are important differences in labour requirements according to fruit variety and the figures do not take account of changing productivity rates. However, using this calculation as a guide, it is possible to obtain a proxy measure of the temporary seasonal employment required to sustain production on a regional basis (Barrientos 1996). The results are shown in Table 5.1.

Table 5.1   Fruit Production and Estimated Employment by Region, 1992–3

Region	Total Area Planted with Fruit (hectares)	Total Area in Production (hectares)(a)	Estimated Permanent Workers Employed(b)	Estimated Temporary Workers Employed(c)
III	6,170	5,150	1,668	10,300
IV	8,390	6,890	2,268	13,780
V	34,060	27,370	9,205	54,740
METROPOL	47,650	37,700	12,878	75,400
VI	59,600	47,000	16,108	94,000
VII	26,510	19,610	7,165	39,220
TOTAL	182,380	143,720	49,292	287,440

(a) Area in production = Area planted – Area in formation (*INE Estadisticas Agropecuarias 1992–93*).
(b) Based on estimation of Venegas (1993) of one permanent worker per 3.7 hectares of total area planted.
(c) Based on estimate of Venegas (1993) of two temporary workers employed in harvesting and packing per 1 hectare in production, excluding ancillary workers (transport, etc.).
Source: Barrientos (1996: 128).

According to this method, there were a total of 49,292 permanent workers and 287,440 temporary workers in the 1992–3 season.

Venegas (1992b and 1993) further estimates that women account for only 5 per cent of permanent fruit workers and 52 per cent of temporary workers. On this basis there were approximately 2,500 women permanent workers and 150,000 women seasonal workers in the 1992–3 season. This shows a clear gender segregation between permanent and temporary work, with women concentrated into less secure, short-term employment. However, it also reflects the fact that temporary work has been increasing relative to permanent employment in agriculture and especially fruit production,[3] and that women have always been more concentrated in the temporary rather than permanent agricultural labour force. The increase in temporary employment was a direct result of Pinochet's agrarian counter-reform policy, but was also facilitated by labour market deregulation following enactment of the *Plan Laboral* in 1979. Female employment as a whole in Chile has been rising generally over the past two decades following deregulation and an increase in 'flexible' employment, of which temporary work is a part (Barrientos and Barrientos 1996).[4] However, the presence of women temporary workers in fruit has been one of the most marked areas of expansion of flexible female employment. Although comparison of official and unofficial estimates is difficult, the broad significance of this can be seen if we compare Venegas' estimate that women constitute 52 per cent of the fruit labour force with the government's estimate that women constituted 31 per cent of the total labour force in the country as a whole (INE 1992). Although traditionally agriculture tended to offer few opportunities for women's employment, fruit now constitutes an important arena for female employment in one of the country's main export sectors.

CONCEPTUALISING THE *TEMPORERA* AND *TEMPORERO*

The heterogeneity of the seasonal labour force within the fruit export sector has been noted by many Chilean writers (Díaz 1991; Rodríguez and Venegas 1989; Valdés 1988; Venegas 1992a). One of the features that many of these writers are concerned with is that the category of *temporeras/os* encompasses a great variety of women and men, working in different places, in different jobs and at different times of the year, which makes any attempt at characterisation of the *temporeras/os* a complex process. The designation of the variety of people involved in temporary work in the export agro-industry as '*temporeros*' clearly stems from their seasonal or temporary work in the rapidly expanding agricultural export sector. The idea of the *temporera/o* has sparked significant debate as it represents a new site for both male and female involvement in waged work. Several studies have been carried out concerning the specific roles women have as seasonal workers and the implications of this for transforming women's lives (Díaz 1991; Valdés 1988 and 1992; Venegas 1992a).

However, producing an agreed description of who can be classed as a *temporero/a* has proved problematic. Various classifications have been put forward, which differ in many respects. PET defines *temporeros* as waged workers without stable employment who work in the fields and packing plants during the harvest season when the bulk of the temporary labour is required. They are mainly women and young people who originate from the urban and rural areas and are seeking an income for the remainder of the year. The *Comisión Nacional Campesina* (*CNC*) takes a more political stance, defining *temporeros* as exploited workers, again mainly women and young people who are unable to organise while the *Plan Laboral* still applies to them (Bee and Vogel 1997; Díaz, 1991). This concept of *temporera/o* also carries a certain amount of political and ideological baggage as it represents the most unprotected sector of workers and illustrates the extreme effects of the neo-liberal model on the labour market. Despite the transition to democracy and the partial reform of Pinochet's labour laws (Barrientos and Barrientos 1996; Marquez 1995), workers in temporary employment are still excluded from the legal right to collective negotiation, and have not benefited from the reform of the Labour Code in the same ways as permanent workers. This affects their pension and social security payments, contracts and job security guarantees, giving employers total discretion to set wage levels and retain or dismiss workers according to their production schedules (Bee and Vogel 1997; Venegas 1993).

These ambiguous definitions help to convey an idea of the difficulties involved in distinguishing a clear sector or group out of the heterogeneity of these workers which make up such a significant workforce within the export sector. It is almost impossible to capture the broad differences among *temporeras* and *temporeros*, between regions and their fruit specialisations in general terms. Both women and men work in different industries at changing times of the year, taking on different jobs as the season unfolds. All these workers consider themselves to be *temporeras/os*: for example, those working in the packing plants and those working in the field carrying out agricultural tasks identify themselves as *temporera/o*s, while seasonal workers producing for the domestic market are also regarded as *temporeras/os*. In some areas the same workers will find employment at different times of the season in both export and domestic production. Some are semi-permanent temporary workers (mainly male), others combine fruit work with periods of non-agricultural employment or more often unemployment, some are students working in the summer holidays. Others still are *campesinas* involved in unremunerated labour who supplement household incomes by working for short periods in the export sector (Bee and Vogel 1997; Rodríguez and Venegas 1989; Venegas 1992a).

It is also not possible to define these workers by their place of residence, as they come from both rural and urban backgrounds. In addition, the different varieties of fruit and the regional specialisation mean that there is some migration from north to south following the harvests and from urban centres to the countryside to take advantage of the wage-earning potential of work in the agro-export sector. This reflects progression of the season from north to south, and substantial regional variation in temporary fruit employment resulting from the different regional concentrations in production. Migration of fruit workers takes place mainly from the centre to the north, where the season takes place earlier and suffers a labour shortage, and where larger companies provide accommodation for the workers. These migrants then return to their own regions to complete the season, so extending their period of fruit employment for up to six months in total. Seventy-eight per cent of this employment is concentrated in the three central regions around Santiago (V, VI and Metropolitan Regions), as shown in Table 5.1. In these regions, there is an intense demand for labour at the height of the season, leading to urban–rural migration in search of fruit employment. Most of this 'migration' takes place on a daily basis, with employers bussing workers out from larger towns, and even Santiago, at the height of the season. Some urban workers stay with relatives or friends in the countryside during the season to take up fruit employment. One study found that 'about 30 per cent of Chile's agricultural work force during the harvest season is urban or semi-urban in origin, a figure that increases to 50 per cent when one includes the country's central valley, the main fruit growing region' (Barham et al. 1992: 65). In effect, there are both push and pull factors prompting migration. The pull factors are the increased employment opportunities in the fruit growing sectors, while the push factors are the poorly paid employment opportunities in the places of origin.

WHO ARE THE *TEMPORERAS*?

The extreme heterogeneity of the temporary workforce with regards to age and family situation leads to significant problems of conceptualisation. However certain characteristics can be determined even within such a varied and complex group of people. The results of several different studies suggest that to a large extent *temporeras* are married with children and that approximately one fifth are household heads. The results of three studies (Bee 1996; Díaz 1991; Rodríguez and Venegas 1991) are shown in Table 5.2. In all three cases, it was found that the majority (between 62.5 and 68 per cent) of women workers are between 20 and 39 years of age. In comparison, Rodríguez and Venegas, who surveyed both men and women temporary workers,[5] found that 76 per cent of men were less than 30 years

Table 5.2   Marital Status and Age of Temporary Fruit Workers

Marital Status (% of sample in each study)

Status	Rodgríguez and Venegas(a) Men %	Women %	Díaz(b) Women %	Bee(c) Women %
Single	65	37	34.0	37.8
Married/cohabiting	29	47	61.5	59.6
Widowed/separated	6	16	4.5	2.6
	100	100	100.0	100.0

Age Range (% of sample in each study)

Age Range Years	Rodríguez and Venegas(a) Male %	Female %	Díaz(b) Female %	Bee(c) Female %
19 and less	34	17	9.1	18.8
20–9	42	38	40.8	38.7
30–9	13	30	27.3	23.7
40–9	6	9	13.7	12.5
50 Plus	5	6	9.1	6.3
	100	100	100.0	100.0

Notes:
(a) Rodríguez and Venegas (1991). Based on a study of temporary workers in six valleys in Regions III, IV, Metropolitan, VI, and VII. Sample size: 220 male temporary workers and 238 female temporary workers.
(b) Díaz (1991). Based on a study of women temporary workers in three localities in the IV, VI and VII Regions. Sample size 44.
(c) Bee (1996). Based on a study of women temporary workers in the Guatualame valley, Region IV. Sample size: 80 women in two villages.

old. Based on her work with Rodgriguez, Venegas estimated that for female *temporeras* the average age was 29 years, which reflected the perception that the *temporeras 'andan en los treinta'* (are around 30) while for male *temporeros* the average age was 24 years (Venegas, 1992a: 102). For both women and men the average age increases if we consider those who work as temporary labour on the export farms and also work on their own farms, or those who combine temporary agricultural work with employment in other economic sectors. However, the average age is lowered in the summer months by the influx of students during the harvest period, using the break from education to earn money (there are no student grants in Chile, and students have to pay fees).

An overall profile of the marital status of the *temporeras* in the Chilean fruit export sector is also shown in Table 5.2. In all three case studies, it was found that a minority of women, ranging from 34 to 38 per cent were single. This compares to Rodríguez and Venegas' finding that the largest proportion of men were single. There is some difference between the case studies in the proportion of women married/cohabiting relative to widowed/separated, but given the small sample sizes, no significant conclusions can be drawn from this. All three case studies found that the largest proportion of women were married or cohabiting (ranging from 47 to 61.5 per cent). Rodríguez and Venegas (1991), whose research was based on the largest sample, found that 16 per cent of women temporary workers were widowed or separated, and that 19 per cent of women were head of household. This is higher than the national figure of 14 per cent female-headed households (Venegas 1992a: 103), and in Venegas' view the majority of female-headed households are accounted for by the loss of a male partner. She found more female-headed households in the urban areas than in the rural areas, and that almost one third of what she describes as '*temporeras múltiples*' (i.e. women temporary workers who take up other occupations out of the fruit season) are heads of household.

Research suggests that the majority of *temporeras/os* are out of work for at least part of the 'blue months' (when fruit is out of season), although this varies according to region, with less unemployment in the centre around Santiago than in the north or south. Male temporary workers are more likely to find alternative employment during this period than women, but according to Venegas (1992a) the majority of women *temporeras* would take up work were it available, giving the lie to the view of many employers that most women work for 'pin money' (PREALC 1990).

Venegas (1992) suggests that certain dynamics of labour supply and demand are peculiar to the Chilean case. The presence of older married women in the workforce suggests that there is no particular preference for young single women, or that any preference that does exist is outweighed by the advantages of employing local, more mature and married women. This relates more specifically to female *temporeras*, given that male *temporeros* are more commonly younger, single men, although the latter could result from the greater availability of alternative employment for men than women. This contrasts with previous studies of export industries in Latin America and South East Asia which have shown that in many cases young, single and often migrant women are preferred as employees over older married women (Arizpe and Aranda 1981; Elson and Pearson 1981; Fernandez-Kelly 1994). That this pattern is not reflected in the Chilean case is partly a result of the fact that the high degree of export specialisation in the central regions stimulates a significant increase in the seasonal demand for labour. Female employment (which is usually for a shorter period than male employment) occurs when the demand for labour is at its height, and employers are restricted in their choice of whom to employ. Married women who return to the home each year have proved to be a very reliable source of seasonal labour, and their repetitive work as annual seasonal labour makes them an experienced group of workers (Barrientos 1996; Venegas 1992a). It is possible that as export specialisation becomes more generalised in other countries (rather than occupying small pockets, as is the case of export processing zones), and as the use of 'flexible' wage labour increases as in Chilean agriculture, there will be a greater tendency to employ older married women in export production, although this is likely to vary from case to case.

GENDER SEGREGATION IN THE AGRO-EXPORT SECTORS

The openness of the labour market under the neo-liberal model does not necessarily bring women greater opportunities within it. Employment segregation and sex-typing remain common and in many areas of work, jobs continue to be strongly segregated. Therefore, the experience of women in the labour market requires an understanding of the gendered character of the market itself. Social norms of behaviour help shape ideas of who is likely to be suitable for certain jobs and these ideas have a strong gender component. As Kabeer and Humphrey (1993: 92) point out: 'Managers have very clear stereotypes of the kinds of work for which men and women are most suited, and workers themselves have very clear understandings of the work they are most suited to and would prefer to do.'

This acceptance and persistence of gender stereotypes within the labour force is demonstrated clearly in the relative importance of male and female employment in different agro-export sectors. In the forestry sector of southern Chile women have to a large extent been marginalised from any new labour opportunities, while in the fruit sector women have come to play a significant, even vital role. The explanation for this difference lies in the specific tasks associated with the production processes in these different export industries. In Chile, research from the early 1980s showed that women's participation in agriculture varies according to regional dynamic, social class and predominant local agricultural activity (Lago 1992: 263). Under the military's neo-liberal model the forestry sector expanded rapidly, especially in the south, and in so doing created a new landless population by forcing many rural families to sell their land to large lumber companies. The production process was then reorganised to increase efficiency, resulting in a decrease in the number of permanent employees. At the same time the increased use of sophisticated technology in the production process has made much of the labour force redundant. Moreover, the forestry sector has not favoured a female labour force because the technology used in the industry has always been associated with men. So the few available employment opportunities in the industry have gone, in the majority of instances, to men (Lago 1987).

This contrasts dramatically with the situation vis-à-vis female employment in the fruit export sector. Many studies have shown that women have become increasingly incorporated into the labour markets associated with fruit export production in Chile because of employer perceptions about their 'feminine skills' in handling delicate fruit (Barría et al. 1985; Barrientos 1996 and 1997; Bee and Vogel 1997; Díaz 1991; Lago 1987 and 1992; Medel et al. 1989; Valdés 1988; Venegas 1992a). Here, direct parallels can be drawn between the labour demands associated with fruit export production and those of certain export industries in South East Asia and Mexico. As we saw in chapter 2, debates around the new international division of labour have highlighted the importance attached by many capitalist enterprises to a range of perceived and often imaginary 'female' characteristics, such as manual dexterity, passivity and non-unionisation (Elson and Pearson 1981). These 'feminine traits', it has been argued, derive from the socialisation women receive in the home and are associated with ideas of the 'traditional' female role. With specific reference to fruit export production in Chile, these ideas have been widely accepted and articulated by employers and have also been echoed in the opinions of the temporeras themselves. Díaz (1991) found that four factors were viewed as being especially important in explaining the employment of women in certain tasks in fruit production and that these factors (however mythical) were accepted by both the *temporeras* and their employers:

1. The majority of the tasks associated with fruit export require little physical strength.
2. The natural and socialised manual dexterity of women is extremely important in export fruit production and forms an important component of the employers' comparative advantage in the market-place.
3. Women have a responsible attitude towards work.
4. Women have a greater respect for authority than men and, coupled with the constraints of the family, are therefore less likely to question their working conditions.

(Díaz 1991: 51).

Díaz (1991) also develops a useful schema for thinking about the range of specific tasks involved in the agro-export labour markets. The tasks have been divided into three sections: tasks and personnel in the fields, tasks and personnel in the packing plants, and tasks and personnel in the refrigeration process. The list of tasks is shown in Figure 5.1. The list is by no means exhaustive, but it highlights the variety of skills required in the production process (for many fresh products) and also to a limited extent begins to suggest how these tasks have become gendered.

A number of studies have found that women tend to be concentrated within the packing plants rather than in field work during the harvest (Díaz 1991; Medel et al. 1989; Rodriguez and Venegas 1989; Valdés 1988 and 1992; Venegas 1992a). An example of the distribution by sex between fieldwork and packing is given in Table 5.3. Women are perceived as possessing greater manual dexterity, which is an advantage in minimising damage to the fruit. Women are also regarded as being able to maintain high levels of quality and productivity on the packing line, which they are able to sustain for longer periods than men. Women tend to be concentrated in certain tasks within the packing plants which utilise these notional characteristics. These tasks within the plant include the cleaning, selection and packing of the fruit, and women are employed almost exclusively for these jobs.

Conversely, certain tasks tend to be the sole preserve of men. For example, the tasks of the *mozo*, which are described as transferring

Figure 5.1   Division of Tasks of the Temporary Workers

A.   Tasks and Personnel in the Fields

1.   Pruning (*Podadores*)
2.   Spraying (*Desinfectadores*)
3.   Thinning (*Raleadores*)
4.   Pinching out (*Desbrotadores*)
5.   Tying (*Amarradores*)
6.   Harvesting (*Cosechadores*)

B.   Tasks and Personnel in Packing

1.   Selection (*Seleccionadoras*)
2.   Cleaning (*Limpiadoras*)
3.   Packing (*Embaladoras*)
4.   Recording (*Anotadoras*)
5.   Weighing (*Pesadoras*)
6.   Labelling (*Etiquetadoras*)
7.   Carrying (*Mozos*)
8.   Sealing (*Selladores*)
9.   Pallet handling (*Paletizadores*)
10. Pallet winchers (*Enhuinchadores*)
11. Controllers (*Tarjadores*)
12. Line supervisors (*Jefes de Línea*)
13. Packing supervisors (*Jefes de Packing*)
14. Statisticians (*Estadísticos*)
15. Assistants (*Ayudantes*)

C.   Tasks and Personnel in Cooling/Refrigeration

1.   Refrigeration supervisors (*Jefes de Cámara*)
2.   Fork lift truck operators (*Horquilleros*)
3.   Machine operators (*Operadores de Salas de Máquinas*)
4.   Temperature controllers (*Temperatureros*)

Source: Díaz 1991: 68, authors' own translation.

the boxes so that they can be filled by the cleaners and then replacing them with empty boxes, are undertaken by young men. Other such 'male' tasks include making the boxes, affixing the lids once the fruit has been packed and loading the boxes ready for transport. However, certain tasks (particularly in the fields such as pruning and attaching the vines to supports) may be undertaken by either men or women.

    The gender segregation of employment in the fruit industry is well illustrated by the results of research in the Limarí Valley in the

Table 5.3   Distribution of the Fruit Labour Force by Sex

Sex	Fields (%)	Packing Plants (%)
Women	28.3	76.1
Men	71.7	23.9
Total	100.0	100.0

Source: Díaz 1991: 50.

semi-arid Norte Chico to the north. Many areas in this region are dominated by the production of export table grapes, a production process with strong evidence of sex-typing and gender stereotypes. Table 5.4 illustrates that certain tasks are undertaken specifically by women and others by men. The results indicate that the tasks involving handling the fruit from harvest to packing are undertaken by women: they are responsible for cleaning, selecting and wrapping the grapes. Men are responsible for the fruit once it has been packed into boxes. The work that appears to be suitable for both women and men includes many of the tasks out in the fields such as pruning, while the technical jobs from tractor driving to running the irrigation systems are the responsibility of men.

The production process in any given export crop is made up of several discrete stages, which require different amounts of labour.

Table 5.4   The Percentages of Women and Men with Specific Jobs in the Grape Economy, 1993–4

Specific Job	Women	Men
Grape cleaning	38.6	0
Grape wrapping	11.4	0
Selection of grapes	10.0	0
Various tasks in packing plants and parronales*	40.0	75.0
Technical work – Irrigation,	0	8.4
Grape cutter	0	16.6

* Various tasks includes a combination of work in the fields and packing plants. e.g. pruning, cleaning, and selecting the fruit.
Source: Bee 1996.

What the evidence appears to show is that, while women are drawn into production at the height of the season partly to meet the shortage of labour, there is also clear gender segregation within that period. Women are more likely to be associated with tasks that prepare the fruit for the high quality presentation required by the export markets. Women have traditionally been associated with the handling, preparation and presentation of food within the household, and as the importance of these tasks has grown in commercial export agriculture, women who have been drawn into waged employment are assigned tasks linked to this socially constructed 'feminine' association. In this respect, women's socialisation in the household, and the gendered labour market, guide women and men towards different tasks within the same production process.

A further consequence of gender segregation is that women tend to have a shorter and more concentrated working season than men (Rodríguez and Venegas 1989; Venegas 1992a). This is both because they are linked to tasks that are concentrated on the final preparation of fruit for export at the height of the season, and because these take place when female labour is essential to meeting labour shortages. This is not to suggest, though, that men do not also experience the significant seasonality of employment opportunities, but their seasonal employment does span a longer period and they are more likely to be employed on a permanent or semi-permanent basis.

The extent of concentration of employment is variable, though, and has a gender dimension. Each particular fruit crop, whether it be table grapes, kiwis or apples, has a peak season labour demand. In areas where several of these crops are grown it becomes possible for *temporeras* to work an extended season by working on different crops at different times. In areas dominated by the production of one fruit crop it is more difficult to combine different types of work unless people are willing to migrate seasonally. However, the majority of migrants tend to be male. The cultural context in which women, especially rural women, search for employment away from the domestic sphere means that family responsibilities may limit their desire and/or ability to migrate. The following chapter explores an example of an area dominated by the production of just one fruit crop, table grapes, where the majority of *temporeras* work a limited season during the harvest (although there is some migration down the valley as the grapes ripen in stages). Chapter 7 discusses a different situation where several fruit crops are grown in the same region and *temporeras* are therefore able to work an extended season. These comparative case studies will demonstrate the variability of employment experienced by women from one area to another, as well as within different regions.

WORKING CONDITIONS

The type of enterprise in which the *temporeras* are employed is variable, reflecting the fragmented structure of production. The direct employment of women as waged labourers in export agriculture can take place in a variety of contexts. It can be in packing plants where the employer is a transnational or national export firm, large-scale farms owned either by export firms or large producers where they might be involved in packing, fieldwork or both, or medium-sized farms which also require female labour at certain times of the year. Temporary workers can have a high turnover of employment during the season, and may work for a number of employers undertaking different types of jobs during each season, while others might work for the same employer year after year. The type of employment available to women and the extent of job turnover will vary both by region and by locality, and will be limited by the degree of mobility of any individual worker, which again affects women more than men (Venegas 1992a).

In attempting to describe the overall characteristics of *temporeras*, putting forward a description of their working conditions is a difficult proposition given the variety of work experiences. Working conditions vary significantly between fields and packing plants, regions, time of year, time of day, between fruit crops and between specific tasks within the production process. The working conditions are also perceived differently by different women depending on their background. For some women accustomed to backbreaking work in traditional agriculture, employment in the packing plants offers a more pleasant alternative. However, many of the tasks associated with the production processes, especially those out in the fields, are considered to be arduous and uncomfortable. Women frequently spend hours moving wooden stools along lines of fruit trees and vines, training or pruning the trees. This is carried out during either very cold or very hot weather, yet still requires significant levels of concentration and manual dexterity. While the conditions in the packing plants are usually more protected from extremes of heat and cold, workers must work at speed, often standing up, for long periods of time.

Some of the most commonly cited problems experienced by *temporeras* are those associated with pesticides and the gases used to treat the fresh fruit before shipping. The export crops are cultivated intensively and require significant inputs of fertilisers and pesticides, which are leading to environmental degradation. Many *temporeras* are exposed to these chemicals over extended periods of time either in the fields or packing plants, and medical complaints ranging from mild headaches and nausea through to more serious conditions are not unusual (Bee 1996; Díaz 1991; Valdés 1992). One study in a regional hospital in Rancagua found that every one of 90 babies born with a range of neural tube defects between January and September of 1993 was born to a *temporera* working on the local fruit farms (Green 1995: 132).

It is not only agro-chemical poisoning that causes health problems for *temporeras*. Standing still for hours at a time may cause postural problems, while cleaning and packing fruit may cause repetitive strain injuries. However, the problems associated with the chemicals used in the treatment of the fruit receive the most attention. Table 5.5 outlines the problems found in one study of health concerns amongst temporary workers, in which nearly half reported they had experienced some form of health problem.

The link between the chemicals associated with agro-export and medical complaints appears to be becoming clearer, and urgent controls on the situation are needed. However, the flexible working conditions and lack of coherent worker organisation means that the implementation of controls is a difficult process. In Chile certain organisations such as *Mujer y Trabajo* (Women and Work) campaign for improved working conditions for *temporeras*, including controlling the use of agro-chemicals (Swift 1997). The issue of fruit workers and

Table 5.5 Fruit Workers and Health Problems Related to Agro-chemicals

Symptoms	No.	%
General health problems	88	47.8
Skin problems	20	22.7
Vision problems	17	19.3
Respiratory problems	9	10.2
Total	134	100.0

N = 300
Source: Adapted from Medel and Riquelme 1994: 77.

their exposure to agro-chemicals is not confined to Chile. In the United States, fruit workers struggled to gain recognition of the dangers of their work through high-profile campaigns and a series of grape boycotts (CEM 1989). Eventually, certain chemicals faced stricter controls or were banned. As campaigns against agro-chemical poisoning and for improved labour conditions gain momentum, it is to be hoped that employers will act to make working conditions for fruit workers safer in all countries, including Chile.

Calculating the hours and pay of temporary workers can be difficult given the level of variability, within a single firm at different times of the season as well as between firms and regions. Given the intensity of production, when the season is in full swing, most *temporeras/os* work long hours. The standard day is 8–10 hours in the fields and packing houses, but overtime can increase this to 16 hours in the packing houses where artificial light allows work to continue into the night, with a six-day week throughout most of the season. Some larger firms have introduced shift systems, especially in the north.[6] As women tend to be more concentrated in the packing houses than in the fields, they often work the longer hours. Work in packing usually starts later in the morning than field work, continuing into the night as the day's harvest must be packed and prepared for shipping.

Pay rates are highly variable, and it is difficult to get precise information for this reason. On the whole, field workers tend to be paid on a daily rate, although in recent years anecdotal evidence suggests there has been a move to employ contract gangs in field work which are paid for the completion of certain tasks by the field. This relieves the producer of direct employment obligations, with the aim of raising productivity. We have no information on forms of payment within contract gangs, most of whose workers probably do not have a contract of employment. In the packing houses, payment varies, with some tasks being paid by day rate, but most tasks being paid by piece rate for fruit that passes quality control. As women are more concentrated in these tasks, they are more likely to receive this type of payment. Table 5.6 gives an example of the rates paid for various tasks in packing in 1993/4, and Table 5.7 provides an estimate of the daily wage a packer can earn by piece rate according to the number of boxes packed.

Experience has shown that on average a woman can pack 200–300 boxes in a full day. For boxes of 8.2 kg this would provide her with daily earnings of CH$3,360–5,040 (US$8.00–12.00). The total number of boxes packed in the plant would have to be in the range 12,001 to

Table 5.6 Wages Earned for Selected Tasks in a Packing Plant, US$, Summer 1993/4

Boxes Packed (thousands)	0–3	3–6	6–9	9–12	12–15	15–18
Job						
Supervisor	5.2	6.1	6.7	7.3	7.89	8.9
Labourer	4.6	5.2	6.1	6.7	7.3	7.8
Pallet makers	5.2	6.1	6.7	7.3	7.9	8.9
Weighers	4.6	5.2	6.1	6.7	7.3	7.8
Secretaries	5.2	6.1	6.7	7.3	7.9	8.9
Selectors	5.2	6.1	6.7	7.3	7.9	8.9

Figure calculated on an exchange rate of US$1 = CH$420.
Source: Bee, 1996.

Table 5.7 Examples of Wages Earned for Numbers of Boxes Packed, US$, Summer 1993/4

Number of Boxes Packed	8.2 kg	5.00 kg
100	4.00	3.00
200	8.00	6.00
300	12.00	9.00

Piece rate per box is US$0.04 per 8.2 kg box, US$0.03 per 5.00 kg box.
Figure calculated on an exchange rate of US$1 = CH$420.
Source: Adapted from Bee and Vogel, 1997.

15,000 for any of the other workers to earn even the lower of these two figures. Through this payment system, income can vary according to individual productivity and the volume of fruit harvested, but it creates the anomaly that the most productive female packers can earn more than male field workers. Fruit wages have to compete with industrial and urban wages at the height of the season to attract sufficient labour. The CNC estimated that in 1993–4 the average earnings of all temporary fruit workers in the country as a whole was CH$57,000 (US$135) per month (Barrientos 1996). This is above the legal minimum wage, which in January–May 1994 was CH$46,000 (US$110), but below the minimum salary required to stay out of poverty and satisfy basic needs, which was CH$65,906 (US$157) in the same period (Leiva and Agacino 1994: 24). However, it must be remembered that this wage can only normally be earned by seasonal workers for 3–4 months, or up to a maximum of six months a year in the case of migrants, and that the majority are largely dependent on this income as they are unemployed for much of the rest of the year. Poverty is thus a significant problem in households dependent on fruit work (Venegas 1992a).

In addition to the instability and seasonal nature of the employment, many employers flout laws requiring them to provide certain facilities such as childcare centres and hygienic toilet facilities. Many *temporeras* are employed without a contract and therefore face the most extreme form of unstable employment and do not receive social service benefits. One study involving approximately 80 *temporeras* from the Elqui valley in the IV Region found that: 'The majority were working without a contract, without social welfare, with hours exceeding the eight to ten laid down by law, with low wages and without payment for overtime (Sundays, holidays)' (Díaz 1991: 133). In another study, Venegas (1993) estimated that overall the number of temporary workers with a contract varies from 70 per cent in the case of large firms and producers with more than 100 hectares, through 37 per cent in the case of medium sized producers, to 15 per cent in the case of small producers. This is not only because employers do not give contracts, but also many workers do not want a contract as, if they have one, 20.6 per cent of their earnings will be deducted for health and pension payments, benefits they are never likely to receive given the insecure and temporary nature of their employment (Venegas 1993).

Union membership among temporary fruit workers is very low. In 1988 it was estimated to be around one per cent of all fruit workers, in comparison to a national union membership of 10 per cent (Falabella 1993). Following the return to democracy, the national level of unionisation increased to 15.5 per cent in 1991, but had dropped back to 13.7 per cent by 1993 (Leiva and Agacino 1994: 46). Although we do not have any reliable figures for the *temporeras/os*, anecdotal evidence from interviews suggests that union membership remains minimal. However, one reason for the lack of union membership since the end of dictatorship is that, despite *Concertación*'s reform of the Labour Code, the legal right to collective negotiation has not been extended to temporary workers, and therefore the benefits of union membership remain extremely limited (Leiva and Agacino 1994; Venegas

1993). Given the highly insecure nature of their employment, many temporary workers are unlikely to risk union membership in the face of employer's historical hostility to unions. Women in particular have no experience of union membership, as they were largely excluded from union membership under the old agrarian system. This is often cited as a reason why they have been preferred by employers to men (Barrientos 1998). The net result is that, relative to the producers and exporters, the seasonal workers remain a highly atomised labour force, whose ability to improve their pay or conditions is limited.

FRAGMENTED PRODUCTION AND AN ATOMISED LABOUR FORCE

We can see that although the fruit sector is based on integration into a highly sophisticated global export sector, dependent on investment in advanced technology for its operation, it is also based on a relatively fragmented production process and a heterogeneous, atomised temporary labour force. In the last chapter we argued that export capital and its partial integration into production represents the dynamics of the industrial accumulation process. It is based on large-scale capital investment, driven by the demands of global market competition and profitability. Yet this accumulation process constantly comes up against the biological constraints of agriculture, the cyclical nature of production and the constant element of risk due to natural hazard and market uncertainty. It is in this context that the export sector interrelates with a more fragmented production process. It is not in the interests of the transnational or large export companies to own a large proportion of production. Through their informal subcontracted relations with a larger number of fragmented producers (over whom they are in a powerful position given their technological and financial superiority), they are able to offset risk and minimise the effects of the cyclical nature of production. From an analytical perspective, the industrial organisation approach (Friedland 1994a) helps to analyse the export and distribution segments of the supply chain, but the industrial analogy is weaker at the point of production. Here natural and seasonal constraints affect the industrial accumulation process within agriculture (Goodman and Redclift 1991). These limit the extent of involvement by large transnational capital, reinforcing the fragmented form of the production process, helping to explain the atomised and gendered nature of the labour force.

For both the exporters and producers, harvesting and packing are the most labour-intensive elements within the sector. Again, these are cyclically determined, but unlike more diversified traditional agriculture, monocultivation has driven them into a highly concentrated period of intense labour activity, during which any risks inherent to this form of accumulation are at their maximum. The atomised, heterogeneous, insecure temporary labour force at this point acts as an essential buffer for producers and exporters alike, allowing them to meet the surge in output needed to meet their global export commitments, while allowing them to offset the effects of any variability in price or output by changing the level of employment or remuneration almost immediately. To some extent these trends have been found in transnational industrial production (through subcontracting and the use of flexible labour), but in the case of Chilean agribusiness, they are very pronounced and determined by the contradictory relationship between accumulation and the constraints of the natural production process.

Within this, gender has come to play a significant role. We have seen that women form over half the atomised, heterogeneous temporary labour force. This is partly due to the shortage of labour. Women, who traditionally have not held paid employment in agriculture, are now being drawn into wage-labour in large numbers as a result of the changing social and commercial relations in agriculture. Their presence is essential to fulfilling the surge in labour demand which monocultivation and export specialisation generate. Their subordinate social position is also essential in that more women than men are forced back into the home during the blue months, due to the lack of alternative employment and their domestic commitments, sustaining them as a reliable, experienced source of labour which can be drawn upon the following season. In this sense the age and marital status of the *temporeras* benefits employers, as their relative immobility increases their reliability as an annual source of seasonal labour.

The gender dimension, however, is also important in terms of job segregation. Women are not only brought in to meet the increase in labour demand, they also tend to be concentrated in the tasks specific to producing the high quality of fruit needed for global export. Traditional fruit production for the internal market does not require such specialised pruning, selection, preparation and packing, and these tasks have been specifically developed by the expansion of export production. Women's concentration into these tasks reflects socially constructed perceptions of their 'feminine skills' and social training within the household. It perpetuates the association of women's role with the preparation and presentation of food, which now takes place on a commercialised global level, facilitating the export of fruit in pristine condition.

In addition, these tasks are performed by women based on the most flexible employment practices in terms of their hours, pay and terms of employment. Women, who have no tradition of union organisation and form a heterogeneous and atomised labour force, largely accept these conditions. Their labour is essential to the production of export fruit with a high value added, yet their pay and flexible employment helps to minimise labour costs and offset risk from variable output or price. Through their segregated employment, women in particular form a critical link between a profitable global accumulation process and the natural constraints of production and risk. The fragmentation of production and the gendered nature of the atomised temporary labour force are thus not coincidental. Their specific form may have been historically shaped under the military's agrarian counter-reform, but their fundamental features have become essential to the functioning of a successful export sector. While the dynamics of this process contain important contradictions, the point we are making here is that the heterogeneity of the *temporeras* is an inherent aspect of the fruit export sector.

Having examined the levels of export, production and employment, we still have one further essential aspect to explore. If heterogeneity and atomisation are defining features of the *temporeras*, then they are having to mediate their atomised work experience with the diversity of their own lives. The form of that mediation is not only important in understanding their role as a sustained and stable temporary labour force – how is it they are able to survive from one year to the next to re-emerge each season as an experienced group of fruit workers? This is also essential to understanding their personal experiences, how they cope with the tensions generated by fruit employment, the impact of this work on household relations, the effect of this work on their position both within the household and society as a whole, and their development from traditional *campesina* to modern, urbanised agricultural wage labourer. Given their heterogeneity, we cannot cover the diverse range of *temporeras*. However, the next two chapters explore the personal perspectives of the *temporeras* from the standpoint of two specific case studies. The first, based on research in the Norte Chico in the IV Region, examines the role of more traditional *campesinas* drawn into fruit employment for part of the year. This represents one extreme of how women mediate their traditional roles with insertion into modern agricultural wage-labour. The second is based on research in the VI and VII Regions, south of Santiago, and focuses on urbanised *temporeras*. This represents the other extreme of how women mediate their insertion into the modern agricultural labour force with the insecurity of survival in a modern urban setting. In both we explore women's employment as *temporeras*, but from their personal perspectives and experiences of coping with this atomised work.

6 Case Study: Rural Fruit Workers in the North

The heterogeneity of the *temporeras* is partly explained by the fragmented nature of the production process, and the partial nature of their integration into fruit work as seasonal workers. It is also a result of the diverse situations from which the seasonal workforce is drawn, ranging from small traditional *campesina* households to urban workers migrating from large cities during the season on a daily basis. This reflects the uneven nature of rural 'modernisation' as agribusiness has extended across the fruit growing regions, with contradictory effects on the women drawn into the sector. However, given their heterogeneity, the specific experiences of women working in fruit exports can vary markedly according to the diverse contexts of their personal situations. In this and the next chapter we explore two case studies which illustrate the different contexts from which women are drawn into fruit work, and the different experiences women have of undertaking this work, both within the same region and across different regions. These case studies help to depict the heterogeneity of the *temporeras*.

This first case study draws on the example of a more traditional situation.[1] It examines the specificities of the situation for the population of the Upper Limari valley, and more specifically the Guatulame tributary valley system, in the IV Region (see Map 6.1). In this semi-arid region, part of Chile's Norte Chico (little north), the transverse river valleys flowing from the Andes have perennially provided irrigation for agriculture supporting a settled agricultural community producing crops such as tomatoes, beans and peppers for the domestic market. As production of non-traditional agricultural exports took off, the Guatulame experienced a truly dramatic increase in the cultivation of table grapes for export. The growth of export production in this area has had ramifications for the local population, and especially women who work in both more traditional agriculture and the export sector.

Rachel and her sister Ximena live in Tome Alto, a small village in the Guatulame valley. From March to November they work on their family land cultivating tomatoes, peppers and beans; between November and February they leave the village to work on the large-scale grape farms

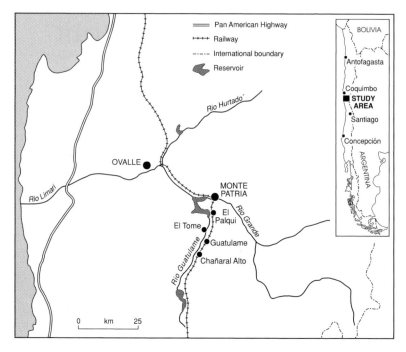

Map 6.1   Map of Case Study Area in the North

(*parronales*) where they clean and pack table grapes for export. While they describe themselves as *campesinas*, for a few months each year they join the substantial numbers of women and men as waged workers in local agribusiness, which is almost exclusively the export of table grapes to the northern markets of Europe and the United States. The very seasonal nature of much fruit export employment means that the majority of workers have some alternative form of subsistence. However, the situation in the Guatulame represents an interesting example of a traditional agricultural area, with the attendant systems of labour organisation and land tenure, which has been overlaid with a dynamic, export-oriented sector. For the people who have traditionally relied on small-scale production for the domestic market this has presented them with a host of new challenges and opportunities that have helped to blur the boundaries between 'traditional' and 'modern', between *campesinas* and *temporeras*.

AGRICULTURAL COMMUNITIES, LAND TENURE AND FRUIT EXPORT PRODUCTION

The Norte Chico region had traditionally been characterised as a relatively poor and underdeveloped region of Chile. However this situation changed dramatically in certain areas of the region where the production of export crops has come to dominate. The dominant export crop in this region is the table grape, which represents one of Chile's most successful fruit exports. Between 1977 and 1986 the international prices of fresh table grapes increased by 50 per cent from US$642 to US$931 (Korovkin 1992). As producers began to recognise the profitability of this particular crop, land under table grape production increased tenfold between 1974 and 1987 with 70 per cent of the total production from this land used for direct export (Gwynne 1991). The particular climatic characteristics allow the grapes from the valleys of the Norte Chico to reach the markets of the Northern Hemisphere approximately one and half months in advance of those from the Central Valley. Thus producers in these areas have been able to capitalise on the higher prices fresh grapes command at the beginning of the season and during the Christmas period.

The Guatulame Valley represents a locality where the production of table grapes for export has expanded dramatically. The majority of the grapes are grown on large-scale estates owned by commercial farmers, who have received financial support from international marketing companies. Producers need to have significant capital to start a grape farm as the total cost for buying land, obtaining water rights and care of the vines until production starts is estimated to be approximately US$35,000 per hectare (Gwynne and Ortíz 1997). The *parronales* have come to dominate the landscape of the Guatulame as increasing amounts of land are brought under export production.

At the same time, the existence of a locally specific organisation of land tenure has impacted on the extent to which export production has been able to expand. The valley is characterised by a variety of landholding systems, including large-scale private properties, *minifundios* and also agricultural communities. It is the latter, communal landholding system that has had an unforeseen impact on the expansion of grape production. In this region the development of the agricultural communities can be traced back to the Diaguita culture of the pre-Columbian era, when the community's social and economic organisation initially revolved around ties of kinship. This system was complicated by favours given to Spanish soldiers, yet as much of the communal land was of poor quality it was not subjected to hereditary divisions and remained more or less intact (Gwynne and Meneses 1994; JUNDEP 1991; McBride 1936). Each community is composed of a fixed number of members (*comuneros*), who hold rights to use the communal land and form the community committee. The number of *comuneros* in each community remains constant, and prior to 1978 communal land could only be exchanged between *comuneros*.[2]

However, in recent years the legal status of the communal land within the communities has been changing and in some instances the communal land has been made available on the open market, while in others it has remained under the control of the *comuneros*. Through a series of laws designed to regularise the land tenure system within the agricultural communities, it became possible for land to be sold to non-*comuneros*, but only if it was agreed by a majority of *comuneros*. Some communities agreed to regularise land tenure and it therefore became possible for *comuneros* to sell their land both to *comuneros* and also more importantly to non-members of the communities. However, the majority of the communities in the Guatulame did not regularise land tenure and their communal land therefore remained inviolate.

The expansion of export production in the Guatulame brought with it a concomitant development of a land market, as large-scale producers sought land for the installation of vineyards. In the communities with regularised land tenure, non-*comuneros* were able to buy land and set up table grape plantations. In communities without regularised land tenure the opposite is the case, as export producers have been unable to consolidate sufficient land for a profitable vineyard. Thus, there appears to be little doubt that the legal status of land tenure within the agricultural communities of the Guatulame has to a certain extent shaped the expansion of export production and with it the organization of working practices in the different communities. To explore these issues we focus on two different villages, Chañaral Alto in the community of Chacarillas, and Tome Alto in the community of El Tome. The community of Chacarillas regularised land tenure in the 1980s and therefore it became possible for *comuneros* to dispose of land to non-members. By 1992 a significant proportion of land rights had indeed been exchanged, with 126 out of a total of 206 rights changing hands (Gwynne and Ortíz 1997). Many of these land rights had been sold to the large-scale producers. In contrast, the community of Tome Alto had still not regularised land tenure in 1997 and the communal land remained intact.

Chañaral Alto, the larger of the two villages (population 2,232 in 1992), is located higher up the river valley than Tome Alto (see Map 6.1). It lies at the end of the main road link from Monte Patria and Ovalle, the capital of the local municipality and major urban centre of the river basin respectively. Traditionally, the economy of the village was based on small-scale farmers (with plots of less than 5 hectares) producing tomatoes, beans, peppers, garlic and melons for urban centres in Chile. However, the community has experienced the effects of the dynamic land market in the valley as a significant number of *comuneros* have sold their land to large-scale grape producers. The village has developed into an important local centre for the grape economy, attracting significant investment directly into export agriculture and also into other areas such as local services. The dynamism of the village economy is reflected in the fact that between 1970 and 1992 there was a 2.7 per cent annual increase in population (Gwynne and Ortíz 1997). The dynamic land market and the expansion of the grape economy into the village have altered certain systems of production; the traditional small-scale producers have to a large extent been marginalised. Yet we should bear in mind that these changes have not completely obliterated the pre-existing systems of agricultural production or community organisation.

In contrast to the situation in Chañaral Alto, Tome Alto has remained relatively unscathed by the expansion of grape cultivation. It is a much smaller village with a population in 1988 of 426, a figure that represented a very slight *decrease* in population since 1960 (Ortíz 1989 and 1990). The village, therefore, has a much more stable population base and does not show the dramatic increase in population seen in Chañaral Alto. The small-scale farmers have a reputation for producing high quality tomatoes, which are cultivated intensively on small, plastic-covered plots known *casetas,* irrigated with water from the Guatulame River. Other crops grown include beans, peppers and avocados. Unlike the *community* of Chacarillas, the Tome Alto community has not yet regularised its land tenure. The communal lands cannot therefore be sold to non-members; this situation exists even in the face of pressure from the grape economy ever-hungry for land for expansion.

SEASONALITY AND GENDERED SPECIFICITY OF LABOUR IN THE AGRICULTURAL ECONOMIES OF THE GUATULAME

The expansion of export production in the Guatulame led to a significant increase in the need for seasonal employment drawing local populations into waged employment on the medium and large-scale farms. This is reflected in the increased involvement of women in some of the new export-oriented industries under the neo-liberal model. The situation in the Guatulame offers a telling example of this process. The arrival of the grape economy in the Guatulame provided women with work opportunities which represent a departure from traditional agricultural work in that they have become highly visible and provide the women with their own personal income. Yet while many rural women of the IV Region have been incorporated into the modern agro-export economy in certain tasks and on a seasonal basis, they have also had traditional agricultural responsibilities on the small family farm. For many women these responsibilities are not neglected but are instead combined with their incorporation into waged work in the export sector. This section explores the gendered nature of work in the agricultural economies of the Guatulame.

The production of high quality table grapes requires significant levels of seasonal labour. The peak of this labour requirement occurs during the summer harvest period. There are also smaller peaks during the winter months for various tasks such as pruning and training the vines. There are some limited opportunities for permanent employment, either for skilled workers such as technicians and agronomists, or on a more casual arrangement for general labourers. Yet temporary labour dramatically dominates permanent labour. The majority of people employed by the export grape industry therefore find that their work is for only one season or various discontinuous periods throughout the year.

Employment in the grape economy is divided between the fields and the packing plants. It is in the packing plants where the gender division of labour is most marked. Research shows that while approximately equal proportions of women and men work in the packing plants during the grape harvest, the work is highly segregated (Bee 1996). We explored some aspects of the gender division of labour within the grape economy of the Guatulame Valley in the previous chapter. In this instance women are engaged in selecting, cleaning and wrapping the grapes in the packing plants. Most of the men's work occurs once the grapes have been packed and includes labelling the boxes, treating them with fungicide and loading them on to the waiting lorries. One of the most important male jobs is the construction of the pallets for the fruit. The only tasks within the packing plants that are undertaken by both women and men is the weighing of the sorted grapes prior to packing, and the various supervisory positions associated with the post-harvest process. There is a much less marked division of labour in the fields, with women and men working together training and pruning the vines. The majority of the female labour is needed during the harvest period from mid-November through to January when women work to prepare the grapes for shipment. It is the packing of the grapes which offers women the greatest wage-earning potential as it is considered skilled and vital to the production process. As we saw in the previous chapter, the piece rates paid to the packers mean that they frequently earn more than the other workers in the plant. In this instance work that is attributed to women is not downgraded; rather, the complex nature of the task and the skills required are recognised and rewarded. The grape packers stand at benches where the grapes arrive on a conveyor belt pre-selected and sorted by colour and size. The women then have to put bunches of grapes into plastic bags before packing them into boxes of various weights. Each box must include the exact weight of grapes and great skill is required to estimate the size of bunches and pack the grapes so that they are not damaged during shipment. The requirements within the packing plants are very specific: each box should contain 8–10 plastic bags of grapes and each bag should contain approximately the same number of grapes, before being wrapped in tissue paper and sealed in the box.

This specific example of women possessing a relatively higher earning potential than male seasonal workers contrasts with the accepted theories regarding female labourers and possible earnings. Examples from both Latin America and South East Asia show how workers in 'naturally feminine' jobs are usually remunerated less than their male counterparts because they are classified as unskilled (Nash and Fernandez-Kelly 1983; Ong 1987). In other industries those working for piece rates may be unable to compete with those paid per hour. In the case of the strawberry export industry in Mexico, workers with higher status jobs and commensurate earnings were paid per hour, while those in lower status jobs were relegated to piece work (Arizpe and Aranda 1986). To a certain extent it is a double-edged sword, in that working for piece rates provides the possibility for a relatively high wage but is also places workers under great pressure to pack consistently and rapidly during the extremely long working hours.

CAMPESINA/TEMPORERA

On the small-scale farms of the agricultural communities the gender division of labour is much less marked than it is in table grape production. Women and men pool their efforts to produce the crops of tomatoes, beans and peppers, and much of this work is extremely labour-intensive and demanding. The responsibilities of rural women or *campesinas* though are manifold and involve more than work on the family farm. Within the family unit of the rural agricultural communities the woman's principal role has traditionally been that of raising children, feeding and giving affection to their family. Based on this, a woman's decisions and responsibilities had, and continue to have, at their root the domestic sphere (JUNDEP 1991). Yet in this context the domestic sphere is an extended one and also includes the cultivation of food for sale or subsistence, the raising of animals and in some instances small business ventures based in the home.

In communities where land tenure has not been regularised, export agriculture has generally failed to penetrate. This is the case in Tome Alto where the majority of villagers dedicate themselves to small-scale production, especially of tomatoes, for nine months of the year. In the IV Region the cultivation season for tomatoes runs from March through to November, when the tomatoes are harvested and sent to market. The summer months of December, January and February had traditionally been months for resting and preparing for the coming cultivation period. They were also the months when incomes all but dried up and many people went in search of temporary employment outside the communities. However, the seasonal demands for labour in the grape economy are such that the majority of the local population are now mobilised for a few months each year. The villagers from Tome Alto, who work in the grape economy, tend to work on the harvest, during the months of December and January. Some may also work for short periods in the fields and a few men have permanent employment on the grape farms. However, not one of the women from Tome Alto who participated in the study was employed as a *temporera* for longer than six months.

The form of participation in the grape economy is in part a factor of the relative robustness of the traditional small-scale cultivation of crops, especially tomatoes. While small-scale agriculture remains the primary concern of the majority of households in the village, employment in the grape economy will continue to be of secondary importance. The land tenure system in the village has perhaps been of

Table 6.1   Seasonality of Female Employment in the Grape Economy of
Norte Chico

Months Worked	Percentage of Women Working in the Grape Economy (1992)		Percentage of Women Working in the Grape Economy (1993)	
	Tome Alto (*n* = 30)	Chañaral Alto (*n* = 42)	Tome Alto (*n* = 29)	Chañaral Alto (*n* = 41)
December–January	73	45	72	46
September–January	13	26	14	22
August–January	13	7	14	4
May–January	0	14	0	15
April–January	0	2	0	7
All year	0	5	0	5

Source: Bee 1996.

Table 6.2   Female Employment in the Grape Economy in Norte Chico

Specific Tasks	Percentage of Women Working in 1992		Percentage of Women Working in 1993	
	Tome Alto (*n* = 30)	Chañaral Alto (*n* = 42)	Tome Alto (*n* = 29)	Chañaral Alto (*n* = 41)
Selecting grapes	17	2	17	5
Cleaning grapes	43	28	52	29
Packing grapes	20	10	10	12
Affixing labels to boxes	3	10	3	2
Various tasks(a)	17	50	17	51

(a)   Various tasks includes work in fields and packing plants, e.g. cleaning,
pruning and packing the fruit.
Source: Bee 1996.

primary importance in limiting the expansion of the large-scale vineyards into the village and the dissolution of traditional systems. Added
to this though, and of pure coincidence, is the synchronisation of the
tomato and grape cultivation calendars. When work on the tomato
crop ends in November, the peak season begins on the grapes. The
specific dynamic which exists in the articulation of traditional forms of
agriculture with the modern, export-oriented enterprises means that it
may be possible for some households or individuals to maintain traditional, albeit intensified, work on the family land with waged work in
the export economy.

In Chañaral Alto the situation is somewhat different from that of
Tome Alto. While seasonal employment still remains dominant, individuals involved in the grape economy may have longer working
seasons than those in Tome Alto. They work for longer periods and
therefore are involved in work beyond the harvest season. For
women the most common form of employment is a mixture of work
in the fields and the packing plants lasting between two and four
months. What emerges is that women in Chañaral Alto experience
longer periods as *temporeras*. While this is certainly not true for all
women employed in the grape economy, a significant minority
(27 per cent of the sample) are employed for a period of six months
or longer. This is work which extends well beyond the harvest season
and supplies waged employment, albeit unstable, for at least half the
year.

The extended periods of seasonal and permanent work coupled
with the greater variety of jobs undertaken on the grape farms reflect
the more fundamental insertion of the population into the grape
economy. In Chañaral Alto there has been a greater local transformation in agricultural production than in Tome Alto. With the expansion of the grape economy, more people have sold land and thus have
been forced to seek work away from their own land, either in work on
the *parronales* or in other sectors of the economy. In a village such as
Chañaral Alto where many peasant farmers have been encouraged by
a combination of factors to dispose of their land, waged work will necessarily grow in importance if rural depopulation is not to become the
dominant process. With regards to the development of seasonal
labour, the pattern emerging in Chañaral Alto more broadly reflects
the patterns in other areas of Chile. As a broad definition, it has been
stated that most seasonal employees, especially women, in the capitalist enterprises, originate in households that have either lost their land
or never owned it (Lago 1987).

How do the patterns of women's employment in the fruit export sector relate to maintenance of small-scale agricultural production? Land tenure has played a role in shaping women's involvement as *temporeras* and their identities as waged workers and/or *campesinas*. In some communities, where land has been sold to large-scale grape producers, the agricultural transformation has been felt more immediately and there has been increased proletarianisation of the population. In Chañaral Alto a significant minority of women work on the grapes for at least six months in any one year, extending their roles as temporary workers and possibly deepening their identity as *temporeras*. Overall though, there has been an incomplete transformation in the agricultural sector – the small-scale producers have not necessarily been marginalised or removed from the landscape. While temporary employment on the grape farms has come to be an important source of income, it may be in addition to the income from their own small-scale properties. Thus the *temporera* labour force remains fragmented, but in possession of long-term strategies for income-generation where small-scale farming continues to be of fundamental economic and cultural importance.

THE IMPORTANCE OF THE DOMESTIC SPHERE IN AGRICULTURAL TRANSFORMATIONS

The availability of work or the demands of small-scale agriculture do not solely condition women's involvement as *temporeras*, household and family structures may also have a strong bearing on a woman's ability to participate in waged employment. These issues have been discussed at a general level in chapter 2 and will be examined more specifically in the following chapter. The particular issue we wish to explore here is that of domestic work, the daily reproduction of the household. The women working in the grape economy frequently work extended hours and also bear the main burden of domestic work. Table 6.3 illustrates in detail the various tasks associated with the domestic sphere and those family members who regularly take responsibility for them.

The information displayed in Table 6.3 corresponds closely to the patterns of divisions of housework which have been documented in many studies, from different parts of the world (Harris 1981). Women either solely, or in combination with other women, are overwhelmingly responsible for the day-to-day tasks involved in the maintenance

Table 6.3   Household Responsibility for Domestic Chores

Task	Tome Alto (n = 45)				Chañaral Alto (n = 83)				
	1	2	3	4	1	2	3	4	5
Cleaning	64	36	0	0	66	24	4	5	1
Cooking	76	24	0	0	80	11	2	5	1
Clothes washing	69	31	0	0	68	22	4	5	1
Shopping (a)	35	7	22	27(b)	39	2	23	19	0
Money management	29	2	36	32	39	1	21	40	0
House repairs	4	0	2	80	4	0	1	81	4

Figures are in percentages.
1 = Main responsibility for task only one woman.
2 = Two or more women share responsibility.
3 = Shared responsibility male/female.
4 = Male only responsibility.
5 = Hired labour.
(a)   Refers to shopping trip outside the village to purchase bulk quantities of goods such as flour and sugar.
(b)   Rows do not necessarily add up to 100 per cent, as some respondents did not go shopping outside the village or undertake household repairs.
Source: Bee 1996.

of the household, such as the daily cleaning, the cooking and the washing of clothes. These are the tasks that require the most constant attention and need to be undertaken daily, or at least several times a week. For this reason women who earn their own money in the grape economy frequently make decisions to purchase, or to save for, household equipment such as washing machines, in an attempt to reduce the number of hours they have to spend on routine housework.

Men's participation in domestic work is markedly different from women's, not simply in the quantity undertaken, but also in the type of preferred tasks. Studies have shown that men have a preference for tasks that are 'functionally specific', that is they have well-defined boundaries and allow discretion in when they are done (Marshall 1994). The results of this study reflect these trends. The most common household tasks undertaken by men, either individually or with other family members, are household repairs, managing the household finances (this includes paying bills and arranging credit), and major shopping expeditions to the local town of Ovalle. The first of these tasks can certainly be described as 'functionally discrete', allowing the men to decide when and how to undertake the repairs and rarely requiring daily repetition. The management of household finances is often undertaken jointly. The women, or even the children, who are habitually sent to the local shop to buy soft drinks or bread, undertake the more everyday shopping. The larger shopping trips to Ovalle usually involve male family members. These trips require at least two people to carry or arrange delivery of sacks of flour, sugar and other foodstuffs. They also require a significant financial output or the arranging of credit with the local supermarkets. Thus while they are tasks that do not necessarily demand male input, they appear to be jobs that recurrently involve male input.

In traditional nuclear and also extended families, the gendered division of labour within the household follows patterns that ascribe certain tasks to certain people. For example in one family consisting of mother, father and four sons, the sons have been encouraged to help in the house. The father helped with domestic tasks when their sons were younger when the woman would be working in the tomatoes. Yet the sons were persuaded to help in the house because they had no sister:

> Sometimes the children arrive from school and I don't have things prepared, so they help because I have to go out very early to work on the tomatoes ..... There are some families where the men never help and in some places the children don't help either and they leave all the work to the mother. But not in my case because I've always taught the children, I tell them, *'You don't have a sister who can help with things or do things, so you have to help me.'* (Maria, Tome Alto)

The organisation of labour within the domestic sphere is slow to accommodate new circumstances, such as women's increasing importance as breadwinners (Morris 1991). Thus while women experience new opportunities for work outside the house, which may bring dramatic changes in their association with the public sphere, the domestic situation lags behind both temporally and in the extent of its adaptation to these changes. The dramatic expansion of the grape economy in the Norte Chico has introduced new labour markets and systems of working within the capitalist production system that are not found within the household division of labour. While nominal efforts are made by men to assume some domestic responsibility normally attributed to women, it is rarely sufficient to relieve significantly the burden of the household from women's shoulders. This leads to the infamous 'double day', which appears to be more pressing when women leave the family farm and associated responsibilities to work on the grape farms. This is mainly a result of the inflexibility of working hours on the grape farms which keep women physically removed from their domestic responsibilities for up to 18 hours a day. This extended separation from domestic chores is most likely to stimulate other members of the household to assume greater responsibility within the house.

The presence of young children in the household is of fundamental importance in shaping women's involvement in work outside the home. In a society that allocates the main responsibility for childcare to women, they have to be primarily concerned with ensuring their children are cared for at all times, and when they go out to work make alternative arrangements. Three possible strategies are generally open to the women of the agricultural communities. They can leave the children with relatives, take them to work or leave them alone in the house. Young children tend to inhibit female work on the *parronales* or packing plant far more than in family production. This represents the separation between what has traditionally been accepted as a *campesina*'s agricultural responsibilities and the new opportunities and problems presented by non-traditional work in the grape economy.

Rural women have perennially combined childcare with their other responsibilities in the extended domestic sphere, which has historically included productive agricultural work. The arrival of local opportunities to work away from the domestic sphere in the grape economy has presented both a continuation of female roles and also a problematic change by introducing a competitor for women's time and energy. It represents a continuation, in the sense that women from the Guatulame have traditionally been involved in agricultural production and, moreover, the tasks they undertake on the grape farms utilise their perceived gender characteristics. The changes are spatial, economic and social in nature. Women work away from home for wages that are paid directly to them, and are integrated into a system of capitalist production in a manner that is distinct from previous experiences. Thus, there exists a conflict between new and more traditional roles, which is frequently manifested in the problems of adequate childcare provision for working women.

The problem of childcare has caught the attention of state organisations (Aranda 1992; Matear 1997). At the opening of a local *Jardin Infantil* (kindergarten) for the children of *temporeras*, much was made of the importance of good childcare for women workers, in that it

provides them with peace of mind and thus leads to improved productivity. Employers are aware of the concerns of their workers with
respect to childcare, yet they themselves have been slow to introduce
childcare facilities into their packing plants. Although one local plant
was supposed to have childcare facilities, none of the people we spoke
to, both male and female, knew of any such facilities in plants where
they worked. The issues of women, work and childcare have generated an arena in which family concerns and strategies have been interpreted by the state and have produced some positive results such as
the new kindergartens and the summer childcare schemes operated in
local schools. Yet the facilities are insufficient, and while alleviating
some of the women's concerns about childcare, they do so with the
express aim of improving the national economy by increasing the productivity of female workers. The role of the state in providing childcare for the children of *temporeras* and the rhetoric associated with
childcare provision are explored further in chapter 8.

NEGOTIATIONS OF HOUSEHOLD GENDER RELATIONS: FIVE INDIVIDUAL CASE STUDIES

This section refers to in-depth interviews with women who have all
been involved to a certain extent with work in the agro-export sector
of the Guatulame. The objective here is to draw out the complexities
of women's experiences in traditional agriculture and export agriculture and to see how household relations and also the extent of transformation of traditional agriculture have shaped these experiences.
Moreover, the relationship between household relations and women's
experiences of work is not a simple or unilinear one. As Lawson
(1995: 424) suggests: 'Women's greater access to incomes ... may lead
to changing divisions of labour in households, with uncertain impacts
on household power relations.' Through a detailed exploration of
individual women's work histories and strategies for negotiation
between workplace and household gender relations, this section
avoids the simple representation of women as passive victims of the
changing agricultural structure of the Guatulame.

Rachel and Ximena, both in their forties, are sisters who live in
Tome Alto. They are married to brothers and work together to the
extent of sharing tomato plots (*casetas*) and many household chores.
The women are not from Tome Alto, but both moved there in the late
1970s when they married. Rachel has three children ranging in age

from 4 to 15. Ximena has no children of her own, but appears frequently to assume responsibility for childcare and thus is a great help to Rachel.

In the neighbouring community, both Rachel and Ximena had grown up working in the grape packing plants during the summer and they wanted to continue once they had married and moved to Tome Alto. They discovered that in Tome Alto there was no precedent set for women to go out to work.

> We were the first women to work in the packing plants. We arrived in 1979 and no women went out to work. The men here were very *machista* and didn't let them. When our husbands met us they knew that we worked in the grapes but we still had to convince them to let us continue. We heard that Don Jaime was looking for workers and so we went together without our husbands' permission to look for work. We were the only ones from Tome Alto to look for work ... then one year they were short of workers and they asked us if we knew anyone. We took some women who wanted to work and now everyone works. (Rachel)

They effectively acted as pioneers, introducing the idea that women could go out to work in the harvest. Yet while there is an acceptance that there is work during the summer grape harvest, the majority of the villagers still regard tomato production as their primary productive activity. Earnings from work on the grapes are either used to make up the shortfall from small-scale production in a year when prices or yields are poor, or to buy consumer goods or extras such as holidays. Ximena described the decisions she made regarding her own expenditure:

> I bought my washing machine with the money from the grapes. Before I had to get up at 6.00 am and do the washing before going out to work. So I decided to save my money and buy a washing machine. (Ximena)

Rachel and Ximena discussed some of the contradictions inherent in the changing systems of agricultural production and labour opportunities. They consider private ownership of their *casetas* to be of fundamental importance and the work on the tomatoes as their primary focus:

> We just work in the packing plants now, because the rest of the year we are working on the tomatoes. (Rachel)

However, they are aware of the disadvantages of this system. Not only are there the practical problems such as the inherent risk in relying on good yields and reasonable prices, but also the incredible amount of hard work required to care for the tomatoes. Yet full-time work on the grapes is rarely regarded as a favourable alternative to work on the tomatoes. Nevertheless, the local availability of seasonal work on the export grapes provides the villagers with a ready source of income which, as a supplement to the income from their own agricultural production, should not be underestimated.

Maria grew up in Tome Alto. In fact, her parents are *comuneros*. She went to school in the neighbouring village of Guatulame until the end of primary school and then went to board in Ovalle until she finished her secondary education. She was unable to study further because her father died and left her mother to take care of the family. For Maria, education beyond secondary standard was too expensive. She met her husband in Tome Alto and they have been married for 20 years. They began to work on the tomatoes as soon as they were married, they had both grown up helping their respective parents when they were young children. Her husband had saved money and they bought a *caseta* when they married. They now work three *caseta*s, one of which is for Maria's mother. In a good year the tomatoes provide all the family necessities and more. In 1992 they had a good crop of tomatoes producing 1,000 boxes and getting a high price at the beginning of the season. In 1993 a late spell of cold weather ruined their tomato crop, and that of many other villagers. This caused problems with repayments on a loan they have from INDAP that they cannot pay off. In total they are in debt to about one million pesos. Maria said that many of the villagers were in a similar situation and that INDAP would have to rethink its repayment policies to avoid trouble. As well as the tomatoes they also have a *parronal*, but its small size and relatively high water demand compared to tomatoes means that they have reduced grape cultivation, although they were considering increasing cultivation of Thompson seedless to cover some of the shortfall in income from the tomatoes. Maria eloquently explained the importance of tomato cultivation in the village, but also emphasised the inherent risk:

> Well with the tomatoes when things are good then it's OK. We buy things. For example, we have a small van that we bought because of the tomatoes, but life is very sacrificial, very hard. The life of the farmers is very hard, and sometimes it's not for profit. For example,

this year was very difficult for us. We lost absolutely everything. We are just waiting and hoping to get work on the grapes, to go and work in the packing. There we will earn a little bit of money. (Maria)

Maria has worked in a packing plant since she was 22, cleaning and packing the grapes. She likes the work because it is clean and done in the shade. As a minimum she earns CH$3,000 (US$7.15) per day and can earn up to CH$7,000 (US$16.70). This is on a good day when she is working on piece rates. The money from the grapes helps buy things for her youngest son and also extras for the house. The money is useful, but she did feel some maternal pressure not to go out to work, though she admits this was generally a self-inflicted pressure:

> I used to worry about going out so as to get things for the children and for school. I have to go out to work to provide my son with things for school. Now it's two years since they started working and they buy their own things. But because I have one [son] who is very young I still have to provide for him. (Maria)

If the harvest in the tomatoes has been poor, the money is vital and Maria notes that there are more village children working alongside their parents in the grape farms to replace some of the lost income. Her two elder sons work cutting and carrying the grapes during the harvest, though her husband does not work outside the family farm. She has about 15 days in February between the end of the work on the grapes and the start of the work on the tomatoes when she rests and sorts things out for the coming year. In her opinion the tomatoes are the focus of their lives, providing all the family's requirements. The grapes are an extra, a way she can earn some money to buy small luxuries for her children, and a safety net during poor yielding years in the tomatoes.

The way in which Rachel, Ximena and Maria combine their work in both the traditional and export agricultural sectors offers a compelling example of the way in which 'traditional' *campesinas* are able to negotiate waged and unwaged work. All three families are traditional in the sense that the women and their husbands agree that the ownership and cultivation of the *casetas* should be the primary source of family income. Any family involvement in the grape economy is seen as a supplement to this. However, the work on the grape economy does bring some material benefits to the household and Ximena's decision to buy a washing machine illustrates the increased control over money it provides for women. Rachel and Ximena were important actors in making it acceptable for women to work seasonally in the grape economy. In the neighbourhood where they had grown up it was accepted that women would go out to work and so once they arrived in Tome Alto, they wanted to continue working. Although originally they went to find work without first asking their partners' permission, it soon became apparent that they could earn substantial amounts of money during a traditionally quiet period in the village and at the same time continue with their domestic responsibilities. In part it is the specific nature of seasonal work that has allowed women to move into the labour market and stay there. For example, the temporary nature of the work in export agriculture is seen as an advantage in that women perceive it as allowing them to combine their traditional role in the home with paid work, and the disruption of their domestic responsibilities is only for part of the year. This 'benefit' is reinforced by the wages they can hope to earn as a supplement to their male partner's income. The roles of *campesina* and *temporera* are therefore juggled by these women on a seasonal basis, although for them their traditional role is the primary one.

Alicia lives in the neighbouring settlement of Chañaral Alto, a village unlike Tome Alto, in that it has been the site of significant expansion of the grape economy. Alicia and her husband sold their own land in the early 1970s when tomato production became unprofitable. Her husband found work on the irrigation system while she stayed at home and raised their five children. Alicia first began to work in the grapes in 1983 and always chooses a farm where there are a lot of local people rather than migrant workers. She views the work in a very positive light for two main reasons. The first is the added financial security the extra wage provides – for example, with her money from the grapes she has been able to buy a washing machine, a radio and clothes. The second is the break in the domestic routine that her work gives her. Although the work is extremely arduous, with long working days, Alicia looks forward each year to her seasonal work:

He [her husband] gives me permission to work because he knows that I relax. I get better because I have all sorts of ailments, I should be worse through working, but instead I feel a lot better. So he leaves me in peace to get on with it. I don't see the children as much as I would like, but you know for my health I work. I feel better when I go to work. (Alicia)

Alicia and her husband now run a bottle shop from the front room of their house, and Alicia has equal responsibility for the ownership and running of the business. In effect she is able to combine multiple roles as housewife, mother, self-employed shop owner and *temporera* in the grape economy. For her the work in the grape packing plants offers a chance to relax and let other family members take over the responsibility for the house. In this respect her husband has been relatively accommodating by helping to take care of the children when they were younger and helping with the household chores. In fact, Alicia feels that her husband is quite enlightened and moreover has learned something of the burden of the domestic routine: 'He realises that the role of mother is not easy, every day the same routine, but I'm lucky because he thanks me for the work I do.'

For Marta, who is 23 and lives with her parents in Chañaral Alto, her work in the grape economy has been economically vital and has become more so now that she has a small son. Her parents were originally from Carcamo, a remote and impoverished village, which still lacks many basic amenities. Her father arrived to work on the tomatoes in Chañaral Alto in 1968 and her mother followed soon after because there was no doctor in Carcamo to care for their children. Marta went to school in Chañaral Alto until year 8 and then followed the normal pattern by boarding in Ovalle. She completed a diploma in nutrition but has never had the opportunity to use her skills in her work. She first began to work on the grapes with a group of girlfriends during the summer school holidays when she was 16. She has always worked for the largest plant in Chañaral Alto. She used to enjoy her work in the packing plants, but recently has been less enamoured of the hard, repetitive and pressurised working conditions:

> I like my job, more or less, but lately I have not been enjoying it as much. I realise that the work in the grapes is the only possibility to earn a little bit more. You're on your feet all day long. Yes, on your feet because if you sit down you slow yourself down. And you can find that you are very, very tired, but you have to put the tiredness aside because if you stop, well it's fewer boxes, and fewer boxes means less money that you can earn, because out of 1,000 pesos, 100 is a lot to lose. (Marta)

In 1990 she became pregnant by a seasonal worker from the south. She is uncertain whether he even knows about his son – he certainly does not contribute to his upbringing. This increased the pressure on her to find employment and during the winter of 1993 she travelled north to Iquique in search of work. Through friends of her sister she found employment as a vendor. In total she was able to earn CH$70,000 (US$167), but this was reduced to CH$56,000 (US$134) after deductions. With the rent and the money she sent back each week to her mother who was taking care of her young son, she was unable to save very much.

She is uncertain about the future, knowing that there is little for her in Chañaral Alto. Marta would ideally like to use her nutritional skills planning meals in a hospital, but realises that her biggest problem will be leaving her son. For her, Chañaral Alto has lost much of its charm. She no longer enjoys going out to parties and discos as she did when she was younger and suggests that there are many more things for men to do than for women. For Marta the seasonality of the work in the grape economy is the greatest problem, as she needs regular local employment to enable her to take care of her son. While she does not have to overcome opposition from a male partner in order to work, she feels keenly the problem of leaving her son behind to search for alternative work:

> There's nothing here for me, so last year I went to Iquique and I still didn't find a job in what I learned and so I became a vendor and it went well. I don't know what I'll do next. They say that there are possibilities to work in the grapes further down the valley. I think it's in March and April so that's where I'll go and look for work, but as long as it's close to my son. Because when I was in Iquique, which is very far away, he lost his affection for me, because he now no longer calls me 'mama', he calls be 'auntie'. (Marta)

Patricia has two children (both girls) and lives with her partner in one of the larger houses in Chañaral Alto. She was born in Viña del Mar in central Chile and came to live in Chañaral Alto when her mother separated from her father. Her mother's family are from the region. Patricia was educated in a technical college in Ovalle and is a qualified nursery nurse. When she finished her education she was pregnant and went to live in southern Chile with her boyfriend who was working for Soprole, a large company making dairy products. They came to visit her mother during one vacation and decided to stay because the village was expanding and there were opportunities to work on the grapes. Her partner works all year on the grapes while she works during the summer harvest, cleaning and packing the grapes. She estimated that during a good week she could earn CH$60,000 (US$143) and in a bad week CH$20,000 (US$48). For the rest of the year she works in the local government office dealing with the electoral roll. Although she earns only CH$1,500 (US$3.60) for a half day's work, she enjoys the security offered by the job compared to work on the grapes. It is also much more sociable and civilised compared to working in the fields all day 'where your face is burned and your hands freeze'. She described the rationale for her decision to work:

> I work so as not be bored, not to waste any time. So with that job [in the packing plant] I have another salary and can buy other things for myself, small luxuries. On the other hand, with the job in the office I have more security, this is a government job so it is more secure. It's more like a job for the future. (Patricia)

Throughout 1993 she was able to combine her work with childcare because her daughter was at school while she worked in the office and they spent the afternoons in the house. The following year presented more problems because her older daughter would be at school out of office hours and she also had to care for her new baby. One solution was to have a female friend, also with young children, come to live with her and between them work out a system for taking care of each other's children while the other worked. Patricia had hoped to set up a childcare facility but was prevented by a combination of government bureaucracy and the opening of a temporary facility for the children of *temporeras* in the secondary school.

Patricia showed a keen interest in and observation of the changes that have occurred in the village. For her the most noticeable change has been the extension of the metalled road into the village making transport of grape trucks much easier. She has also seen the way the young people have increased their consumption of alcohol and 'soft' drugs. In her opinion though it is very much a problem introduced into the village by the migrants. But the local women are also involved in taking drugs and alcohol: 'The more mature women and the young women, they all take it, it's like a vice. So that also came with the grapes. A type of decline came with the grapes'.

At the same time positive changes have occurred, especially in the material condition of people's lives and also in the freedom that women have to go out to work, gaining independence and increasing family income:

> Well the women here aren't as feminist as in other countries. You know, as recently in some countries women can live alone and do almost anything. It's not exactly like that here, but the women are

not totally confined to the house. In spite of everything, the woman can have her own money and buy her own things. She can decide what to buy rather than relying on the men to give her money and tell her what to buy. (Patricia)

For Patricia her work on the grapes represents a possibility for an income when other work is not available. She has been fortunate in obtaining regular employment in the government sector, although she still harbours hopes of setting up her own childcare facility.

For Alicia, Marta and Patricia, the strategies they employ to manage their domestic responsibilities and wage-earning opportunities are complex. For all these women the grape economy is just one waged activity they undertake. Alicia runs the *botelleria*, Patricia works in the government office and Marta has had a variety of jobs. Yet none of these women mentioned having any traditional responsibilities in small-scale family farming. While the parents of these women (or in the case of Alicia, her husband), had originally earned their living from small-scale tomato production, it appears not to be an option that is now considered by the women. This contrasts dramatically with the opinions expressed by Rachel, Ximena and Maria, who view traditional small-scale production as the central aspect of their income-generating activity and the grapes as an additional opportunity to earn their own money. In Tome Alto the women still regard themselves as *campesinas* first and foremost, and their role as *temporeras* as being of secondary importance. This contrast between the women from the two villages highlights the heterogeneity of the temporeras.

CONCLUDING REMARKS

It is difficult to summarise the situation *vis-à-vis* employment in the modern agro-export sector for the populations of the agricultural communities. It represents both a new possibility for employment in an area traditionally characterised as having very limited job opportunities. It has also provided rural women with a new wage-earning potential and the freedom to move beyond the domestic sphere and traditional agriculture. However it has bought with it dramatically new systems of labour organisation, especially in areas where agribusiness dominates, or indeed has marginalised, traditional production and labour systems.

The contradictions inherent in seasonal work in the agricultural sector of the Guatulame are experienced by both women and men. The very limited duration of much of the work in the grape economy means that it offers few meaningful opportunities for personal advancement. The work is arduous, repetitive and poorly paid; it is also the only alternative source of income outside small-scale traditional agriculture. The women, especially those working in the packing plants, have the burden of the double day and extremely long working hours. On the other hand, the work provides income during periods of severe work scarcity in traditional agriculture. For many women it is the first opportunity they have had to earn substantial amounts of money and have it paid directly to them. It also allows them to escape the routine drudgery of the home. To this extent it has the potential for empowering women through increasing their independence, if only for a short period each year.

In both Tome Alto and Chañaral Alto the changes brought by the grape economy have been evident in the social life and organisation of the villages. The alterations in land tenure and labour organisation have had ramifications that cut deep into the social fabric of the traditional agricultural communities. While in one village small-scale production has continued with only superficial changes, the other has experienced the development of an active land market and many small-scale producers have disposed of their land and become more reliant on waged labour. In both villages there has been a fundamental reworking of labour market organisation with large numbers of both women and men being incorporated into the export grape economy as either permanent or temporary waged workers. With the importance of female labour to the successful production of high quality products, women have been leaving the domestic sphere and family farm to undertake predominantly seasonal paid work.

This has had ramifications for the organisation of household production and reproduction, frequently physically removing women from the location of much of their regular responsibilities, especially domestic work and childcare. While the women may be preoccupied with the problems of neglecting their children and work an extended double day, it also accustoms men to female family members working and may sometimes spur them to take up some of the slack by helping out in the household. The composition of the household and the level of household income are important factors in determining women's labour force participation. However, it is apparent that these factors are closely intertwined with the cultural perceptions of gender roles and how both partners interpret these.

The heterogeneity of the *temporeras* is underlined in this case study by the combining of traditional and modern, both in terms of income generation as *campesinas* and household responsibilities. This reflects the uneven and partial integration of modern agribusiness into this region of rural Chile, providing an example of the way production for the domestic market is interwoven with export activities. The seasonality of output and variations between the peaks of output of different produce facilitate the multiple roles of women combining different types of agricultural work and their domestic responsibilities. However, women are caught at the interface between the traditional and modern, and at the interface between production on the land and the industrial process of the preparation of fruit for export. This has contradictory effects on the women themselves as they juggle their multiple roles and identities. At one level the burdens on them are increased, but at another there is an element of empowerment as their ability to generate independent income is enhanced. How individual women mediate these contradictions depends to a large extent on their personal circumstance. However, changes in gender and social relations through the extension of agribusiness have been only partial, perpetuating traditional aspects of the subordination of women in ways that facilitate their permanent availability as a seasonal workforce when required by the agro-export sector.

7 Case Study: Urban Fruit Workers in the South

The diversity in the backgrounds of the *temporeras* is illustrated by the fact that they are drawn at the one extreme from traditional rural households and at the other extreme from urban areas. The previous case study explored some of the ways in which women from the Norte Chico region have mediated the tensions between their traditional roles as *campesinas* with their insertion into modern agricultural wage labour in the grape economy. In contrast, the case study in this chapter draws on research in the VI and VII Regions, to the south of Santiago, to explore the situation of *temporeras* from more urbanised backgrounds. These women are engaged in similar processes of change and mediation, combining seasonal waged employment in modern agribusiness with the more traditional demands of home and family. However, these women must cope with the added pressures of ensuring the survival of their households in an urban environment where income-generating options outside seasonal employment in agribusiness are few and far between.

We focus on the *temporeras'* perceptions of their work in agribusiness, exploring some of the differences in working conditions and employment opportunities they each face, as well as the precarious nature of their dependence on wage-labour in agribusiness. We then examine the women's motives for working, the effects on household relationships, as well as the ways in which they negotiate the tensions of the double day. Following this, the chapter will examine the changing nature of gender relations within the workplace as women are brought into contact with new and complex issues of sexual harassment and worker organisation through their paid employment. Finally, the complex and contradictory questions regarding the potential for women's empowerment will be discussed.[1]

AGRIBUSINESS IN THE VI AND VII REGIONS

Both the VI and the VII Regions have a long-established history of agricultural production, with advantageous soil and climatic conditions in the valleys which have favoured the cultivation of a wide range of fruit species (Murray 1996). Nationally, the VI Region has the greatest concentration of land dedicated to fruit production, amounting to 59,600 hectares in the 1992–3 season. This accounted for 33 per cent of Chile's total fruit growing area. The VII Region has less land dedicated to fruit production, although this amounted to 26,510 hectares in the 1992–3 season (INE 1992–3).

A wide range of fruit species are cultivated in the VI Region, including table grapes, apples, pears, kiwis, cherries and plums. The most significant in terms of production levels are red and green apples, which accounted for 46 per cent of national exports in 1994–5, nectarines, 36 per cent, kiwis, 25 per cent and table grapes, which accounted for 25 per cent of exports in the same period (Asociación de Exportadores 1994–5: 125). In the VII Region, a similar range of fruits are cultivated. Again, red and green apples are the most significant, accounting for 43 per cent of exports in 1994–5 (Asociación de Exportadores 1994–5: 125). Other significant fruit export species in the region include kiwis, pears, table grapes and cherries (see Table 4.2 on page 67 for regional export figures).

The case studies are drawn from in-depth interviews with women from very different communities within these two regions, shown in Map 7.1. The first location lies in the VI Region, is the small settlement of Las Mercedes in the *comuna* of Graneros. The municipal town of Graneros is situated in the province of Cachapoal, VI Region. The regional capital, Rancagua, lies approximately 50 km to the south. Graneros is an area with a well-established agribusiness sector, with table grapes, apples, pears and peaches as the principal species cultivated. A more recent development is the cultivation of onions and garlic for the international market.

Las Mercedes is situated about 7 km to the west of the urban centre of Graneros. This represents a community of approximately 20 households which depend on wage labour in agribusiness, despite its proximity to an urban centre. There are no public transport links from Las Mercedes to Graneros and an unpaved road is the only link between the settlement and the metalled highway. The isolation of the settlement means that it retains a relatively traditional rural way of life. However, the extent of agribusiness in the area means that few households own and beyond a family-sized plot, making them dependent on wage labour in agriculture in order to survive. Thus, while agriculture may offer a few permanent employment opportunities to men, the women of the settlement rely on seasonal employment

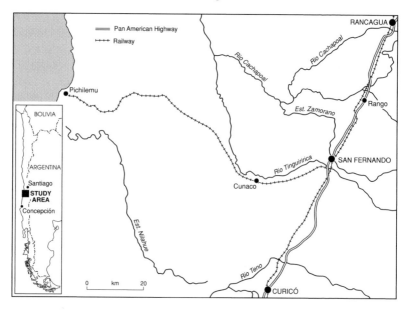

Map 7.1   Map of Case Study Area in the South

in agribusiness to provide a wage income that is vital for ensuring the survival of the household through the winter months. There are relatively few packing plants in the immediate area, and the women seem reluctant to venture further afield to find this type of work. However, the extent of export agriculture is such in this sector that there is a range of work available in the fields and orchards within walking distance. The second location is the city of Curicó, the capital of the province of the same name in the VII Region. This represents a large urban centre, which nevertheless, is also largely dependent on agribusiness to provide employment. Many of the service industries in the city are based on agriculture, providing employment for a substantial proportion of the regional workforce (Murray 1996: 246). This means that although alternative employment opportunities may exist, seasonal employment in agribusiness provides the central wage-earning activity for many households, particularly those from low-income neighbourhoods on the outskirts of the city.

In both regions, the expansion of agribusiness has meant a movement away from the traditional rural relations of household-based production towards an insertion into a modern wage-based economy.

The dependence on a wage income to obtain goods and services has led to the increased poverty of households where a single male income is no longer sufficient to maintain a family. In this situation, the adult members of a household, including women, may find themselves obliged to seek work as seasonal labourers, often the only available employment opportunity, in order to alleviate the effects of poverty. As we have explored, the demand for specifically female labour in agribusiness has led to a transformation of gender relations at a social level, in order to allow women to be brought in as an essential labour force, while there has been a corresponding shift in gender relations at the household level, as women become wage-earners whose income is essential to the survival of the household.

Gender relations also play a significant role in ordering the labour market within agribusiness. Previous chapters have discussed the extent of gender segregation of tasks in agribusiness and the employment opportunities that are available to women. In the two regions under study here, the specific tasks carried out by women vary according to the range of fruit species cultivated. However, the general separation of activities in both the fields and packing plants follow the lines of gender segregation outlined in chapter 5. Field tasks such as the pruning, thinning and pinching out of peaches, apples and grapes are deemed to be 'female' tasks due to the delicacy required to minimise damage to the fruit. In the packing plants, the same gender division of tasks applies, with predominantly women being employed in the cleaning, selection and packing of the fruit, whether it be kiwis, grapes, apples or peaches. All these tasks require a relatively high degree of expertise, and *temporeras* often become 'professional' in a particular task, seeking the same type of work season after season.

The systems of remuneration vary from activity to activity, although there is a general tendency for field tasks to be paid by the day (*al día*), and packing to be paid by the piece (*a trato*).[2] However, the majority of 'female' tasks tend to be paid *a trato* or piece rate, a system that extracts high levels of productivity from women who need to maximise their earnings, while minimising labour costs. Nevertheless, piece work offers women potentially high earnings, bearing out the observation made in chapter 4 that women are concentrated in those activities with a greater earning potential than men. This is an indication of the ways in which a simultaneous reworking and reinforcing of gender relations at all levels plays a central role in securing a cheap, flexible, yet highly skilled labour force to carry out key tasks within the production process.

Despite the difficulties and disadvantages this type of work involves, the movement away from the isolated domestic role into a wage-earning one may offer a potential empowerment to these women, in a similar way to that experienced by the women in the Norte Chico. They are collectively drawn into new sets of relations in the workplace, where traditional gender relations are subverted, yet reinforced. Although this has contradictory outcomes, the opportunity to move away from the isolation of their homes into new collective relations of production may provide women with a common experience on which to base collective action. Moreover, the earning of a wage income which is paid directly to them has an effect on the power relations within the household, challenging traditional expectations of gender roles. Through their mediation of these tensions, women may be able actively to renegotiate traditional gender relations within the workplace and households and gain a degree of power for themselves.

The following individual case studies have been selected to give an insight into the lives of five women who combine paid work as *temporeras* with their family roles as wives and mothers. These women have all worked in agribusiness during the season for a number of years, in a variety of activities which represent the range of employment opportunities available to women in this sector. The case studies provide an insight into the contrasting situations of these *temporeras,* both in terms of the types of activities they undertake and the nature of their incorporation into the agricultural labour force. Through an exploration of five women's experiences, the heterogeneity of their working experiences will be drawn out, together with the effects of their employment on the gender relations within their households. Their attitudes towards their paid work in agribusiness provide further insight into the active ways in which women mediate these complex and contradictory roles.

INDIVIDUAL CASE STUDIES

In this section, five women's different experiences of employment in agribusiness will be explored, based on in-depth interviews (see note 1). Three of the women live in Las Mercedes in the VI Region, while the other two live in Curicó. Despite the differences in the nature of their insertion into the modern agricultural wage labour force, all five women mediate similar tensions in their changing roles within the workplace, the community and the household. All the women interviewed have resident partners and children, so their employment in agribusiness must be combined with carrying out their domestic responsibilities, and, in a traditional *machista* society, they must also negotiate with their partners in order to gain permission to work outside the home. However, the heterogeneity of household relations means that each woman negotiates these tensions in different ways, and their experiences of working are shaped by these relations.

The demographic characteristics of the interviewees shown in Table 7.1 indicate that they are married with children, and range in age from 23 to 42. This fits with the general profile of the *temporeras* discussed in chapter 4, although the variety of the women's backgrounds and family situations emphasises again the heterogeneity of the *temporeras* and the variety of people who are drawn into the seasonal labour force. In three of the cases, the women come from households that rely on seasonal waged labour, as their husbands are also *temporeros*. In one case, the household has one, year-round, stable income, as the male partner has permanent employment in agriculture. In yet another case, the male partner is not employed in

Table 7.1 Demographic Characteristics of the Interviewees

Name	Age	Years of Schooling	Marital Status	No. of Children	Husband's Occupation	Type of Household and no. of Members
Las Mercedes						
Luisa	23	7	Married	2	*Temporero*	Extended (5)
Berta	25	7	Married	1	*Temporero*	Extended (11)
Ruth	38	4	Married	2	Permanent agricultural worker	Nuclear (4)
Curicó						
Anita	29	8	Married	2	*Temporero*	Extended (5)
Clara	42	9	Married	2	Self-employed mechanic	Nuclear (4)

Source: Vogel 1997.

agriculture at all, but is a self-employed mechanic with his own workshop. However, this income is also variable.

Ruth, Berta and Luisa live in Las Mercedes, in the community where they have lived all their lives. Agriculture is the main activity in the area, providing the principal employment for the people in the settlement. Ruth's husband has permanent, year-round employment, albeit poorly paid, while Berta's and Luisa's households depend on seasonal work in agribusiness. None of the women continued their secondary education, as there was only a primary school in the relatively isolated settlement. Financial constraints, together with social attitudes towards women's education, made it difficult to continue their education. All three women work as *temporeras* in different activities within the local agribusiness.

Anita and Clara live in separate low-income neighbourhoods on the outskirts of Curicó, a city where they have also lived all their lives. As has been discussed previously, agribusiness provides a significant source of employment in the city, and both Anita and her husband rely on seasonal work in agribusiness to maintain their family. Clara's case is different again, as her husband owns a small metal-workshop. However, this is an unstable living and Clara has worked for many years in agribusiness to supplement this income. Both women have more years of schooling than the women from Las Mercedes, indicating that residence in an urban centre may facilitate women's access to secondary education. However, it seems that financial constraints also prevented them from continuing their studies.

Employment in agribusiness offers many women the opportunity to earn potentially high wages, as has been mentioned. Table 7.2 shows the average monthly earnings of the *temporeras* and their husbands, as well as their total earnings for the 1993/4 season. In all cases, the women were able to earn more than their husbands through their employment in agribusiness, indicating the vital contribution they make to household income. It is important to bear in mind that only Ruth's husband has a year-round income; for the other households, the average earnings apply only during the season when work is available. Similarly, Clara's husband has only sporadic earnings. As the earning potential of both partners only exists for a few months of the year, the cycle of employment and unemployment has serious implications for the economic security of those households dependent on wage-labour in agribusiness. The case studies forcefully illustrate this insecurity and the hardship of surviving the winter months when there is no work available.

Table 7.2 Average Weekly Earnings of the *Temporeras* and their Male
Partners, CH$(US$),[3] 1993/4 season

Interviewee	Total Earnings for Season (total working period in season given)	Average Weekly Earnings During Working Period	Male Partner's Average Weekly Earnings
Ruth	$302,400 (US$720) 4 months	$10,800 (US$26) Dec.–early Jan. $24,000 (US$57) through Jan. $15,000 (US$36) Feb.–end Mar.	$15,000 (US$36)
Luisa	$309,600 (US$737) 4 months	$7,200 (US$17) Nov.–late Dec. $13,200 (US$31) late Dec.–mid-Jan. $42,000 (US$100) mid-end Jan. $15,000 (US$36) Feb.–through Mar.	$12,000 (S$30)
Berta	$117,600 (US$280) 2 months	$13,800 (US$33) Feb. $15,600 (US$37) Mar.	$14,910 (US$35.50)
Clara	$320,000 (US$762) 8 months	$10,000 (US$24) Nov.–through May	$10,000 (US$24)
Anita	$268,800 (US$640) 4 months	$16,800 (US$40.00) Jan.–though April	$10,800 (US$26)

Source: Vogel 1997.

Las Mercedes

The women from Las Mercedes tend to work mainly in the orchards
and small and medium-sized packing plants which are situated close
to their homes. The extensive availability of nearby employment
means that they are able to juggle the demands of their work and
family roles relatively successfully, while long-standing social relationships within the community tend to ensure their employment in the

same activities season after season. This means that employment relations tend to be informal, based on good-faith agreements. Moreover, the women from the community often work together, which helps to reduce the opposition from husbands.

Ruth

Ruth (aged 38) has worked in the same peach orchard near her home for the same boss for nine years since before she was married. Her husband is an agricultural worker with stable, albeit low-paid work all year round, and while Ruth did not work for a period while her children were young, economic necessity has prompted her return to this job. Her husband's income of CH$15,000 (US$36) a week is not sufficient to maintain their family. During the season, Ruth earned weekly between CH$10,800 (US$26) and CH$24,000 (US$57) per week – a significant contribution to the household income.

Ruth is skilled in the delicate task of pruning peach trees and this has helped ensure her job year after year. This is known as *raleo*, and involves removing the smaller fruit buds in order to allow the strongest one to mature. The delicacy of the task means that women's smaller hands and lightness of touch are among the perceived characteristics which suit them to this job. However, it is regarded as relatively heavy work by the *temporeras*, as wooden benches and ladders are used to reach the fruit on the higher branches of the trees. This bench is carried from tree to tree down the line, involving a high degree of physical exertion. This provided Ruth with work for 2–3 months, from November to January. During this period, she earned CH$1,800 (US$4.29) for a day of approximately eight hours. Although Ruth's *patrón* had her sign 'everything', she was not sure whether this meant she had a contract, but was not unduly worried as the good-faith agreement with her boss has ensured her employment every season.

In this activity, Ruth worked six days a week for a wage of CH$10,800 (US$25.71) with no deductions for her social security contributions. This was a relatively low wage in her opinion, but one that had the advantage of being guaranteed for the whole two-month period. In other seasons, Ruth has sought further employment in the apple orchards. This year, however, she obtained relatively well-paid employment harvesting onions destined for export, which had been cultivated for the first time near to Las Mercedes. This activity provided employment for many people, both men and women, from the surrounding locality, including Luisa.

The first job in the onion harvest involved following the lines of harvested onions and cutting off the root and the stem, *desmochadura*.
This was by far the best job in that season as it was paid by the piece.
Ruth calculates that her average earnings were about CH$24,000
(US$57.14) a week in the *desmochadura*. However, this lucrative work
lasted from January to February only, as so many workers arrived
from the immediate surrounding area to take advantage of the high
wages.

There was more work available in the onion fields through March
clearing up the leavings from the harvest. In both the *desmochadura*
and the clearing, work began at 8.00 am, with the arrival of the
workers checked by list. The pace of work was steady during the
desmochadura, although the temperatures were high during this
period and there was little shade in the open field. Lunch was at noon,
when workers would find a shady spot to eat food brought from home.
The absence of facilities was one of the disadvantages of working in
the field mentioned by both Ruth and Luisa: there was nowhere to
wash the mud from their hands before eating lunch and there were no
toilet facilities, which was a problem as they were working alongside
men: 'There was a cornfield and we all had to go together and guard
one another' (Ruth). However, the *desmochadura* was so well paid
that it was possible to earn a day's wage by three o'clock in the afternoon, and many of the women would ask permission to leave early
and return to the more comfortable facilities of their homes.

Neither Ruth nor Luisa received a contract for the work in the
onions, although it seems there was an attempt to draw up contracts:

> One day there were some people, they came to sign contracts with
> us; I, at least, didn't get it back, another lady did, but they hadn't
> signed it with the *patrón*, they were badly done, they had the names
> all wrong, so they were no good! The only thing was that he did pay
> the end-of-contract settlement. (Ruth)

This lack of clear contractual relations is a common feature of work in
the fields. *Temporeras* are often asked to sign blank contracts, as well
as blank end-of-contract forms. This clearly jeopardises workers, particularly in terms of their wage levels, which can be altered several
times during the course of a single job. However, in this case, the
workforce was drawn mainly from the local community and, as the
employer wished to cultivate onions there again the following year, he
observed the workers' rights to a certain extent in order to maintain
good relations within the community.

In the *desmochadura,* there was no apparent segregation of tasks along gender lines. Women and men worked together in the fields, and of approximately 80 people working in the field, the majority were men. However, during the clearing, there was a marked gender segregation of tasks, with the women picking up the leavings and the men filling the bins at the end of the lines. There was also a differentiation in the remuneration, with men being paid piecework rates and women paid a daily rate of CH $2,500 (US$5.95). In Ruth's opinion this was discriminatory and reduced the women's earning capacity:

> They said that putting the onions into the bins was too heavy for us, and yet we filled a truck quicker than they did. But afterwards, they just kept the men on, and they paid them a lot more, they paid us per day and they paid them piecework, and we worked faster than them. (Ruth)

Evidently, women were eventually marginalised from this activity. This is only one example of the contradictory ways in which gender stereotypes are first subverted in order to ensure a supply of labour at peak times, such as during the harvesting and preparation of the onions for shipment, only to re-emerge as a justification for paying women lower wages and laying off the female workforce when it was no longer needed.

For Ruth, work in agribusiness is important as it enables her to provide for her children and to meet the secondary needs of the household. Ruth indicates the ways in which their incomes are put towards different aims as she gives her reasons for working:

> To help in the house, to buy things for the children, and to keep things for the winter; because with what my husband earns it's only 15,000 pesos a month and you have to buy them [the children] extra things, that's why I work. ... Because sometimes you guarantee things with what he earns, you make sure of the food, all those things. But if it's about a pair of trousers, a pair of shoes, that's when I put in more. (Ruth)

Although Ruth indicates that her husband is the main breadwinner, she recognises that her contribution is important and the economic situation of the family has been improved through her paid work:

> I bought clothes for the children, and sometimes extra things so that we can eat better in the time when one is working. ... I bought some cement to fix up the outside [of the house] and we bought sugar to keep for the winter, flour, things like that. (Ruth)

Through Ruth's contributions to the household income, essential structural repairs were made to their dwelling, and she was able to stock up on food staples for the winter. Nevertheless, Ruth's perception is that she is only a contributor to the family income, a helper. In spite of the fact that she earns more than her husband during the season, he is still the indisputed head of the household:

> Because he always made sure that he had a job, even if it was only a little, but he has always worked to maintain us all .... That's why I think he should be the head of the household! (Ruth)

However, this season, the increased availability of work meant that she was able to make a substantial contribution to the household welfare. Moreover, there is usually some money left over for savings and for personal spending:

> Yes, there is enough. At least this year I didn't save any money, I just bought things. Other years when I didn't have the little ones, I would save, but not now! Yes, it's enough to give yourself some small luxuries! (Ruth)

For Ruth, the main motivation to take on paid work lies in being able to improve the situation of her children and her home. She enjoys working as it enables her to leave the house; however, this involves a significant disadvantage in terms of her domestic obligations:

> When I've worked, I've felt good, I've got out of the house more, but ... of course, then you get home and you have to do more things. The work in the season is double for me, because you have to do all things in the house and work outside. ... Not like the man, who works out there and then comes home and everything is ready. ... It's not as difficult as what one has to do, one has to do one thing and then another. (Ruth)

Ruth's home and family are the most important, and she will only work if it does not cause too much disruption to her domestic routine:

> I have never worked further away, I don't like going out very much. Also, I like to come home at midday. I always try to leave as much done as possible when I work. The house is always the most important, I think. (Ruth)

The problem of childcare is a recurrent one for *temporeras*. As temporary workers, they are not entitled to claim the statutory childcare provided by employers to permanent workers, although there has been some attempt to address this problem on the part of the state. SERNAM organises childcare centres for the children of *temporeras* during the season (Matear 1995). However, although SERNAM ran a childcare centre in Graneros, this was too far away for the women of Las Mercedes. Instead, Ruth's mother, who lives next door, takes care of the children while she is at work, highlighting the importance of female family members in allowing mothers to take on paid employment.

In Ruth's case, traditional gender relations within the family remain basically unaltered: although she has succeeded in extending her role to include working outside the home. However, as her rationale for doing so is to provide her children with some extras, she remains within the boundaries of her role as mother. This explains why her husband, who initially opposed her working, no longer does so: 'At first he didn't like it, but now he knows that I work for the little ones' (Ruth).

This season, the increased availability of work meant that Ruth was able to make a substantial contribution to the family welfare. Ruth's income is clearly important in ensuring that the secondary needs of the family are met. This prompts Ruth to desire to work all year round, in spite of the disadvantages she perceives in terms of her family role. This would alleviate the poverty of the winter months when there is little work available in the countryside. As the only available work lies in agribusiness, the future is uncertain. Ruth fears that next year she will have to look further afield for work, as the local fruit appears to have been damaged by a fly infestation, compromising her domestic responsibilities further. If she is unable to find work nearby, the economic security that was gained through her efforts this year will be lost.

Luisa

Luisa (aged 23) had never worked before the season as she had been taking care of her alcoholic father before her marriage and, subsequently, her two children. Her husband works as a temporary agricultural labourer with an unstable income. She has always wanted to work, but her husband had not allowed her to do so on the grounds that the children would be neglected. However, once the youngest child began walking, Luisa was able to convince her husband that the children were old enough to be left with their maternal grandmother. She began to work at the end of November, pruning vines in the field. This work involves a variety of tasks, such as removing long shoots from the vine, and removing the smaller fruit buds. The first task was paid by the day and Luisa received CH$1,200 (US$2.86) for a 9-hour day. The second was paid by the piece and Luisa was able to earn between CH$2,000–3,000 (US$4.76–7.14) a day in this task. She worked about two months in the vineyard. Piecework was paid daily, while the day tasks were paid every 15 days: 'I had never earned so much before, the only trouble was it didn't look as much because we were paid every week' (Luisa).

After working in the vineyard for November and December, Luisa went on to work in the onion harvest with Ruth, where she earned a higher average of CH$42,000 (US$100) per week. As both men and women were employed in this activity, Luisa's husband joined her in the work on the onions. Luisa's main reason for wanting to work was the low income earned by her husband, who is also a temporary worker. His average weekly earnings are CH$12,500 (US$30), although this is earned only during the months of the season. For Luisa, it was important for her to make a contribution to the household income: 'There were so many things we needed in the house, things for the house and for the children and what he earns just isn't enough' (Luisa).

She also felt she was wasting her time being at home when there was ample work available:

> It's just that being here, doing the things that need to be done, you don't get anywhere, but working you can get money to buy the things that are necessary. (Luisa)

Luisa also enjoyed working much more than being at home: 'I like it because you do just one thing, while in the house you have to do so many things!'

There were specific items she wanted to purchase and she did not want to wait for her husband to have enough money to give her. In an environment where many of her neighbours were working, she felt there was no reason preventing her from doing the same. Luisa used her income to provide her children with clothes and school articles, as well as purchasing a quantity of food staples for the winter. She also bought household goods and glazing for the windows of her house, which she eventually put in herself. This latter item represents a necessity rather than an 'extra'. As in Ruth's case, this is an important structural improvement to the dwelling which enables the family to consolidate their economic security. Luisa decided herself how to spend her money, and she was careful to leave a little extra to buy some items for herself: 'Yes, at the end, I bought myself some under-wear, some cosmetics, I had my hair cut, I bought shoes and clothes' (Luisa).

This was evidently an important measure of her own independence, particularly as she was able to fulfil the goals she had set herself regarding household expenditure, as well as setting aside a proportion of her wage income for personal expenses. Thus, through her wage income, Luisa was able to make a substantial improvement in the standard of living for her family, especially as their economic situation deteriorated in the winter when both she and her husband were unemployed.

For Luisa, making alternative domestic arrangements for her first season as a *temporera* proved difficult. Her mother was able to take care of the children some of the time, but, when she also went to work during the season, Luisa faced problems with her youngest child and was obliged to take him to work with her in the fields:

> I didn't have anyone to look after the children at times, there is a need for someone to look after the children here in the summer. ... Sometimes my mother works in the summer, so when she works, it's a problem because I didn't have anyone to look after him. ... I would take him with me, but the heat, sometimes it gave him a fever. (Luisa)

However, there was no alternative if she was to continue working. Moreover, Luisa did not receive any help with the domestic respons-ibilities at home, and she was unhappy that her husband did not help her, despite the fact that they were working together. This proved to be a source of tension:

> I, when I got home in the evening, would be doing everything, so I was bad-tempered; I had to do the cleaning, prepare the meals, and sometimes I would come home to make bread and I baked at 12 o'clock at night and I went to bed late, so I was angry and I didn't want to talk. (Luisa)

Luisa's case illustrates the extent to which attempting to combine domestic responsibilities with paid work can present a significant double burden of work, particularly if other members of the house-hold do not help. This indicates the persistence of the traditional gender relations, where Luisa, as the only female member of the household, is solely responsible for the domestic tasks. Nevertheless,

Luisa perceives that the role of mother and housewife is fully compatible with that of *temporera*. The main problem she faced was opposition from her husband, but that was overcome through her organisational skills. She feels there is enough time to do both – look after her family as well as work during the season. However, this is achieved through taking a considerable double burden of work upon herself, and it is the temporary nature of this employment itself that makes it difficult for her to negotiate a more equitable distribution of domestic responsibilities with her husband, as the inconveniences of the double burden need only be borne for a period of months.

The jobs that Ruth and Luisa took during the season are a good illustration of the type of work available to women within the range of field tasks. As agribusiness is well established in this region, there were ample employment opportunities and both the women were able to find work within half an hour's walk of their homes, for four and three months respectively. The proximity to their homes seemed to compensate for the inconveniences of working conditions and both expected to work in similar activities in the following season. There is also work available in the few nearby packing plants, but Ruth was unwilling to explore this possibility, even though she is aware that it is possible to earn higher wages in the packing plant, as it would compromise her domestic responsibilities further. However, for Luisa, her first experience as a *temporera* proved to be a positive one overall, and she expressed a firm desire to venture further afield during the next season.

Berta

Berta (aged 25) also lives in Las Mercedes, in an extended household of 11 people, where the men are also dependent on employment in agribusiness. She has worked for a number of years in the apple orchards and vineyards nearby, as well as in packing plants. This season, Berta had worked for three months. The first job was in the vineyard where she was arranging the bunches of grapes prior to the packing process. This was paid by the piece and lasted only a few days. Berta earned an average of CH$2,300 (US$5.48) in a day of eight and a half hours. She worked six days a week and took home CH$13,800 (US$32.86). The pace of work was not unduly strenuous, although each worker carried a bench along the lines of vines, which made the work heavier. As with the work in the onion field, there were no facilities and workers ate lunch brought from home to eat in the vineyard. There were no contracts given for this work. From this job, Berta passed into the packing plant proper. Here she was employed as a *limpiadora*, one of the early stages in the packing process, cleaning bunches of grapes. Any leaves and damaged fruit must be removed from the bunch, it is clipped into shape before being packed. The plant was a large one, employing around 200 people. The majority of them were women and there were three lines with 130 women in total. Berta regards the work in the packing plant as being hard. The *temporeras* work standing for long hours, with the pace of work imposed by the mechanised production line. This work was also paid by the piece at a rate of CH$60 (US$0.14) per box. The day began at 9.00 am and finished between 7.00 and 8.30 pm, until all the grapes that had been cut that day had been cleaned. However, as well as an hour for lunch, there was an official break at 6.00 in the evening, when the firm provided the workers with a snack and a drink. This work enabled Berta to earn an average of CH$2,600 (US$6.19) a day. Berta worked in the packing plant for a month through March and, although she worked only two months, her total earnings for the season came to approximately CH$117,600 (US$280).

Berta's motives for working are similar to those expressed by the other women. She works in order to improve the situation of the family. While her husband was working, he earned an average income of CH$14,910 (US$35.50) a week, which is sufficient to cover the daily needs of the family. Berta's earnings are divided between food, dry goods for the winter and items for her child and the house: 'Something for the food and something to buy. This year I bought a bed, and things for my son' (Berta). However, as Berta lives in a large household with her husband's extended family, the costs of food appear to be met by the incomes of the men in the family, while her contribution is an 'extra'. Berta retains a larger proportion of her income for her own expenditure than either Ruth or Luisa do, only contributing to food costs if necessary. Berta herself does not view her income as essential to the family's welfare; they could survive on her husband's income alone. This causes problems as her husband is opposed to Berta's working; however, she continues to work in spite of this:

> My husband tells me not to work, but I work anyway, the money is always useful. My husband is a little jealous! ... I like working, I'm used to it. (Berta)

It may be that her husband's opposition is not enough to prevent Berta from working as she does not face the same domestic disadvantages as the other women. Her son is looked after by her mother, who lives in the same household, while the domestic responsibilities within the household are carried out by her sister-in-law. In addition, the wide availability of work in the sector means that Berta has become accustomed to earning her own money during the season, enabling her to provide herself and her family with 'extras' which improve their standard of living. Next year, she intends to work again, and she intends to find better-paid employment.

Berta's case illustrates how living in an extended household may make it easier for women to take on paid work outside the home. The presence of other female members to take on a significant share of the domestic responsibilities, as well as childcare, means that Berta faces considerably less tensions when she has to work. However, as it appears that her contribution to household income is less important than that of the other women interviewed, she faces continuing opposition from her husband. Despite this, the extensive availability of nearby employment prompts her to take advantage of her wage-earning capacity in order to improve the material conditions of her family.

For the women of Las Mercedes, the proximity of the employment opportunities often means that the disruption of the women's domestic responsibilities is minimised, while the work schedule allows them a degree of flexibility to return home during lunch breaks, or to leave work early. This may compensate to some degree for the less than adequate working conditions inherent in field tasks. Moreover, on one hand, this flexibility enables them to negotiate the tensions between their productive and reproductive activities with relative ease, while, on the other hand, minimising the impact of their paid work on the still traditional gender relations within their households, so avoiding undue conflicts with their husbands. However, this is won at a considerable physical cost, as women take on an onerous double burden of work during the season.

Nevertheless, the three women view their work as important in that it enables them to make up the shortfalls in expenditure that cannot be met from their husbands' incomes, particularly in providing necessary articles for their children and homes. However, as gender relations are only partially and temporarily modified, the perception that they are working for 'extras' is reinforced, leaving traditional gender role expectations and the division of labour within the household basically unchanged.

Curicó

We have seen that the women from Las Mercedes were able to find employment in close proximity to their homes, in tasks carried out in fields and orchards. By contrast, the women from Curicó work in large packing plants, where employment relations are more formalised, and production is carried out in a modern, mechanised line. While the packing plants may not be a great distance from their homes, travel to and from work takes time, and the work schedule does not permit them to move between work and home as some of the women from Las Mercedes are able to do. This means that, for these women, there is a greater separation between reproductive and productive activities, at least during the season. Moreover, the dependence of these households on employment in agribusiness, whether directly or indirectly, seems to have a significant impact on gender relations within them.

Clara

Clara (aged 42) has been in a dual-earner household since her marriage. Her husband's income from his metal workshop has never been sufficient to support the family, so she has worked as a *temporera* for 15 years, as well as taking on other jobs. The range of export fruit species cultivated in Curicó means that there is a degree of continuity in employment through the season. She had worked for the same packing firm for almost ten years. This firm also incorporated a refrigeration plant and this enabled her to work for eight months a year, from November to May. Work began with the selection of cherries, passing on to the freezing of strawberries, followed by plums, peaches and concluding with apples, the final fruit of the season:

> They didn't let people go because as the strawberry finished and the plum started, then they began to send people to the packing plant, the same people from the refrigeration they sent them to the packing plant to start on the other fruit. That's why you were able to work eight months continuously. (Clara)

Clara has now been working for five years in another packing and refrigeration plant. During the previous season, she worked as a calibrator, again from November to May, a task which was paid by the day for which she received CH$1,600 (US$3.81) a day plus lunch and transport. This was stipulated in the contract that all the workers in her firm received. However, although this is an improvement in the contractual conditions experienced by the women in Graneros, the contract does not guarantee security of employment as the firm retains the right to lay off workers without notice should the schedule require it.

The shift begins at 7.00 am and ends at 4.00 pm, with half an hour for lunch. At the start of the season, there is a high volume of fruit to be packed and the shift can be extended from 12 up to 18 hours until all the order has been packed. Furthermore, at the start of the season, *temporeras* work seven days a week, which only reduces to six towards the end. Workers are paid overtime, at a rate of CH$280 (US$0.67) per hour. However, as Clara points out, this is a low rate for overtime, considering that a shift can extend into the night, with no breaks for the workers:

> Sometimes, when there is a shipment or an order and it has to be got out, they get it out, I mean, they don't worry too much about the people. Because with just one meal, people can't be there that many hours. Afterwards they give you a cup of tea, that's all, and nothing more until the next day, when you have another tea in the morning. And you have to spend the whole night with nothing, and in that cold. Imagine! (Clara)

Clara would take home approximately CH$40,000 (US$95.24) a month, including overtime, which brought her earnings for the season to approximately CH$320,000 (US$762); at times this was considerably more than her husband's earnings. However, for Clara, the conditions in the packing are too hard, particularly the cold, so she is looking for work in the fields and orchards for the next season. For Clara, her income is essential for improving the quality of life for her family, enabling them to live beyond the mere satisfying of basic needs:

> In order to get ahead a little, because when one works, then you can renew the mattresses, the sheets, everything, what else can you do? At least I bought the television, I've bought some things in order to fix up the house: we bought sheets of zinc, we had to buy fifty sheets of zinc ourselves, and in that way we can try to live a little better. (Clara)

Although the delineation between the uses of the two incomes are similar to that of the women in Las Mercedes, Clara does not consider herself to be earning money for 'extras'. Her income is essential if the family is to have a home and a minimum standard of living:

> It's very important. Because with just … what the husband earns, it's well, it's practically nothing you can do for the house. So, when one works … at least you can eat a little better, and at the same time, buy something else for the house. Because … that money we use to buy something that will be of more benefit, or at least it's there as a memory: I bought that with my money. (Clara)

The higher demand for female labour in the season means that Clara's daughter also works a *temporera*. As Clara's husband's workshop is next to the house, he helps out with the household chores when Clara is working, together with Clara's youngest daughter. This situation contrasts with the husbands in Las Mercedes who suffer their wives to work so long as there is minimal disruption of the domestic regime. As Clara's husband's income is sporadic, it is necessary for him to take on some of the burden of the domestic responsibilities in order to allow her to take advantage of the greater opportunities for female employment. Moreover, as she has worked throughout her marriage, their expectations of gender roles have been modified. Clara's husband does some cleaning and cooking while he works, and he took an active role in childcare when the children were young. The necessity of maintaining both partners in the labour market has meant that there is an important reworking of the gender division of labour in Clara's household.

When Clara is working, she is able to earn more than her husband. The unreliability of her husband's income means that at times, Clara is the main earner. In spite of living in an urban centre, there seem to be few employment opportunities outside export agriculture for either men or women. The extent of this dependence on seasonal work is highlighted by the fact that her husband has had no work due to the neighbours' lack of resources. This situation has been exacerbated as there appears be less demand for labour this season and there have been difficulties in finding work:

> At the moment, we are bad, economically we are in a bad way because my husband's work has been bad. … There has been no work for us in the season … and for him, well, they say that everyone is like this, with no money, that's why he doesn't get any work

either, not even little soldering jobs. So we have had days when we haven't had enough even to buy bread ... today we are bad. Waiting to see if something turns up and nothing does. (Clara)

Although working as a *temporera* provides Clara with an opportunity to earn a relatively high income in a few months of the year, the seasonality of the work creates many difficulties. In Curicó, this type of work represents the livelihood for many households, rather than an opportunity for the wife to work for 'extras'. This is reflected in the critical financial situation which is experienced by many households during the winter months when no work is available. In spite of having made material advances during the season of work and having the minimal security of owning their house, the real poverty of the winter creates a cycle where economic security is rarely gained. It is for this reason that Clara would gladly take a lower-paying job that lasted all year round:

I would like to have been a good hairdresser, but I can't do a course or something, as I would like ... I would like any job, but one that is stable, a job that you have all year, even though it might pay less, but that you have it all year round. Because it's very sad, sometimes, in the winter, to not even have a heater, to be warm, nothing. If one could have a job all year round, then you'd live that much better. (Clara)

This conveys vividly the very real poverty that Clara's household experiences during the 'blue months' when there is no work available. Despite the fact that Clara's husband has a separate income-generating activity, the extent of the dependence of their neighbours on work in agribusiness affects his business directly.

Anita

Anita (aged 29) lives in another neighbourhood on the outskirts of Curicó and both she and her husband work as a *temporeros*. They have had joint responsibility for maintaining the family since they married seven years ago. Anita earns an average wage income of CH$16,800 (US$40) a week, while her husband earns an average of CH$10,800 (US$25.71). However, it is only possible to earn this during a few months of the year. The types of jobs that Anita and her husband take on during the season reflect the gendered division of the labour force. Anita works in the packing plants where it is possible to find work for extended periods, while her husband tends to find more work in the fields. Anita has worked as a packer for seven years in plants in the surrounding area, packing strawberries, apples, kiwis and grapes. Packers are paid by the piece and as making a good wage depends on the skill and speed of the individual, Anita has become 'professional' in this activity. This season, Anita worked from January to April packing kiwis. Anita prefers to work the night shift as the conditions of work are a little easier. Only the line supervisors are present and there is more tolerance when workers become too tired to work at the pace of the machine:

> Because when a person gets too sleepy, they move you, they put you in a part where it's slower, a machine which is slower. But you still move all night long, but it is a bit slower. (Anita)

The night shift begins at 9.00 pm and ends at 8.30 the following morning. There was only one break during the shift, of 15 minutes. The rate was approximately CH$2,800 (US$6.67) per shift, and Anita took home CH$69,000–$79,000 (US$164–$188) a month, for seven shifts a week. She had to miss a few days as her mother was very ill at this time. Other workers were able to earn as much as CH$97,000 (US$231) a month. Anita's total earnings for the season were CH$268,800 (US$640) – more than her husband. Owing to the extensive availability of employment for women in agribusiness, Anita is the *de facto* principal breadwinner. However, Anita perceives herself to be a joint breadwinner. Both their salaries are essential to the survival of the family as neither of them will have work during the winter:

> It's always to get ahead with one more little thing. But we always do it in the good time. For example, if we want to buy something, we can do it between December and January, because in February and March it's just for the kids and school, and to save money for the electricity and the water; then at the end we start to just save money. (Anita)

Anita's income is not dedicated to a particular set of uses in the same way that the women from Las Mercedes dispose of their money. Anita and her husband organise the family budget on a joint basis: 'We leave one salary for the house and for paying the debts, and the other we use to buy things, to start improving our standard of living' (Anita).

Nevertheless, as both partners are dependent on temporary work in agribusiness, their living is precarious; during the winter months, survival is often extremely difficult. Occasionally, Anita can find work in the refrigeration plants in the winter, or else she is able to take in laundry or work as a maid. These represent some of the alternative job opportunities that arise as a consequence of living in an urban centre. The women of Las Mercedes have none of these alternatives owing to the isolation of their settlement. Anita's neighbours often help out with food or small loans, as Anita returns the favours when she is in a better financial position. This helps to alleviate some of the hardship experienced during the 'blue months' when there is no work.

As Anita's family rely on temporary waged work for their livelihood, it is crucial that either of the partners be free to work as soon as it becomes available. This has led them to develop a very egalitarian distribution of domestic responsibilities:

> When he's working and I'm not, I don't let him do anything. But when we're both working then we fit together well, because we always look for different shifts. For example, he is bad at staying up late, [so] I go to work at night and he works by day, so he does the night-time things. ... He washes at night, and leaves the ingredients prepared for the meal. When I come home in the morning, I just have to finish it, that's all. When only one is working, either one of us [does the chores]. He's like a woman for doing the household chores. (Anita)

This division of the domestic tasks means that Anita has less to do at home when she is working, in contrast to all the other women who face a 'double shift' during the season. Anita's situation is that of a true joint breadwinner. Both she and her husband have reworked traditional gender roles within the family in order to take advantage of the temporary labour market conditions. If one partner is out of work, then that one becomes responsible for carrying out the domestic chores, while if both are working, they divide the responsibilities in a pragmatic and flexible manner. They even succeed in ensuring that one parent is at home when the children come home from school, as, by working the night shift, Anita stays at home during the day and is thus able to take care of the children in the afternoon. In this way, Anita and her husband ensure that they are maximising their earning potential in order to maintain their family and to gain some improvements in their standard of living. The reworking of gender relations within Anita's household leads her to have very different expectations of gender roles from the traditional. Anita has a clear opinion on how the division of labour should operate within the household:

It was on that condition that I started work ... that both of us would have to do the chores, both of us would help. Just because I'm a woman it doesn't mean that I'm going to do all the chores in the house, no. The husband has to be a good partner, both of you are human beings, he has to help. (Anita)

For Anita, one of the most important aspects of taking on paid work is the change it provides from the traditional female role:

I liked having more friends, it's another environment when one works, and I like the work I do, being *embaladora* [a packer]. ... That's why it's lovely to work, it's important for the woman to work, because she leaves the routine of the home, everyday, the food, the housework ... I get bored, you miss your friends, you shouldn't shut yourself up in the house all day. (Anita)

Anita is of the opinion that all women ought to work – one salary is not enough to maintain a family nowadays. Also, for her, taking on paid work is an empowering experience for all women:

It's because we are oppressed when we try and do things, we can't do anything, wherever you go, they say. 'She's a woman, she can't do anything.' That's why it's good for you to work, it's desirable that a woman should work. (Anita)

It seems, then, that in both Anita's and Clara's households, the dependence on wage-labour in agribusiness in order to maintain their families has had a lasting impact on gender relations at the household level. These households depend for their survival on the income from both partners, and the traditional gender division of labour has been modified to accommodate this economic reality. Instead of taking on a double burden of paid and domestic work, these responsibilities are shared and carried by both partners in a departure from traditional gender norms.

The case studies discussed in this chapter illustrate the extent to which female labour is an essential component within agribusiness in Chile. Women are incorporated throughout the process to carry out a wide range of tasks, providing rural women with employment opportunities that previously did not exist. This is particularly the case in more isolated rural areas such as Las Mercedes, where there are no alternative employment opportunities for women. However, even in urban areas, such as Curicó, where there may be alternative employment opportunities, working in agribusiness also forms the principal option for large numbers of women. The dependence of the whole region on agribusiness works to exacerbate the precarious situation of low-income households during the 'blue months', a situation which is forcefully illustrated by the case studies.

In both Las Mercedes and Curicó, the income gained by the *temporeras* is vital in order to alleviate some of the effects of the poverty experienced in the winter months when there is no work. Over the summer, money can be saved, food can be bought to store over the winter and material improvements made to homes. However, the seasonal cycle of work followed by unemployment means that these gains are made only in the short term. The income from temporary work never seems to be sufficient to gain financial security or build towards a future, with households often reaching the end of the winter with the same economic problems as the year before.

Despite this dependence on a precarious livelihood and the cycle of poverty endemic to seasonal work, paradoxically, these particular women seem to have been empowered by their work in agribusiness. The importance of female labour within agribusiness means that their earning potential is crucial to the survival of the household, particularly in the absence of alternative employment opportunities. As the case studies make clear, this has enabled the women to make gains in terms of increased financial control over household resources, as well as personal gains in terms of increasing skills and self-confidence. This in turn has had an effect on gender relations within the household, reworking traditional expectations as the women mediate the tensions between their paid work and their domestic work in varied ways. At times, this has resulted in modest reworkings of traditional roles, while in others, there has been a radical transformation of the gender division of labour within the household, as the women have become 'permanent' temporary workers. This tension between the traditional and modern, which we have observed elsewhere, is further complicated as women are drawn into new sets of relations within modern employment which are nevertheless cross-cut by traditional gender and class relations. In the next section we explore how these relations, and the resulting tensions, are negotiated by the *temporeras* within the workplace.

LABOUR RELATIONS IN THE WORKING ENVIRONMENT

As the *temporeras* are drawn into these new kinds of employment relations, they must not only mediate tensions at a household level, but
also those tensions which arise out of their specific situation as women
workers, in particular where traditional gender relations conflict with
new labour market conditions. As women are drawn out of their
homes, they enter new types of power relations within male-
dominated workplace hierarchies. This can often lead to sexual
harassment, as traditional *machista* gender relations continue to
operate. Furthermore, as the formal avenues for collective bargaining
are restricted within agribusiness, *temporeras* must find new strategies
to negotiate hierarchical employment relations and attempt to
increase their control over conditions and pay.

Sexual Harassment

In all the working environments discussed above, women workers tend
to be supervised and directed by men in positions of authority. This
situation, coupled with *machista* perceptions of women, raises the
issue of sexual harassment in the workplace. This is a particularly
important issue in Chile, where patriarchal culture predefines the
dominance of men over women in social relations. This means that
the issue of sexual harassment is one that has only recently begun to
be recognised and discussed as the numbers of women in the labour
force increase.

Sexual harassment has been interpreted by feminist theory as an
expression of power, the power that patriarchy gives men to control
women (Brant and Too 1994; Délano and Todaro 1992). However, it
is important to take into account the cultural context and locality
where the sexual harassment takes place. The context here is the
workplace, where sexual harassment has been defined as taking place
when one or more of the following conditions are present: when submission to the harassing behaviour becomes an explicit or implicit
condition of access to employment; when the submission, or the
rejection, of such conduct by an individual becomes the basis for decisions which will affect that individual's employment; when the harassing conduct interferes with the performance of the worker, creating
a hostile or intimidating work environment (Délano and Todaro
1992: 24).

This definition incorporates the element of consent and the dimension of a *quid pro quo* exchange which are integral to instances of sexual harassment. It highlights the key idea that sexual harassment is a power issue rather than a sexual one – consent cannot be given on an equal basis as one individual is in a position of power over the other. Furthermore, the power to refuse an approach of this nature is conditioned by the awareness of the reward offered (Brant and Too 1994: 17). This is the type of sexual harassment most commonly experienced by *temporeras*, where entry to a job or the wage level is frequently dependent on informal, personal relationships, which can mean an individual's willingness to submit to a boss's sexual advances.

The extent of sexual harassment within agribusiness remains hidden as there has been little investigation, and the delicacy of the issue prevents women from talking openly about it. Nevertheless, some *temporeras* were prepared to talk about sexual harassment in their workplace. The informality of the employment relations in export agriculture means that there is ample opportunity for bosses to take advantage of women seeking work. It is usual for bosses to ask younger women for 'dates' in return for guaranteeing their employment, although one interviewee mentioned that this type of attention was indiscriminate, and married women with children also suffered this type of harassment. However, it appeared that the women who consented to the bosses' advances were often the most vulnerable, for example, single mothers in need of employment, or the women with little working experience.[4] This would be consistent with the definition of sexual harassment discussed above, where the most vulnerable women are in a subordinate position of power *vis-à-vis* the boss, and where their refusal to consent would cost them a valuable employment opportunity. It is these most vulnerable women who may become partners or co-habitees of a boss for the duration of the season, an apparently common situation.

These situations are often viewed with tolerance and considered a part of working life by both women and men. Anita points out:

> The bosses bother you more than they check the fruit! And when there are pretty women, well then they work things out another way; bosses who fall in love are everywhere, in every job. (Anita)

In Anita's opinion, attention from bosses is a nuisance, but no more threatening than that. This is due in part to the cultural context of patriarchal gender relations which, to a degree, permit men to focus attention on women in public, attention that is often interpreted as a compliment by both parties. This interpretation confuses the boundaries of acceptable behaviour of men towards women, disguising the extent of the harassment taking place. However, awareness and recognition of this problem are becoming more widespread. Clara is able to identify explicitly certain behaviour as sexual harassment, and she also highlights the practical problems that result when women workers are harassed by male supervisors in the packing plant:

> I think they should give women more opportunities as supervisors because for one, in the first place, the men take more advantage of the *temporeras* when they are bosses, because they say to the girls, to the young ones, they start to say, 'you'll have a job for longer if you come out dancing with me tonight', or something like that. ... that's sexual harassment. ... When I was working in the Co-operative, they had more posts for female supervisors, they generally put various female supervisors so that the work would always be in order because with just male bosses it didn't work. (Clara)

The fact that unwanted attention from male supervisors has practical repercussions in terms of productivity brings into question the nature of traditional, patriarchal gender relations. These gender relations must be reworked in order to ensure the smooth functioning of labour relations within the workplace and maintain productivity, bringing the issue of sexual harassment to the fore as a real workplace issue, rather than a cultural issue. This means that specific measures can be taken by both *temporeras* and employers to deal with the problem. In this way, the expansion of agribusiness again has unexpected outcomes in terms of modifying traditional gender relations, opening up a new arena for their renegotiation.

Nevertheless, there are still very few complaints or charges made by *temporeras* against bosses. Many women refuse to submit to the demands of the boss and almost certainly lose their jobs, while those women who do press charges find that the process of law is slow. There was a case mentioned of a local boss in Graneros with four charges of sexual harassment pending in one season, who nonetheless was never prosecuted. In addition, the women who do make accusations against their bosses will often be branded as troublemakers and will face problems in obtaining another job in the area. This highlights the shortfall that exists between rapidly changing social relations of production and attitude changes in wider society.

'Cruzando los Brazos': Negotiating for Higher Wages

The lack of union organisation to represent workers' interests in the agro-export sector further complicates the problem of sexual harassment, perpetuating the informal nature of labour relations. This in turn leaves *temporeras* vulnerable to the threat of sexual harassment, influencing their access to employment in this sector. Moreover, the absence of formal avenues for negotiating pay and conditions means that *temporeras* must employ other strategies in order to gain improvements for themselves. However, in the absence of any collective negotiating powers, it is quite common for *temporeras* to attempt to influence the level of the tariffs paid per box through wildcat strikes. This belies the stereotype that women are a docile and passive workforce. *Temporeras* seem to have a clear perception of the vital importance of their labour at this one point in the global chain that is agribusiness and they do not hesitate to exert the limited power this affords them. Traditionally, the lines of workers only have to cross their arms, *cruzar los brazos*, and let the fruit just roll along the line. This stoppage is generally successful depending on the number of workers participating, the urgency of the shipment and the rates being paid in other plants. Also, the strength and mobilisation of community and friendship networks from outside the workplace are often pivotal in bringing about a successful stoppage.

For the *temporeras* from Las Mercedes, the majority of the people were relatives and friends from the settlement. However, there were still workers present who had migrated from other areas, and it was these 'outsiders' who undermined attempts to strike within the packing plant. Nevertheless, in Berta's plant, they had three successful stoppages during the season, in spite of the lack of solidarity from the workers from outside the area:

> Sometimes when we want to stop so that they pay more per box, they [the outsiders] don't want to stop working, they don't want to support. ... They drag their feet. It's that some of them are supervisors, or else they have work all year with the *patrón*, they don't want to stop. ... This year, we stopped three times and he would put it up straight away because he knew that he was paying too little. (Berta)

In this case, the community and friendship networks between the workers were strong enough to overcome opposition from workers outside these networks and enabled the *temporeras* to gain higher wages. Nevertheless, the heterogeneity of the labour force means that unifying relations dissolve with the end of the season, severely constraining any attempts to use this as a basis for more formal labour organisation.

CONCLUDING REMARKS

The case studies presented here highlight the importance of this employment opportunity for the women interviewed. In spite of the difficulties imposed by less than adequate working conditions, the poor job security, as well as the arduousness of the work, it remains a means of generating essential income for the households of the *temporeras*. Moreover, the case studies highlight that the *temporeras* themselves value their work, in spite of all the difficulties they face. It enables them to gain a degree of financial independence, which they do not hesitate to exercise. Through this, they can make substantial improvements in the standard of living of their families. The sense of self-worth and empowerment which this fosters emerges clearly from the interviews. Their continued employment year after year also presents the potential for reworking gender relations within the household, while further opportunities for collective action within the workplace are also present. However, the potential for empowerment at both the household and workplace level remains varied within the different sets of household and social relations which exist in this heterogeneous workforce.

In Las Mercedes, the growth in export agriculture and the corresponding demand for female labour has provided employment opportunities for the women who would not otherwise have worked. The relative ease of obtaining work in the locality has meant that women from households with a stable income from a husband or male partner can take advantage of the opportunity to earn 'extra' money during the season. The motive for working expressed by these *temporeras* is principally to buy items for the house and 'get ahead' in material terms. Their expenditure is directed towards buying clothes for their children, foodstuff for the winter and perhaps consumer goods, which represent an improvement in their standard of living. This reinforces the perception that they are working for 'extras', rather than making a joint contribution to household income together with their husbands.

In a social context where attitudes towards gender roles tend to be very traditional, the temporary nature of the work in export agriculture is an advantage for some women in that they can earn a significant level of income as a supplement to their male partner's income without too much disruption to their domestic responsibilities. In these families, the traditional gender roles and the division of labour within the household remain basically unchanged: women have to get up earlier and carry out their domestic tasks faster if they are also working. Extra responsibilities such as childcare are usually taken on by other women in the household such as grandmothers or elder daughters. By contrast, in those households entirely dependent on work in agribusiness, the temporary nature of the work is a disadvantage. These women need to maximise the period of time they are earning and their domestic responsibilities become an impediment. The most significant restriction remains childcare. In the absence of established childcare facilities, children are left with grandmothers or neighbours, and in extreme cases, elder children are withdrawn from school to look after the younger ones. Sometimes they are even taken to the field to work with their mother and help add to her wages for that day.

Given the constraints of the 'double day' faced by most women when they have to work, the question of the potential empowerment of women through this employment remains. We have seen that some women have achieved a greater degree of independence, both financial and personal, and that this has had some effect on gender relations at the household level. However this independence has a high price, physically, mentally and emotionally, as the women carry the burden of the conflicting demands of their paid employment, domestic chores and paid work. Within the workplace, we have seen that at the height of the season, *temporeras* are able to take advantage of their central role in order to improve wages, but what are the real possibilities for sustaining this co-operation? As we discuss in chapter 4, this heterogeneous labour force is only brought together during the season by the global processes of agribusiness, which also relies on its subsequent dispersal out of season in order to maintain profitability. In the light of this, while the *ad hoc* strikes of the *temporeras* belie the stereotype of docile women workers and show that some power can be exerted, the prospects for continued collective action seem remote. From this exploration of individual and household experiences of work in agribusiness, we now turn to the role played by the state in this process in order to assess how the *temporeras'* access to better pay and conditions might be achieved. The following chapter will discuss the ways in which state policy has negotiated the conflicting goals of responding to the real needs of this fragmented, vulnerable yet vital workforce, while maintaining the smooth functioning of the equally vital agricultural export sector, particularly in a context where a concern over social equity has increased.

8 State Policy and the *Temporeras* in the Transition to Democracy

The expansion of the fruit export sector and with it temporary female employment really took off under the neo-liberal military regime. The state at this time played a minimal role in terms of promotion of the fruit export sector, and the privately owned *parceleros* and larger export companies provided the momentum for its expansion. During the period of dictatorship, the state took an ideological stance that promoted the role of women as home-maker, wife and mother. However, as we saw in chapter 3, a paradox of the neo-liberal period was that the military's economic policies had the contrary effect of increasing female employment. This was seen most clearly in the case of the *temporeras*, whose entry into the seasonal fruit labour force as waged workers was a direct consequence of the government's policy of agrarian counter-reform, combined with deregulation of labour markets. However, the military government, in line with its ideological and political stance, provided no support for these workers. They had to fend for themselves as isolated and unorganised individuals, reinforcing their heterogeneity and atomisation. When military rule ended in 1990, the new government took a somewhat different stance. The democratically elected government continued to promote the neo-liberal economic model, within which the fruit export sector was central. But this was combined with a policy of promoting greater social equity, and promoting the interests of marginalised groups, particularly women.

It is clear from the evidence in the case studies of *temporeras* from different regions, that the export-oriented economic model in Chile has produced both positive and negative effects at the level of individual *temporeras*, their households and the region in which they live. In this chapter we shall examine how measures taken by the government to improve the working conditions of the *temporeras* have produced complex, paradoxical and often unexpected results. Under democracy, successive governments have struggled to strike a balance between the twin goals of growth and equity, which has involved mediating between competing and conflicting interest groups without destabilising Chile's economic success. In the fruit sector these interest groups have included the *temporeras* themselves and feminist civil servants who have aimed to improve the equity and working conditions of these seasonal workers through a range of initiatives inspired by Caroline Moser's work on gender planning (Moser 1993). On the other hand, the vested political and economic interests have opposed any measures that might prove detrimental to the profitability of the agro-export sector. This particular combination of growth based on export-oriented development and equity implies that, for women, government policy should address more than practical gender needs. However, this dual policy has revealed the contradictory nature of shifting relations between modern export and the goal of improving gender equity, which will be explored next.[1]

GENDER AND THE STATE IN RURAL CHILE IN THE 1990s

While Chilean society has undergone profound changes in recent decades, perhaps the most visible transformation has occurred in the roles which both rural and urban women play. Not only did the military regime push women into the labour market, it also provided many women with a reason to become politicised and increasingly active in social organisations.

In July 1986, at Punta de Tralca in the V Region, the *Departamento Femenino de la Comision Nacional Campesina* (CNC) elaborated the *Demanda de la Mujer Rural*, which called on rural women to organise and mobilise for democracy. They argued that 'only under a democratic government will it be possible to fulfil all the demands of rural women.'[2] Their demands were wide-ranging and showed that rural women in both the traditional and modern sectors had suffered severe neglect under the military dictatorship. They called for legal equality with men, particularly in the areas of employment and social security rights, the right to land, and access to housing and rural infrastructure. They also called for recognition of the vital role which women played in social and economic life. The late 1980s were a particularly dynamic period of political change in Chile and women's organisations were able to take advantage of the fact that the state was in flux and the political parties were realigning themselves in the transition.

Blueprints for policies with a transformative gender dimension were formulated by the *Concertación de Mujeres por la Democracia*, a section of the women's movement with links to the non-governmental organisations and the political parties which emerged with considerable political bargaining power during the transition to democracy. They elaborated a highly technical report,[3] which included an analysis of the situation of rural women, and they formulated a political programme for women to be implemented by the future democratic government.[4] In particular, the *Concertación de Mujeres* recommended that women and gender-specific issues should be incorporated into public policy at all levels, to take account of the diversity of women's needs and demands.

During the transition to democracy the Chilean state continued a free market non-interventionist approach in relation to most parts of the economy, including the fruit export sector, but it has made certain exceptions to this approach, including the promotion of policies on gender issues. Indeed, throughout the developing and developed world, governments have adopted an increasingly active role in incorporating gender into the development process and into public policies. In recent years, an increasing number of countries in Latin America and elsewhere have followed United Nations recommendations, and have created state institutions to plan and/or implement specific policies. In Chile, there are currently two state institutions, the *Instituto Nacional de Desarrollo Agropecuario* (INDAP) and the *Servicio Nacional de la Mujer* (SERNAM), which plan and implement policies affecting women living or working in rural areas. SERNAM, which was created in 1991, aims to improve the condition of women in society by addressing immediate gender needs such as access to employment, housing, education or credit. Its long-term objective is to improve the position of women in society *vis-à-vis* men by eliminating institutional forms of discrimination, alleviating women's responsibility for the home and childcare, and ending the sexual division of labour. Also in 1991 INDAP, which is part of the Ministry of Agriculture, created the *Area Mujer* specifically to address the issues facing rural women which were not covered within its mainstream programmes. The latter were focused on alleviating extreme poverty in rural areas and on meeting the demands for training and technical assistance, which had gone unmet during the dictatorship.

At an institutional level, linking gender and development in a political programme combines two theoretical issues – the social, political and economic status of women, and the nature of development (Kardam 1995). How the causes of gender inequality are defined and the development goals pursued will affect the policy recommendations and outcomes. What is crucial in this debate is the way in which interpretations of gender and development interact at the level of discourse and mainstream policy-making. If the mainstream policies emphasise economic growth, the gender policies are likely to focus on women's potential contributions to economic development and the initiatives taken may involve employment training and skill acquisition. If the policies emphasise equity, the gender policies are likely to seek ways of combating the feminisation of poverty with such initiatives as access to credit for micro-enterprise schemes. If state policies have empowerment as a goal, then the gender policies may aim to increase women's choices by resolving childcare or emphasising the importance of redistributing the workload within the household from women to men (Kardam 1995).

This analysis is particularly illuminating when applied to the formulation of policies with a gender dimension in Chile in the 1990s. On one level, it demonstrates how permeable the state can be to the introduction of policies that respond to the needs of newly organised social groups, such as women. Yet, on another level, it reveals the difficulties involved in reconciling political and economic interests and the limited manoeuvrability of the state within the dominant economic model. The programmes of the *Concertación* government have focused heavily on modernisation and economic growth. This has been in order to dampen fears among the former regime, the right-wing parties and the business sector that the Chilean economic miracle, in which fruit exports played a fundamental role, would be threatened in any way. This emphasis was not incompatible with the government's proposals for women, which focused on increasing the number of women in employment and maximising women's comparative advantages in the labour market. Government programmes have also focused on the repayment of the social debt and the eradication of extreme poverty. The model of intervention emphasised the empowerment of specific groups, including women, which suffered social disadvantage, not with welfare benefits but through employment and social investment. This approach was pursued through a 'top-down' strategy rather than grassroots activity, and there was also no intrinsic incompatibility between these objectives and an analysis of the factors which often make women poorer than men.

In the area of employment rights, the government's social project has clearly clashed with the economic model pursued. Reforming the legal system was a priority for the first government of the *Concertación* and one of the key tasks for SERNAM. The impulse for the state to intervene to further the interests of temporary workers, and the *temporeras* in particular, came from a series of meetings between the preparatory commission for SERNAM, social organisations and rural unions that aimed to identify and prioritise the needs of the *temporeras*. Changes to labour legislation were the first legal reforms to be approved by Parliament under the first government of the *Concertación*, and some of the *temporeras'* demands were in fact met. SERNAM contributed to the bill to reform the Labour Code, which became law in September 1993.

The case studies in chapters 6 and 7 provide a weighty testament to the lack of protection which the temporary workers face, and underline the need for government intervention and increased regulation of working conditions in the fruit export sector. In this respect, the reform of the Labour Code was a welcome advance, given that it contained specific provision for the seasonal workers in the fruit industry. It required employers to provide hygienic facilities for food preparation, transport to the fields or packing plant, and sleeping accommodation for those workers who required it near the place of employment (Venegas 1993). However, only a minority of *temporeras* are migrant workers, as the vast majority tend to find employment locally or near their place of residence to travel daily to the plants. Overwhelmingly, migrant workers tend to be male. In any case, changes in the law alone are not sufficient to improve working conditions – there must also be some means of enforcing such regulations and applying sanctions if employers are found not to be meeting their obligations. In Chile, this task falls to the *Dirección de Trabajo*, a unit within the Ministry of Employment, which covers safety in the workplace and working conditions. However, it is under-resourced and there are added difficulties in monitoring conditions for a highly mobile, temporary workforce.

Other demands which would have incurred costs for the fruit producers or the state were not addressed. These included forcing employers to meet their legal responsibilities on safety standards, encouraging unionisation among temporary workers and providing social security covering the 'blue months'. The legislation did nothing to address the problems which the *temporeras* face most frequently. Temporary contracts or, as occurs in many cases no contracts at all, prevent these women accruing the necessary time in a job to have entitlement to maternity benefits, sickness pay and other social security provision. There is ample evidence of women suffering sexual harassment in the workplace. There are clear limitations for furthering women's interests when the state limits itself to piecemeal reforms of the legal system rather than radically overhauling it to end the institutionalised forms of women's subordination.

In Chile the most frequent infraction of women's rights as workers must surely be employers evading their legal obligations on childcare provision by never contracting more than 19 female employees on full-time contracts, when 20 (or more) requires crèche provision to be available (CUT 1992). Although this legislation was intended to provide a degree of protection for female workers with children, it has proved to be a double-edged sword. If it is enforced, this legislation can actively discriminate against women, because only female employees have the right to childcare rather than parents of either sex. Consequently, employers faced with the additional costs of employing women with children are often tempted to opt for employing a maximum of 19 women regardless of whether they have children under the age of two. Moreover, this provision in law does not address the long-term needs for pre-school childcare because it does not resolve the problem for the children of working parents between the ages of two and five. Paradoxically, this law reinforces women's responsibility for childcare, disadvantages them in the labour market and does nothing to redistribute responsibility for children within the family. In any case, the existence of such legislation does not benefit temporary workers.

Although advances have undoubtedly been made in incorporating a gender dimension into state policy for rural women, this has been somewhat hindered by the process of institutionalisation itself which has revealed tensions between traditional and innovative forms of policy-making. The former has imposed rather artificial and restrictive bureaucratic structures to accommodate the new departments within the traditional model of the state. This runs counter to the aim of integrating gender into policy at all levels. SERNAM failed to establish formal mechanisms for sectoral work with INDAP until 1994 – a full four years after it began operations.[5] The lack of attention to the rural sector was, in part, due to SERNAM's budget restrictions, which meant that areas had to be prioritised, as the team of sectoral representatives was gradually pieced together.[6] Within INDAP, the *Area Mujer* (Women's Unit) was staffed by women with a long history of participation in the women's movement and in NGOs (often specialising in rural issues) during the dictatorship. Consequently, this may have been one area that it was relatively uncomplicated for SERNAM to leave uncovered.

The division of responsibilities and policy-making between SERNAM and INDAP assumed that there was a clear distinction between *campesinas* and *temporeras*, and that the two categories did not overlap. The complex reality clearly does not support this assumption and, consequently, the assignment of tasks between the institutions was unsatisfactory. First, SERNAM's actions were biased towards urban women or women working in rural areas, through its Childcare Programme for the Children of *Temporeras*. As a result, it was assumed that the *campesinas* and non-urban *temporeras* did not have difficulty in obtaining childcare facilities or that their work was not perceived to be productive as it was not integrated into the modern capitalist sector. By not having contact with the Childcare Programme, they also risked being marginalised from other mainstream policies, such as employment training or micro-enterprise support, which were channelled through SERNAM to the various ministries. Consequently, their needs might not be identified or represented. The *temporeras* were targeted in SERNAM's proposals for the Labour Reforms and also through the Childcare Programme. The women who benefited were wage workers in the modern agricultural sector, who travelled daily to the fields from the urban periphery. The reason for this was that the Childcare Programme used municipal infrastructure in small and medium-sized towns in the place of residence, rather than install nurseries at the packing plants or in rural shanty towns. In this way, urban dwellers benefited more than women living and working in rural areas where provision was minimal.

SERNAM's actions to benefit peasant women were limited to the regulation of land rights that facilitated their access to credit facilities and other benefits available to producers. The population of the traditional rural sector has long been marginalised from mainstream policies and the benefits associated with the modernisation process, and few women have legal rights to land. SERNAM was established to incorporate all women into the process of national development, yet rural women were inadequately included in its sphere of action. Conversely, INDAP's remit is restricted to the peasant population. This institutional limitation circumscribed INDAP's ability to act in benefit of those rural women temporarily employed in the fruit export sector. The *temporeras* fall outside INDAP's remit since they are not small-scale producers but are a rural semi-proletariat.

WHO WILL LOOK AFTER THE CHILDREN ...?

According to official statistics, approximately one third of women in Chile are employed. Although participation in the labour force tends to correlate with levels of modernity and development, female employment in Chile is below the regional average for Latin America. The principal obstacle for many women to entering, and remaining in, the labour market is the lack of affordable childcare. Moreover, this is the demand that the *temporeras* most frequently cite as a priority, usually above working conditions and wage levels. Childcare provision, whether through the state or the private sector, varies according to the age of the child, the needs of the parents and whether the focus is primarily on the children's education or on relieving women of their caring role to take up paid employment. The state provides pre-school care in *salas cunas* for infants aged 0–2 through the *Junta Nacional de Jardines Infantiles* (JUNJI), but this reaches only 2 per cent of children in this age group.[7] There is also state provision in nurseries run by the JUNJI for children aged 3–5. These facilities were originally established with the aim of reducing infant mortality, preventing malnutrition and preparing children from low-income families for entry into the education system. There was little recognition that such provision could also be beneficial to the mother and by extension the rest of the family unit, by enabling her to earn an income. Indeed, despite the reality of women taking on paid work, the prevailing ideology within the state still assumes that women are primarily responsible for bringing up children. This is evident in the opening hours of the state-run centres, which bear little resemblance to the average working day and close at 4.30 pm. The coverage of pre-school education by income quintile can be seen in Table 8.1.

The overall coverage of pre-school education through the state and private sector reaches slightly more than one child in every five. However, urban areas enjoy more facilities than rural areas and there is also a marked variation between income brackets, as the coverage in the highest income bracket is double the coverage in the lowest. Children in rural areas are therefore doubly disadvantaged because of location and because they are more likely to be poor. Only 174,673 children (17.3 per cent) in the poorest 40 per cent of the population receive pre-school education yet this is precisely the group which has the greatest social disadvantages including less stimulation, poor motor skills and literacy problems (MIDEPLAN 1993: 75). There are many advantages to increasing coverage for this group,

Table 8.1   Coverage of Pre-School Education by
Income Quintile

Income Quintile	Pre-school Coverage
1	16.6 per cent
2	18.1 per cent
3	21.9 per cent
4	25.7 per cent
5	33.8 per cent
Total	21.0 per cent

Source: Adapted from MIDEPLAN (1993: 74).

including improved nutrition (and by extension releasing some of the family budget to improve the nutrition of other members), and it is widely acknowledged that early entry into the education system can compensate for social disadvantages. Furthermore, the increased coverage would enable more low-income women to have paid employment, thereby increasing the total household income and benefiting the children.

Without a gender perspective at the level of policy-making, it is often assumed that the problem of childcare is resolved when children begin school. Yet, the school day is quite out of line with the typical working day. In urban areas with high population density and insufficient schools, children can only attend classes either in the morning session or in the afternoon/evening session. As we have seen, many of the *temporeras* are of urban origin and travel to the fields on a daily basis. Further, given the peak season for fruit picking coincides with the summer school vacation, the provision of childcare provision was central to the *Temporeras* Programme run by SERNAM.

Childcare provision for workers in the fruit export sector is a relatively recent phenomenon in Chile. A study in 1992–3 indicated that, just over 40 per cent of centres providing childcare had been in existence for one season only, and that 52 per cent had been functioning for two seasons (Herrera and Zúñiga 1993: 15). As women entered the seasonal rural labour force in increasing numbers during the 1980s, a significant gap grew between the demand for childcare provision and the facilities available (Herrera and Zúñiga 1993). In areas where there are few employment opportunities during the winter months, and where the wages earned in the peak season often have to keep the family for the rest of the year, economic necessity forces women to work shifts of up to 18 hours a day. There is evidence that in 1990–1, as many as 70 per cent of the *temporeras* worked for six days per week in the peak season and 20.4 per cent worked a seven-day week. In addition to the time spent at work, it is important to add the journey between home and the packing plants (as many as one third of *temporeras* travel daily from urban areas; Díaz, 1991: 97). The lack of childcare provision means, in effect, that children are often left alone, in the care of older siblings or neighbours, or taken to the fields and packing plants. These unsatisfactory solutions result in above-average incidences of injuries, malnutrition and juvenile crime (SERNAM 1993).[8]

Public policies are a product of the specific configuration of social circumstances, a power structure and a political programme. In some cases these may be the products of vertical decision-making by elites, while in other cases they are the expression of demands which actors in civil society have brought to the state (Guzmán et al. 1994). In the case of state-run programmes for the children of the *temporeras*, their origins lay in a pilot scheme in the province of Talagante in 1991, which had participation from local government, unions, the employers and SERNAM. This experiment in co-operation between the public and private sectors at the beginning of the transition to democracy demonstrated that collaboration between the state, the business sector and the beneficiaries could provide an innovative solution to practical needs without necessarily hitting an ideological impasse. In the 1991–2 season, SERNAM, in conjunction with other participating state institutions and the private sector, operated 22 centres in the III, IV, V, VI, VII, and Metropolitan Regions which were attended by 1,837 children and 1,074 women. The following year, this provision had increased to 42 centres in 38 localities in the same regions, benefiting 3,795 children and 2,011 women (SERNAM 1993: 15–16). In the peak season of 1993–4, the programme had 50 centres in 46 localities and, in addition to the same regions as before, they also had a presence in the VIII Region (SERNAM 1994). The centres operate between December and March, which is the peak season for fruit picking and packing and which also coincides with the summer school holidays. Childcare for children under the age of 2 is, in theory, covered by the Labour Code, so SERNAM concentrates its facilities on children between the ages of 2 and 12.[9] Because of limited resources in the public sector, it was necessary for SERNAM to make optimum and innovative use of existing facilities in the various state institutions which work with children, and municipal facilities which were empty during the school holidays. The programme was implemented in the fruit export regions that provided childcare for the *temporeras* during the peak season (December–March).[10]

The programme's objectives underwent significant transformations as it became more extended throughout the fruit-growing regions. In the first season of 1991 and 1992, the programme aimed to provide and co-ordinate resources to provide childcare facilities and to foster collaboration between the *temporeras*, the employers, the state and the local community in resolving such problems. Indeed, childcare was perceived as one of the problems affecting the *temporeras* that could be resolved by negotiation and through their own organisation. It is significant that in the early stages, the issue of provision was presented as the collective responsibility of the *temporeras*, the employers and the state (SERNAM 1993). Yet, by the following season, the objectives set by the programme differed significantly in both tone and focus from the previous year. The programme's principal objective was still to provide childcare facilities that would enable women to enter and remain in the seasonal agricultural labour market during the school summer vacation (SERNAM 1993). However, it also acquired other specific aims that focused primarily on the children of the *temporeras* rather than on the women themselves. These aims included reducing the accident rate and malnutrition among the children of *temporeras*, making better use of their free time through sport and recreation, and preventing social problems, such as juvenile crime and drug abuse, which might result from a lack of supervision.

Although the women's insertion into the labour market and the value of the *temporeras'* productive role remained central to the programme, the *temporeras* were targeted less as workers and more as mothers who were vulnerable and in need of state protection. There was no analysis of the underlying causes of the potential social problems that the children of temporary workers might experience. These include the poverty that results from underemployment beyond the peak season, erratic and low wages during the season and a lack of investment in infrastructure in poor peripheral urban or rural areas. Nor was there any analysis of where the responsibility for such neglect might lie. The initiatives such as the creation of resources and spaces for negotiation, organisation and participation were removed, as these were issues that the state was not in a position to promote. Temporary workers were not encouraged to become unionised and

Table 8.2   Regional Childcare Centres

Region	No. Centres	Province	Municipality
III	3	Copiapó	Copiapó (2), Tierra Amarilla
IV	4	Elqui	Vicuña, Paihuano
		Limari	Ovalle, El Palqui
V	11	Quillota	Quillota
		San Felipe	S. Felipe, Sta. María
			Panquehue, Putaendo
		Los Andes	Rinconada de los Andes
VI	11	Cachapoal	Malloa, Machalí, Olivar, Graneros, Rancagua, Rengo, Peumo, San Fco de Mostazal
		Colchagua	Chimbarongo, Sta. Cruz, S. Fernando
VII	5	Talca	San Clemente, Culenar
		Curicó	Curico, Teno
		Linares	Longavi
RM	13	Santiago	El Bosque
		Cordillera	Puente Alto
		Chacabuco	Colina, Lampa
		Maipo	Paine
		Melipilla	Melipilla, Alhué
		Talagante	Talagante, El Monte Peñaflor, Isla de Maipo

Source: Adapted from SERNAM (1993: 14).

the government faced pressure from the right-wing parties and from fruit exporters not to amend the law if, by doing so, it put in jeopardy the economic success of the fruit export sector by increasing labour costs. Consequently, the social content of the original proposals was lost. Goals that might be characteristic of modernisation and demo-cratisation, such as empowerment, participation and organisation, were sacrificed for a more traditional and paternalistic approach. Significantly, the reduced scope of the programme did not encourage the *temporeras* or their communities to play an active role.

Financial responsibility for the programme was intended to be covered by a tripartite arrangement with the involvement of state institutions, the municipalities and the private sector. However, employers demonstrated little formal commitment to the programme, and they did not perceive that their responsibility for and contribution to the provision of childcare facilities should be commensurate with the benefit they received from this. The employers were not obliged to make any formal contribution to the programme, but were requested to contribute with finance for additional personnel, operational costs and donations of fruit and vegetables to supplement the children's diet. More than half made an economic contribution (58 per cent) and more than one third (38 per cent) donated fruit (SERNAM 1993). The bottom line on the employers' contribution was that they knew the programme would go ahead with or without their contribution and, while they benefited from increased productivity when the workers were relaxed about their children's safety, the problem of childcare was not theirs but the *temporeras'*.

However, despite the employers' lack of firm commitment to funding the programme, this does not seem to correlate to any reluctance to employ women with children. Indeed, there is evidence that employers may even prefer workers with children since they can supplement the demand for labour at extremely short notice by taking their children to work. Moreover, while female heads of household are often the most disadvantaged group in terms of employment opportunity, they do not appear to be discriminated against as temporary workers. Since they are the primary or sole source of income for

Table 8.3   Employer Contributions by Region in Pesos

Region	Contribution	Per cent
III	None	0.0 per cent
IV	274,000	3.7 per cent
V	310,000	4.0 per cent
VI	2,986,000	39.9 per cent
VII	505,546	6.7 per cent
MET REG	3,405,270	45.7 per cent
TOTAL	7,480,816	100.0 per cent

Source: SERNAM (1993: 26).

the household, their need for stable earnings means they are less likely to leave mid-season to take up employment elsewhere. Female heads of households were more likely to be employed in the summer and sporadically throughout the winter, as they supplemented this work with other activities such as domestic service (Rivera 1993).

PARTICIPATION AT THE GRASSROOTS

SERNAM has raised the need for the *temporeras* to have a more proactive role in planning its childcare programme and participating in workshops and meetings. During the working day SERNAM cannot have access to the women in the plant and, after a long and intensive day, the women have little time or energy for participation. When the season ends, the women have greater freedom, but their cohesive identity as temporary workers has been lost and they are difficult to contact. Yet, as the GIA study of childcare centres showed, the grass-roots participation of women can be important, and the temporeras played an active role at three key stages of the process:

1. rallying support for centres to be established initially;
2. involvement in the internal planning and co-ordination; and
3. assisting SERNAM in specific tasks such as registration, promotion and assisting the staff with the children.

This level of practical participation appears to be valued among the *temporeras*. This raises the question of whether SERNAM's emphasis on workshops and discussions of 'gender issues' may not indicate a lack of awareness of the linkages between gender and social class and adds yet another burden to the *temporeras'* already heavy workload. Despite the rhetoric of empowering the *temporeras* with information through the workshops, there is a danger that they may see the women as potential receivers of a truth which 'enlightened', middle-class feminists in central government wish to impart. Participation in such activities would be more effective and undoubtedly more attractive during the winter months. However, it requires the adaptation of the methodology of the Childcare Programme to suit the needs and lifestyle of the *temporeras* and recognition of those practical areas in which the women already play a role. More significantly, it requires a tacit recognition by the government that the *temporeras* continue to exist beyond the end of the season and that the challenges they face may be different but no less arduous.

Separately from direct state childcare provision for *temporeras*, other activities also exist, some of which involve SERNAM, to support seasonal workers at a more grassroots level. As we saw in chapter 5, formal trade union organisation among all seasonal fruit workers is very low. This partly reflects the level of union repression in existence under the military during the period of expansion of the fruit sector. But it also reflects to some extent the difficulties traditional, male-dominated, rural unions have had in addressing the needs of seasonal workers in export agriculture, especially those of women.[11] The problems faced by the *temporeras* not only include those relating to their pay and working conditions, but also childcare, the 'double day' and lack of alternative employment during the 'blue months', which traditional work-based unions are ill-equipped to address. In addition, during the season when the *temporeras/os* are working flat out, they have little time for union activity, but during the winter months they no longer have a connection with work-based unions. However, a significant fact in low levels of unionisation is that temporary workers still have not received the legal right to collective negotiation under the transition to democracy. Attempts to extend collective negotiation rights (enjoyed by permanent workers) to temporary workers have met with stern resistance in Congress and from employers in the agro-export sector. Despite its policy of equity with growth, the government so far has succumbed to this resistance.

Lack of union organisation, however, has been compensated in some areas by local community organisations, often supported by NGOs or the Church. Grassroots activity often has much greater success in addressing the needs of women, by taking up not only problems arising during the working season, but also providing support during the 'blue months' for those who are unemployed. In some areas, where funds have been found, community centres have been set up providing services such as crèches, information, education, a meeting place and other support facilities (Falabella 1993; Venegas 1993).[12] However, community organisations tend to be fragmented, with little co-ordination between them, and have the limitation of only reaching those seasonal workers who are resident within a particular area, not those who are bussed in. Women often play a much more active role in community-based organisation, and the needs and voices of women specifically can be raised within this type of forum, enhancing the potential for their empowerment (Barrientos 1998). At times, they have also provided a focal point for co-ordination between NGOs, trade unions and the state.

SERNAM's regional offices made attempts to incorporate other members of the community into its programme including local business, NGOs, community organisations, regional branches of the CUT and neighbourhood associations. However, there is evidence that in one third of the centres run by SERNAM, the social organisations which had been present at the start had withdrawn from the programme because of conflict (Herrera and Zúñiga 1993). The organisations considered that the state failed to appreciate their efforts and that, in reality, there was little commitment to developing organisations to represent the *temporeras'* interests. Relations between SERNAM and the Women's Secretariat in the CUT remained informal, although the potential for co-ordination did exist through the *Temporeras* Programme.[13]

SERNAM, therefore, has made few inroads into the low level of organisation and unionisation among the *temporeras*. To the contrary, there was evidence that centres that attempted to participate actively in the government programme met with resistance from SERNAM (Herrera and Zúñiga 1993). SERNAM implemented some small-scale actions at regional level by visiting women in fruit-packing plants and industry with information on employment rights, sexual discrimination and sexual harassment.[14] Although beneficial in themselves, these actions at micro-level are clearly no substitute for sectoral policy with active input from the state, the unions, community and women's groups. The lack of co-operation is particularly worrying, given trade unions and social organisations are weak in rural areas and their ability to pressure employers or the state on behalf of their members is limited. Therefore, while grassroots participation and co-ordination have some potential, there are clearly contradictions between this approach and government policies. The government has addressed the issue of the *temporeras'* practical gender needs during the season, especially when that facilitates export production, but has not been prepared to address their strategic gender needs. At heart, state-led strategy in support of temporary workers is being pulled by the requirements of export-led growth, which often conflict with the equity needs of women seasonal workers.

In reality, SERNAM'S childcare programme was a practical initiative which reached a relatively small number of the *temporeras* who required such a facility, and it involved relatively few resources. It undisputedly provided a solution to the problem of inadequate or unaffordable childcare, a factor that more frequently than any other excludes women from the labour market. However, it raises issues that go far beyond the scope of the programme itself, in particular, regarding how women's strategic gender interests have been subverted by the dictates of capital. There are several reasons why childcare was provided specifically for the *temporeras*. In part, the special provision could be explained by lower coverage of nursery places in rural areas. However, many *temporeras* are not of rural origin but travel to the packing plants from urban areas on a daily basis. Moreover, the programme uses municipal schools, and therefore the centres are located in small and medium-sized towns rather than rural areas. Therefore, the SERNAM programme does not make a significant contribution to meeting the demand for childcare provision in rural areas. A second possible explanation may be that the programme is necessary because the peak period of employment for the *temporeras* coincides with the summer school vacation. Yet, other sectors of the economy continue to employ women during that period without making any special provision. Clearly, these explanations alone are insufficient to account for the state's provision of childcare to support women entering paid employment in privately owned enterprises. We must conclude, therefore, that because the *temporeras* are central to the success of the fruit export sector, without their labour in the peak season the economy would suffer. Furthermore, it is essential that childcare provision does not extend beyond the peak season as this would enable the women to seek other employment. These workers must permanently remain as seasonal workers, available year after year to resume their tasks in the packing plants and in the fields. The government's programme is structured accordingly and SERNAM's team of personnel which runs the programme also disperses until the following season. It is a temporary programme for temporary workers, who unfortunately have rather more permanent needs of earning a wage and caring for their children.

The 1990s have seen coalition governments of the centre and the moderate left, which have steered a difficult course of intervention on behalf of certain groups (women included) within the neo-liberal economic model which was introduced under the military government. Within the fruit export sector, this dichotomy of political and social democracy versus economic liberalism has had clear implications for the state's commitment and ability to channel resources in order to improve the working conditions of the *temporeras/os*. The result has been an almost constant tension between government policies that aim to redistribute resources more equitably, and the opposing logic of the market that tends to concentrate resources among those groups that have an initial advantage.

As we have seen in this chapter, the changes in employment legislation affecting temporary workers responded to very real practical needs. However, the potential for the law to advance more fundamental strategic interests of temporary workers was severely circumscribed by the internal and external economic pressure to maximize profits at the expense of workers' rights and conditions of employment. By providing places where children could be looked after and fed, SERNAM alleviated the double shift for women so they could seek employment albeit temporarily. However, because the provision was linked to a particular type of seasonal employment, it did not remove the structural obstacle to women seeking any form of employment in equal conditions to men. Indeed, by specifically focusing on female workers with children, the programme failed to challenge the prevailing gender ideology by presenting childcare as a joint responsibility for both male and female workers, employers and the state. The objectives of the childcare programme for the children of the *temporeras* owed more to the immediate needs of capitalist agriculture and to serving the neo-liberal economic model, than to any project of empowering women or advancing their gender interests in the long term. Despite the failures of the *Concertación* in addressing the interests of the *temporeras*, the process of globalisation itself has opened up possibilities of working directly through the supply chain to improve the wages and conditions of fruit workers. This final paradox is explored in our concluding chapter, which draws together the many strands of our analysis.

9 Global Policies for Temporary Workers in Agribusiness – Conclusion

The global dimension to the expansion of Chilean fruit is an aspect we have explored in relation to production and exports, but which also has potentially important implications for the *temporeras* themselves. Whilst the *temporeras* are a heterogeneous, marginalised group of workers, they are at the same time integrated into a global market. Despite fragmentation at the point of production, within Chile there is increasing concentration in the export sector. At the retail end within many developed countries to which they export, there is also a tendency to increased control along the supply chain by large supermarkets. This is a phenomenon which has taken place in the agro-food system generally as globalisation has proceeded (Ward and Almas 1997). Since the mid-1990s in many northern countries there has been an increased consumer awareness of the problems of poor labour conditions among export workers in developing countries. An anomaly of globalisation is that, whereas national democratic governments such as *Concertación* in Chile have failed to act in the interest of seasonal agricultural workers, foreign multiples are increasingly moving towards introducing codes of conduct to protect labour standards among their 'third world' suppliers. The global supply chain could thus, in the future, prove a new route for improving the labour conditions of the *temporeras*. In this chapter we shall examine the potential of global policies to help the position of women working in agribusiness, which at the time of writing were still at an early stage of development. In a concluding section, we shall summarise the main features of women working in agribusiness, as exemplified by our own case study, pointing to further avenues for research in this important new area of female employment.

THE GLOBAL SUPPLY CHAIN

The growth of both agribusiness and female employment internally in Chile were linked to the transformation of the rural sector and

185

commercialisation of agriculture. Externally, as we saw in chapter 4, they were linked to the expansion of the global fruit market and changing consumption patterns in developed countries, which stimulated the sales of fresh produce throughout the year, independent of season. Connecting internal production and external distribution and marketing is the export 'funnel', which is increasingly dominated by large transnational firms as the global fruit supply chain has expanded. These firms play a central role in facilitating the year-round supply of fresh horticultural produce to northern consumer markets, sourcing homogeneous fresh products from different locations around the globe as seasons change.

In many ways the global fruit supply chain replicates the supply chains of industrial consumer goods. Large corporations and transnational capital play a dominant role, and a high level of investment in sophisticated transport, communication and distribution systems is required. The trend to outsourcing and flexible production methods in global industry has increased the analogy with agribusiness, which in the Chilean case is also based on a form of 'outsourcing' in which a large number of producers link into a more centralised export structure. As a result there are parallels between female employment in agribusiness and the industrial sector. But we have argued there are also specific traits inherent to agricultural production which affect the terms and conditions of employment, and its gender dimension in agricultural export production. Female workers enduring insecure, flexible and poorly paid employment act as a 'buffer' between the global integration of commercial capital and a more fragmented production system which is subject to relatively high levels of risk and volatility. Agribusiness draws on and reinforces the subordination of women to meet its own ends, and temporary agricultural workers continue to be one of the most marginalised sectors of the Chilean workforce.

Despite the marginalisation and fragmentation of the *temporeras,* they are nevertheless integrated into a global supply chain. The dichotomy between fragmentation and globalisation has generated new forms of production and supply relations, with potential implications for the *temporeras* themselves. One feature of global supply chains is that, despite outsourcing and flexible production methods, computerised control and communication systems have facilitated high level monitoring along the supply chain from one company to another. This has reinforced the dominant position of the larger corporations and transnational companies within the chain, who can control production without direct ownership. Hence, although there is fragmentation along the chain, there is at the same time an increased degree of integration in the supply relations between companies. In chapter 4 we examined how distribution of fresh produce is increasingly taking place through large supermarkets (multiples), and they are exerting greater control along the chain up to the point of production, ensuring the produce meets their precise specifications.

Chilean fruit exports integrate into what has been defined as a 'consumer-led' global supply chain, in which the final product is destined for retail usually (though not only) in developed countries (Gereffi 1994). Other examples of consumer-led supply chains outside food are clothing and consumer durables. This is in contrast to producer supply chains, such as automobile parts, in which the product is destined as a production input, usually in developed country manufacturing. In the case of food, the increasing dominance of multiples has been combined with changing consumption and shopping patterns. Many consumers now opt for 'one-stop' shopping on a once a week basis, often going by car to an out-of-town store to load with groceries and many other household goods.[1] Many working women in developed (and developing) countries have been able to benefit from the expansion of supermarkets, through more efficient concentration of time on shopping, and sometimes through turning the shopping trip into a 'family outing'. To some extent supermarkets have displaced the traditional image of the 'caring mother' in the home preparing the meal for the family (Barrientos and Perrons 1996). This trend is being reinforced by competition between multiples, which is leading to a drive for customer patronage through loyalty card schemes and other enticements. The result has been a concentration of shopping in fewer outlets, and greater identification by consumers with specific supermarket chains.

A particular feature of food is that it is for direct consumption or physical ingestion by the consumer, and a contaminated food product could seriously damage health. Increasing the time and distance between point of production and final consumption through expanding the global supply of fresh produce increases the risk of contamination, and along these chains great attention has to be paid to maintaining hygiene and limiting deterioration of the product. Suppliers to most large supermarkets now have to meet stringent conditions regarding their standards of food handling and preparation, which are closely monitored by the supermarkets themselves. This is in addition to specifications often laid down regarding other factors such as product quality, packaging and presentation. However, global distance does not hinder monitoring by supermarkets, and European fruit buyers from multiples often visit producers and exporters who supply them in Chile and many other countries. Despite fragmentation of production, therefore, globalisation has simultaneously facilitated greater integration along supply chains, including fresh produce. The changing relation between consumers and multiples also has other implications for the supply chain and ultimately the *temporeras*. The 'caring image' of supermarkets, designed to attract and maintain customer loyalty, extends not only to practical customer needs such as hygiene and quality, but also to the consumer 'conscience'. This has been reflected both by the concern by supermarkets for meeting environmental standards, and more recently by their adoption of codes of conduct to cover the labour conditions of their suppliers in developing countries, with potentially important implications for marginalized groups of workers such as the *temporeras*. The expansion of global supply chains have thus facilitated the extension of international labour standards by large corporations as a potentially important area of labour market regulation in the era of globalisation.

LABOUR STANDARDS AND THE *TEMPORERAS*

The *temporeras* have gained a number of benefits from paid employment, but at the same time continue to endure many burdens. They are a heterogeneous, marginalised group, with little union organisation, lack of labour rights, poor pay and working conditions. As seen in the previous chapter, despite the transition to democracy in Chile, there has been little substantive improvement in the labour rights of temporary workers. Although trade unions have been legalised, in the case of workers such as the *temporeras* unions have no legal right to collective negotiation. Given adherence to the neo-liberal export model, the ability of the state to regulate at a national level is inherently limited if the model itself is to be successful in a competitive global environment. The high degree of international competition means there is a constant drive towards lowering costs and/or raising productivity to retain a competitive edge. An inherent failure of the democratic government's strategy of 'growth with equity' is that when proposed regulation to improve labour conditions compromises the interests of producers and exporters, the needs of the latter take precedence over those of the temporary workers in the pursuit of export growth.

This problem is evident in many developing countries trying to maintain their competitiveness within an export-led growth strategy. Structural adjustment and economic liberalisation have reduced both the role and the power of the state to act as a national regulator of labour markets. Simultaneously they have encouraged falling real wages and increased insecurity of employment. There is thus a tendency in the global economy for the lowest common denominator regarding labour conditions to prevail among competing countries. This affects all export sectors, and increased female employment across many developing country industries has been linked to the reduction in labour costs and conditions of employment (Afshar and Dennis 1992; Elson 1991; Standing 1989). It has also been a factor in labour-intensive sectors such as agribusiness, where women like the *temporeras* have been drawn into new forms of employment through the process of trade liberalisation and global integration. However, globalisation has also produced new potential avenues for extending the campaign for labour rights beyond old national boundaries. These include the increasing use of consumer-based campaigns in the North in support of labour standards in developing countries, and campaigns for the inclusion of social clauses in trade agreements (such as the European Union, World Trade Organisation and North American Free Trade Area). These have increasingly been seen as a means of countering the global downward pressure on pay and conditions (Sengenberger and Campbell 1994; Shaw 1996; Michie and Grieve-Smith 1995; LeQuesne 1996).

CODES OF CONDUCT

Over recent years, a growing number of large companies have become more receptive to consumer pressure relating to environmental and labour standards. There is now greater emphasis on business ethics as part of the new 'social agenda'. This is largely a result of the success of consumer-based campaigns led by a number of northern Non-Governmental Organisations (NGOs), as well as a reaction to the excesses of corporate greed and individual self-interest, which predominated following the onset of neo-liberalism during the 1980s. Information is more easily accessible through the media and global communication systems, and some large corporations have had their 'clean-cut', consumer-friendly image tarnished by revelations about sweatshop conditions or environmental damage in their supply chains or production operations. There has also been a realisation that ethical trading can be profitable, as demonstrated by the success of niche companies such as The Body Shop in the UK.

In a highly competitive global market, oligopolistic competition between the 'big players' has displaced more fragmented free market competition, and ethical trading is a potential method of non-price competition between large firms. In this market, large corporations have become increasingly aware of the potential of consumer power. Traditionally, consumer campaigns have often been weak, partly because consumers are a very heterogeneous fragmented group and partly because shopping was a diverse activity spread over a large number of firms and retailers. As concentration has increased amongst producers and retailers, so that fewer firms are responsible for a larger proportion of market share, individual firms have become more exposed to consumer campaigns. At the same time as there has been a diminution in the role of the state there has been a growth in importance of NGOs and other pressure groups, able to co-ordinate consumer campaigns against individual producers. The campaign against the dumping of the Brent Spar and its effect on Shell sales in Germany in 1995, for example, sent shock waves through many large companies about the potential damage a successful consumer-based campaign could incur. As a result many large corporations became aware of the potential impact of social and environmental campaigns. The shift to a more 'ethical' corporate culture could be a temporary phenomenon, and there is a wide gulf between stated intentions and actual implementation (the so-called 'ethical deficit'), but it is a tide which companies cannot ignore.

Ethical trade itself is not a new phenomenon. There has long been a network of alternative trading organisations, producing, importing and selling ethically produced goods (Barratt Brown 1993). Organisations such as the Fairtrade Foundation, set up in the UK in 1992, have also provided a Fairtrade mark for products meeting specified ethical conditions in their production (Fairtrade Foundation 1995 and 1996).[2] Increasingly, fair trade products (for example Café Direct) have been successfully sold in mainstream retail outlets and large supermarkets. Over recent years, under pressure from consumers and NGOs, a growing number of large commercial companies have introduced their own codes of conduct covering labour and environmental conditions along their supply chains in developing countries (NEF and CIIR 1997). These companies initially tended to be in manufacturing-based, consumer-led commodity chains, and clothing companies such as Nike and Lévi Strauss ranked among early firms adopting codes. But other producers and retailers have joined an increasing number of firms adopting more ethical sourcing practices. This largely reflects the success NGO and consumer groups have had in campaigning against the poor labour conditions under which much production outsourced to developing countries takes place (especially the worst examples of child labour and unpaid female labour). Large firms have been keen to avoid adverse publicity which a consumer campaign can draw, preferring to promote a conscientious corporate image in a competitive consumer market. The cumulative effect of this trend led in the UK in 1997 to the formation of a joint initiative to set up a single organisation to co-ordinate codes of conduct implemented by the larger firms. The Ethical Trading Initiative, launched at the beginning of 1998, was composed of private companies, trade unions, NGOs and organisations such as the Fairtrade Foundation, New Economics Foundation and Catholic Institute for International Relations, with the support of the UK government Department for International Development.[3] The aim is to 'develop and encourage the use of a widely endorsed set of standards, embodied in codes of conduct ... which will enable companies to work together with other organizations outside the corporate sector to improve labour conditions around the world' (ETI 1997: 1). Its purpose, therefore, is to establish best practice among third world suppliers, and develop agreed monitoring and verification procedures.[4] By companies joining together, it is hoped to avoid some of the problems experienced in establishing environmental standards, when companies were implementing different standards with no common agreement. The standards under development by the ETI are based around core International Labour Organisation (ILO) conventions (ETI 1997). Core ILO conventions cover issues such as freedom from discrimination in employment and occupation, equal pay, freedom of association, the right to organise and collective bargaining, abolition of child labour, and often occupational health and safety.[5] The extent to which these would be used was still to be established in early 1998. Similar initiatives are also underway in the US and other European countries, with the potential for communication and co-operation between them. By the end of the 1990s, therefore, there was clearly a discernible trend towards more ethical practices among many larger corporations, with moves to improve labour conditions along their supply chains from developing countries.

Supermarkets have also been subject to pressure to improve their sourcing policies (Arnold 1996; Christian Aid 1996). Some of the larger UK and European supermarkets have moved towards extending codes of conduct covering labour and environmental conditions to own-brand suppliers along their supply chain, with the possible inclusion of fresh produce (Christian Aid 1997).[6] A number of factors have stimulated multiples to follow the trend taking place elsewhere in the retail sector: The desire to avoid any adverse publicity, commitment to the principles of ethical trade by many of their employees and shareholders, and a desire to be part of rather than left behind what is clearly a growing trend. Changing consumption patterns and the increased concentration of multiples have affected the relative power of consumers in contradictory ways. At one level the individual consumer is minuscule relative to the giant multiple, but at another level, the increased purchasing potential of each consumer cannot be ignored by multiples, especially in the battle for market share.[7] In the contemporary food retailing market there is much greater consumer awareness and demand for information, which in the world of global information technology is also more easily obtainable.

Food scares, such as over salmonella, 'mad cow disease' (BSE) and E. coli, have increased consumer awareness of the need for vigilance and alerted the food industry to the risks of a loss of consumer confidence. The large multiples already impose strict conditions covering aspects such as quantity, quality, product specification, labelling, methods of production, hygiene, animal welfare, and the use of chemicals and pesticides, which all their suppliers have to adhere to. These are monitored by the large supermarkets through periodic inspection and their own independent systems of quality control. Suppliers have to agree to meet the standards set by the supermarkets, and if they fail to comply, have to agree a plan for implementation or can be struck off as a supplier. Setting labour and environmental standards would be an extension of the standards they already demand, and in-house monitoring procedures which exist could form part of a mechanism of enforcement. They would extend the 'caring' image of the supermarket as looking after the interests of the consumer, not only in terms of the quality of food available but the 'conscience' of how it is produced.

Within the UK, the Co-operative Wholesale Society (CWS) and Sainsburys initiated the move by supermarkets in 1996 by announcing a policy of developing a codes of conduct or 'ethical sourcing' in conjunction with the Fairtrade Foundation for all own brand suppliers (*Guardian*, 20 May 1996). Their initial aim was to adopt codes for their 'own-brand' producers and suppliers relating to labour rights and conditions. In 1997, as the trend to more ethical trade progressed, the CWS and Sainbury's joined the move to set up the Ethical Trading Initiative with the aim of establishing codes of conduct across suppliers (Christian Aid 1997), and were joined by other major multiples, including Asda, Safeway, Somerfield and Tesco (ETI 1997). At the time of writing it was too early to say what specific form the multiples' codes of conduct, monitoring or verification would take. Large multiples, through their increasing share of sales and their increasingly dominant position within the supply chain, are in a prime position to implement a code of conduct. With the tendency towards increased multiple dominance in the UK and to a lesser extent in Europe, their ability to influence the sector is likely to grow in the future.

Fresh produce is nominally counted as 'own brand', even though it does not always carry the supermarket logo, and sometimes carries the producer's or exporter's label. It is thus likely that fresh fruit will be covered by supermarket codes of conduct. The advantage of a code of conduct applied from the retailer end of the chain is that it would apply to all Southern Hemisphere suppliers of fresh fruit to the relevant multiples, and not discriminate between them, based on country of origin. This is important in achieving a positive movement to promote the consumption of ethically produced fruit from all countries.[8] Given poor labour conditions and levels of organisation among non-traditional agricultural workers, this could be important in strengthening local campaigns to improve labour rights and conditions in all supplier countries. It might thus have important implications in the future for women workers such as the *temporeras* in Chile.

The Chilean fruit sector, as we have seen, is relatively heterogeneous, particularly at the level of production. There is very little government regulation of the sector, and low levels of enforcement of that legislation which does exist. In the previous chapter we examined the failure of the democratic government to introduce substantive legislation to improve the labour rights and conditions of the *temporeras* given resistance by the producers and exporters. A code of conduct could be another avenue by which such an improvement could be initiated. It is a paradox of globalisation, therefore, that while the democratic government has failed to make substantive improvements for temporary workers, in the interests of maintaining 'national competitive advantage', NGO and consumer-based pressure on large concentrated retailers is stimulating a potential improvement in labour conditions through the external supply chain. Within Chile it is possible that the bigger producers and multinational exporters, who are more likely to adhere to existing legislation and provide better pay and conditions of work, will find it easier to implement a code. But if all relevant multiple suppliers have to implement a code, it could have an impact on raising conditions of employment across the sector.[9] Adopting codes of conduct would raise the issue of labour rights and conditions within the Chilean fruit sector as a form of business enhancement – a way of maintaining sales, raising prices and promoting Chilean produce in a competitive global market. This is in clear opposition to the prevailing ideology among many national producers and exporters, cultivated under dictatorship, that profitability and business 'prowess' depend on minimum labour costs and conditions of employment. In the *macho* world of Chilean agriculture, the extension of ethical trading to the Chilean fruit sector to include the *temporeras* would be quite a culture shock!

However, there are a number of potential problems with codes of conduct and their potential impact should not be overestimated. Clearly, to have any real effect codes would have to be adopted by a large number of suppliers in Europe and the US, and to date this is some way off. There are issues relating to designing the content of a code of conduct, and how it is to be monitored and verified, which have been under discussion between many companies and NGOs, including within the UK Ethical Trading Initiative. One of the main concerns is how labour representation of southern workers, and especially more marginalised groups such as women, can be ensured. Should the companies implementing codes or independent organisations undertake the functions of monitoring and which independent organisations should undertake verification or both functions to improve the effectiveness of codes from the standpoint of labour? One of the more contentious issues in implementing codes is likely to be freedom of association and union representation, especially in sectors where this has been lacking to date. Female seasonal agricultural workers are very atomised, with weak union organisation, but their interests must be represented in the process if codes are seriously going to address their needs, and it is not clear how this will be facilitated. However, codes could help those campaigning for better organisation and representation of groups such as these.

There could be immense problems implementing codes of conduct down a supply chain which is as fragmented at the base (where much of the employment takes place) as the Chilean fruit export sector. Not only are there a large number of producers feeding into each export firm which would have to be monitored, but the labour they employ is seasonal and highly mobile, making consistent monitoring and verification from the standpoint of labour more difficult. Further, as we have seen, the producers and to a lesser extent the exporters who actually employ the *temporeros/as* are often in a weak position to improve labour conditions, as they themselves are being squeezed along the chain by the pricing structure and methods of payment. The producers particularly are subject to high levels of risk from both adverse natural conditions and market volatility, and many operate on a close line between solvency and insolvency. Unless changes take place within the supply chain linking Chile to multiples operating codes of conduct, many smaller producers will find it even more difficult to continue production.[10] Finally, many of the real problems of women *temporeras* do not relate solely to specific labour and environmental standards, but broader issues such as childcare, the double burden and out of season employment. Codes of conduct which only address labour conditions within paid employment are thus limited in that they do not address many of the problems of reproductive and domestic responsibility specific to female workers. Complementary policies would also be needed too if women are really to benefit.

Despite their limitations, there is little doubt that codes of conduct represent a progressive move, particularly in the case of marginalised women workers such as the *temporeras*. Addressing the issue of labour rights and conditions through the supply chain provides another avenue for improving temporary employment, which national legislation has failed to address. It also provides a forum through which more specific gender issues can be raised, as the gender dimension of global horticultural production becomes more exposed. The commercialisation of food production and retailing globally has led to the significant integration of women into paid work in the sector, but they remain an atomised group. Some of the main problems faced by the *temporeras* relate to combining their dual roles as productive and reproductive workers, and their long periods of unemployment out of season, which codes of conduct are unlikely to address. But improving labour rights and conditions of the *temporeras* within the context of the global fruit chain could enhance their organisation and ability to campaign for improvements elsewhere.

Another avenue for improving labour conditions being opened up under globalisation is the issue of social clauses within trade agreements. There have been proposals that organisations such as the World Trade Organisation (WTO) should adopt social clauses, based on International Labour Organisation (ILO) Conventions, with the ILO playing an important role. The social clause would then commit all signatory governments to a trade agreement to guarantee minimum labour standards based on these conventions. An example of a social clause was that introduced in the side-agreement of the North American Free Trade Area (NAFTA). However, as originally negotiated when Mexico joined NAFTA, this is a minimal social clause, simply requiring each country to enforce its existing labour and environmental legislation, and enforcement of the clause is cumbersome and weak (LeQuesne 1996). However, the possibility of more general adoption of social clauses in trade agreements is a long way off, and there is fierce opposition to such a move from some developed and developing countries, especially the Asians. They see this as an affront to their 'competitive advantage' of cheap labour, and a disguised form of protectionism by the US and Europeans. Social clauses are thus quite a contentious issue, and it is beyond the scope of this chapter to explore all aspects of the debate.[11] One argument behind supporting social clauses is the extension of ethical trade to labour and environmental conditions, reducing 'unfair advantage' gained from lowering these. There are also moral arguments for social clauses as a means of extending human rights and basic labour rights, to groups of workers, such as women, who have traditionally been denied such rights (Women Working Worldwide 1996). In an era of trade liberalisation, when female employment is expanding, this could provide a means of promoting the improvement in the labour conditions of women workers (Joekes and Weston 1994).

The implementation of codes of conduct at the time of writing would appear to be much more likely than a comprehensive social clause. Unlike a social clause, codes of conduct operating through the production and distribution chain would not directly address government failure to change or improve the existing legislation with which producers would have to comply. Although the accompanying publicity might possibly have an effect on a government keen to promote a positive image of one of Chile's key exports abroad. Unlike social clauses, codes of conduct are not comprehensive and do not apply to non-multiple suppliers (who could market themselves on cheapness to undercut the multiples). Despite these limitations, codes of conduct might be a stepping stone towards the implementation of a social clause, which would be enhanced if the multinationals applying codes of conduct saw the removal of unfair competition as being in their interest. Codes of conduct and social clauses are thus not counterposed. They are different ways of approaching the issue of human rights and labour conditions among fruit workers at different levels and pursuing ethical trade. As such they are potentially complementary policies.

Social clauses and codes of conduct could provide a twin-track approach to improving labour conditions in the context of a global economy. Codes of conduct would enforce labour conditions within segments of specific sectors, and social clauses would be a means of enforcing legislation (which ultimately only government is in a position to implement) across sectors of competing nations. Both could facilitate an improvement in human rights and labour conditions. The problems of women workers result not only from lack of rights and poor labour conditions, but also from unequal gender relations and women's dual role as reproductive and productive workers. Social clauses and codes of conduct only directly relate to their latter function as paid workers. But any improvement in the ability of women workers to organise collectively and campaign for their own interests would enhance their empowerment. In many respects globalisation has had a negative impact on women, but it is also a contradictory process containing some potential benefits which these combined global policies might help to enhance.

CONCLUSION

The expansion of the Chilean fruit sector has clearly been linked to a global process, which could continue to affect the process of change in the future. The integration of *temporeras* into fruit exports, despite their atomisation as a group, has clearly also been linked to this global process. This book has attempted to demonstrate the complex ways in which rural transformation has taken place in Chile, and the often contradictory effect this has had on women temporary workers. In this section we conclude by drawing together the various threads of the book, and summarise their links to the global picture.

A radical transformation has taken place in the Chilean countryside over the past 25 years as a result of the commercialisation of agriculture and expansion of the agro-export sector. This has affected the lives of all women in the rural sector, and especially the *temporeras* drawn into fruit export employment in the central regions for 3–6 months each year. We have traced the shift away from the *hacienda* as the dominant form of agrarian system, to commercial fruit farming based on the *parcela.* The specific form this process took under the military dictatorship's policy of agrarian 'counter-reform' led to large numbers of *campesinas* being displaced from the land into rural towns and larger cities. They now became dependent on wage labour for survival, and in many cases job insecurity and poverty forced all able members of the household to seek paid employment when it came available. As monocultivation expanded through specialisation in the production of specific varieties of fruit for export, agribusiness became increasingly dependent on the mobilisation of a large seasonal workforce to meet its labour demands. Large numbers of rural and urban workers, 250,000 or more, are drawn into this employment each year. Given the degree of export specialisation in the regions, for many this work is their primary source of earned income throughout the year, and there is a lack of other forms of employment especially out of season.

The effect of this transformation on traditional gender relations in the countryside has been profound. Under the previous agrarian system, women usually worked as unpaid labour on the household plot, and any work carried out on the *hacienda* was under the contract of the husband. Some women worked as paid seasonal labourers, but these were the most marginalised group within the hierarchy of rural work. The dominant role of women in this context was within the household, rearing children and undertaking domestic responsibilities. This role, confined to the private sphere, was seen as subservient to that of men who undertook the paid employment, held any rights to land tenure, and whose primary functions were located within the public sphere. While the workload of rural women was often heavy, it was largely invisible. A paradox of dictatorship was that, despite emphasis on a *machista* ideology in which the place of women was deemed as in the home, increasing numbers of women were drawn into paid employment in the context of economic liberalisation and deregulation of the labour market. In the rural sector, where the sway of traditional ideology was often stronger, affecting women more adversely than in the urban sector, the expansion in female employment was the most rapid (Barrientos and Barrientos 1996). Women now represent approximately one third of the total labour force in Chile, but within the fruit sector they represent over half the temporary labour force.

Agrarian counter-reform under the military led to the commercialisation of the farming sector based on the *parcelas,* setting the framework for the production of fruit. Professional farmers bought up *parcelas*, and with the profitability of fruit production, the rapid expansion of an indigenous fruit export sector took place. Important factors contributing to this were previous investments under the Fruit Plan in infrastructure and technology, the availability of a large cheap seasonal labour force, the free market export model and Chile's early entry into this expanding area. Initially, many of the export firms were nationally owned, but as the sector integrated into the global fruit market, transnational capital became increasingly dominant within the export funnel. However, the integration of transnational capital did not become extensive within the production process itself. Most production has remained in the hands of a relatively large number of domestic producers, who feed into the more concentrated export segment of the fruit chain. None the less, there is a distinction between ownership and control, and by the 1990s many producers were in a relation of financial and technological dependency on the exporter they serve.

These features of the Chilean export sector partly reflected the specific form commercialisation of the agrarian sector took in Chile under the military. To some extent the structure of Chilean agribusiness reflects trends in global manufacturing, in which large exporters and transnationals outsource production to smaller formally independent but largely captive smaller producers. However, we have argued that these features of the Chilean fruit export sector also reflect inherent aspects of agriculture as it has expanded into the global market. Despite advances in biotechnology and production methods, agriculture remains subject to natural constraints and risk. The most important of these are the temporal constraint to production of the season, the risk of climatic variation throwing production schedules into disarray, and potential market and price volatility. The risks of infestation by pest and disease also persist, despite the intensive use of advanced agro-chemicals, and indeed when they strike, the effect can be devastating given specialisation in specific varieties of fruit under monocultivation. Transnational export capital can offset the adverse effects on profitability of these inherent constraints and risks through its relation with smaller domestic producers. The degree of transnational integration into the production process itself has thus remained limited, and the latter has remained relatively fragmented in comparison with the more concentrated export funnel. Finally, this has been reinforced by globalisation of the fruit sector. Large transnationals can source fruit for the north all the year round by rotating supplies around the globe as the seasons shift, locking into domestic production in different locations at specific points in time through the year.

This is the sectoral context within which employment of the *temporeras* has expanded. Agribusiness and the commercialisation of production has led to a high level of dependence on a seasonal workforce to meet the annual surge in labour demand. In the fruit-growing areas, nearly all available able labour is drawn into temporary fruit work at the height of the season. Female labour is a crucial element within this, and the ratio of *temporeras* to *temporeros* is approximately equivalent to the ratio of women to men in the population at large.[12] However, female labour is a preferred labour force by many employers for certain tasks. The concentration of women in the packing sector reflects the belief that women have the dexterity to undertake delicate work without damaging the fruit. In other words, their socially imbued skills are drawn on to maintain the high quality of output demanded by the export sector generating a gendered segregation between female and male work. Women are also considered by many employers to be a more reliable and subservient labour force. This partly reflects their traditional lack of union organisation (due to their exclusion from much paid work), but also reflects the persistence of *machista* ideology within modern agribusiness, and exploits women's traditional role within the household. Female labour is also the more 'flexible' in terms of duration and security of employment as well as means of payment (piecework being more prevalent in tasks predominantly undertaken by women than men). Female labour thus helps to provide a buffer for employers between the exacting demands of export to meet tight production with high quality output, and the risk of variation in those schedules due to natural conditions or market volatility. Agribusiness takes advantage of traditional gender roles, while at the same time subverting those roles, if only temporarily each season, by drawing in and ejecting women from the paid labour force to meet its pattern of labour requirements. Agribusiness thus reinforces the insecurity and marginalisation of its seasonal female labour force as an essential element of its profitable operation at a global level.

The effect on women themselves is both complex and contradictory. Paid seasonal work compounds the burdens of many *temporeras*, but at the same time provides opportunities for them. Many rural women are now able to move beyond their traditional role within the household by taking up fruit work, enhancing their empowerment, yet by the nature of the work this can only be partial and disjointed. The problems borne by the *temporeras* as a group are immense. They are very heterogeneous, coming from both rural and urban backgrounds and a variety of personal circumstances. Some combine traditional work as *campesinas* with temporary work in the fruit. Others rely totally on fruit work as their sole means of survival. They endure long arduous hours of work during the season for poor recompense, with their health often suffering through strain and exposure to chemicals. Most have families and carry the double burden of combining their employment with household responsibilities in the season. Many women confront tensions in the mediation of their multiple roles of wife, mother, housewife and fruit worker. Poverty among this group of workers is significant, and most face long periods of unemployment out of the season.

Yet despite all these problems, the potential for their empowerment has been enhanced through entry into agribusiness. At a personal level, the ability to take up paid work, often for the first time, increases their independence financially, and for many improves their bargaining position within the household. Their sense of worth and self-esteem is raised, and the inequity of their traditionally subservient position is undermined. At a social level, the *temporeras* have the basis for greater social interaction and contact enhancing their empowerment through strong social relations. They may be a heterogeneous group, but once a year they come together to work in large numbers providing new experiences and interaction. Their work may be marginalised, but it is no longer invisible, and gradually there has been a greater recognition of their role. In terms of their collective organisation, union membership amongst *temporeras* is very low. But this could well reflect the inability of traditional rural unions to meet their needs as seasonal women workers as much as their fragmentation as a group of workers. There have been many instances of NGO and community organisation amongst the *temporeras* enhancing their ability to participate in activities to address their needs. However, these tend to be localised with little unity and poor resources, although the *temporeras* themselves are often very aware of their potential strength, without any formal organisation. At the height of the season when production is at full tilt, they simply 'cross their arms' to pressurise managers and employers into giving concessions (although these might often only be temporary). Lack of formal organisation is thus partly compensated by the collective power they can acquire through working together. Despite their partial integration into paid work, and their weak organisation, agribusiness has thus enhanced the potential empowerment of the *temporeras*, and a number of studies have shown that given the alternatives the majority like the work they do (Díaz 1991; Venegas 1992a).

In the context of the transition to democracy in Chile, government policies to support the *temporeras* have been limited. The government has pursued a dual strategy of 'equity with growth', yet the temporary fruit workers been more affected by the strive for growth than a genuine improvement in their position of equity. They have not been included in many of the benefits which have been extended to permanent workers, especially the legal right to collective negotiation, which could have provided a stimulus for union organisation. Unlike most other groups of workers, though, the *temporeras* have been the recipients of a government childcare programme administered by SERNAM, which has also supported some joint initiatives such as setting up local centres for them. These are clearly beneficial, and are to be welcomed. But these policies also help to facilitate the availability of women fruit workers during the season, supporting this important export sector and its contribution to the Chilean economy. The benefits of the childcare policy only last the duration of the season, reinforcing the necessity for women to return to the home and poverty out of season. Government policy thus concurs with the partial insertion of women into the agricultural labour force. It has failed to enhance the ability of women to challenge the all-embracing power of agribusiness through the right to collective negotiation, and has thus done little to genuinely improve their position of equity. In the face of the export-led model, the requisites of growth have taken precedence, and the *temporeras* remain a largely marginalised group of workers.

Within the context of globalisation, however, new possibilities are emerging which could help to improve the position of seasonal agricultural labour in Chile and elsewhere. The trend towards greater concentration along the export sector of the supply chain has been complemented within the globalised consumer market in many developed countries by an increasingly dominant role played by supermarkets. Suppliers to supermarkets have to meet high standards in production and quality of supply, which are monitored in different ways by the multiples. Supermarket buyers now have tighter relations with importers and exporters along the supply chain, and often visit the point of production. Supermarkets themselves have also come under increasing pressure by NGOs and consumer-based campaigns to improve the labour conditions amongst their suppliers in developing countries. This has formed part of a general move towards more ethical trading policies by many large corporations in the later 1990s. An outcome is that many northern supermarkets are now introducing codes of conduct to cover labour conditions amongst their third world producers.

This trend is only at an early stage at the time of writing, but it is likely that existing ILO Conventions on labour and safety standards will form a common element within these codes. The core ILO conventions cover sex discrimination, equal pay, banning child and forced labour and freedom of association and collective bargaining. The latter are likely to prove the most contentious in the formulation of supermarket codes of conduct, given the low level of union organisation amongst agricultural workers, and the active disdain by many employers for unions. However, a code of conduct which denied these workers rights enjoyed by many other groups of workers internationally would have little meaning, and many northern trade unions and NGOs concerned with ethical trade are pushing for their insertion. If comprehensive codes of conduct were successfully implemented, there is little doubt they would strengthen the hand of marginalised women seasonal workers, and their chance of gaining an improvement in labour conditions. A paradox of globalisation, therefore, is that where national policy has failed to help temporary workers in export production, new channels and opportunities are emerging along the global supply chain through which pressure can be exerted to improve their employment rights.

Even if successfully implemented, however, codes of conduct would have limitations, and should not be seen as a panacea. This is especially so for women workers in agribusiness, who by nature of the sector are only partially integrated into employment, and often a very heterogeneous marginalised group. Codes would only apply to producers supplying multiples, and only relate to the period of employment, which in agriculture is often only a few months. There are also important issues relating to how women's views and needs in developing countries are going to be represented in the design, monitoring and verification of codes of conduct applied by northern multiples, which to date have barely been addressed. Social clauses in trade agreements could be more comprehensive, but arc lcss likely to be implemented given a lack of international consensus on the issue. However, both policy approaches only cover conditions of workers while in employment in the export sector, ignoring domestic producers and other forms of employment which seasonal workers pursue to eke out multiple incomes needed to survive. They do not address the important needs of women workers in having to combine paid employment with childcare and domestic responsibilities, and cannot be a substitute for national and local support policies in these areas. They are top-down policies, which might contribute to the empowerment of women workers, but are not in themselves directly empowering.

Despite their integration into a global export sector, and the actual and potential opportunities seasonal work generates for them, the *temporeras* remain a fragmented and marginalised group. Their work is insecure, arduous and poorly paid with little alternative. The experiences of women seasonal workers in Chile are similar to those of groups of workers in agricultural exports in many other countries – Mexico, Argentina, Brazil, Columbia, South Africa, Kenya, Zimbabwe, India, to name just a few. Research in this area to date has been limited, and much further work is needed to understand and analyse in a more comprehensive way the gender dimension to non-traditional agricultural export production. Much emphasis is placed by international organisations, such as the World Bank, on the success of non-traditional agricultural exports. But as this case study shows, along with many others which are emerging, this is a 'success' which has two sides. Hopefully, this book has contributed to exploring the other side – that of the women seasonal workers who have helped to underpin the Chilean economic 'miracle'. As a marginalised group their voice, and even their existence, so far has been largely ignored. Despite the opportunities this work can open up, these workers also bear the brunt of the costs of export success and of sustaining a global consumer market in fresh produce. In future the inequity of their position must be addressed, and their voices heard.

Notes

CHAPTER 2

1. The term 'traditional' is often given different interpretations. In the context of this book, we do not use the term in the sense of pre-capitalist relations, but to describe an era when social and economic relations combined subsistence production with a market economy. This is in contrast to our use of the term 'modern' in which social and economic relations are dominated by capitalist production and employment, there is a high level of integration into the global economy and subsistence production has been marginalised.

2. The 'first food regime' in contrast was the period prior to the Second World War, when agricultural trade was characterised by colonial links, and supplies from settler estates and plantations to the industrialising countries of Europe and the US (Friedmann and McMichael 1989). There is a large body of literature which analyses the evolution of agribusiness and the food system generally, which we will refer to only briefly here, given our main concentration is specifically on non-traditional agricultural exports. For more detail see Bonanno et al. 1994; Fine and Leopold 1993 and Fine et al. 1996; Friedland et al. 1991; Goodman and Redclift 1991; Jaffee 1993; Le Heron 1993; McMichael 1994; Ward and Almas 1997.

3. We recognise that using the term 'non-traditional' still carries problems, in that some countries (for example, South Africa) have exported this produce for a long time. However, it is only in the past two decades that fresh produce has become widely available at low cost in northern markets throughout the year, hence the inclusion of (2) in this definition. At some point, once this trade is long established, a different term will have to replace 'non-traditional'.

4. The ability to lock into this type of trade requires a specific combination of circumstances, and is not open to everyone. A location must have the right natural and environmental conditions to produce the varieties of produce for which there is demand, it must acquire (either domestically or through transnational investment) significant technical expertise and capital investment in production methods, packing plants and equipment; a seasonal labour force able to produce high quality produce must be available; sufficient infrastructure and transport facilities are necessary; and the right economic and political environment is relevant.

5. Evidence from outside Latin America also suggests widespread female employment in non-traditional agriculture. In South Africa, 230,000 workers in total are employed in the Western Cape fruit industry, 53 per cent of the women (Kritzinger and Vorster 1996). The failed attempt by Budd to establish production in Senegal also involved

widespread female employment (Macintosh 1989), and anecdotal information from Kenya, Zimbabwe and India also suggest a similar significant level of female employment.

CHAPTER 3

1. State planning in the rural sector first began with the Agrarian Plan of 1945 and the Plan for the Development of Agriculture and Transport in 1954.
2. Perhaps the clearest example of this would be post-revolutionary Mexico where, for ideological reasons and for political gain, the state committed itself (usually rather half-heartedly) to agrarian reform and the creation of a communal system of land holding in many regions. Yet it simultaneously pursued an economic model which favoured capitalist, large-scale farming in other areas which enjoyed preferential access to state support (Hamilton 1986).
3. These were technically known as the *Sociedades Agrícolas de Reforma Agraria*.
4. The CEMAs had existed since the late 1930s when they were encouraged in poor urban areas by the Catholic Church. Later, during the 1940s, the number of mothers' centres continued to grow (Valdés and Weinstein 1993; Valdés 1993).
5. The *Unidad Popular* came to power in the 1970 elections. It was a broad coalition incorporating six of the main political parties from the left. The *Unidad Popular* was committed to 'the peaceful road to socialism' and aimed to transform society and the economy into a socialist state (Roxborough, O'Brien and Roddick 1977).
6. The increase in inequality is shown by the rise in the Gini coefficient of family income. In 1969–71 it was 0.493; in 1979–81 it measured 0.523; and in 1982–84 it measured 0.543 (Meller 1991: 1).
7. This situation was compounded by the fact that the *parceleros* also acquired liability for the debts of the pre-reform *asentamiento* lands (Yotopoulous 1989).
8. CEMAS were now renamed CEMA-Chile.
9. The figure for rural female heads of household in employment in 1990 was 21 per cent, well below the national average (MIDEPLAN 1993).
10. Chile's main traditional export had been copper. This continued, but was now supplemented by fruit, fish and timber, leading to an increase in export diversity.

CHAPTER 4

1. The research for this chapter was based on the use of trade literature and publications combined with interviews with professionals working in the trade at all points along the supply chain in Chile, Holland and

the UK. A total of 12 in-depth interviews were carried out by Stephanie Barrientos during 1994 and 1995 with producers, exporters, freight executives, importers, supermarket buyers and marketing specialists involved directly with Chilean fruit. In addition interviews were carried out with a number of academics and other professionals with knowledge of the trade. For reasons of confidentiality no specific references are made to either the interviewees or their companies. The research was made possible by a University of Hertfordshire research grant.

2. This is a relative levelling off of growth during the 1990s compared to the dizzy heights of the 1980s, but despite increased pressures on Chilean fruit, the volume of exports has been sustained in the 1990s.

3. Chile also grows a large number of grapes for wine production, but these are excluded from fresh fruit production and export figures.

4. Each group is represented by their own association. The main producers association is FEDEFRUT, and the main exporters association is Asociación de Exportadores.

5. The use of hormones in production play an important part in ensuring the right quantities of fruit are ready for harvest at the right time to meet planning schedules.

6. As UK handling facilities for fresh produce have improved at Dover and Sheerness (*Eurofruit*, various issues), the quantity coming directly to the UK is likely to grow.

7. Kiwi exports grew rapidly from the late 1980s, and Chile challenged the dominant position of New Zealand as the main Southern Hemisphere supplier of kiwis. Until 1991/2 kiwis were grown for export only, and most Chileans were unfamiliar with this fruit. Following a slump in the world market, kiwis were sold internally, and Chileans have now had to become accustomed to eating kiwis, which was nicknamed 'gringo fruit'.

8. If we compare Chilean exports with other developing countries, the figure is much higher. In 1990, for example, Chilean grape exports accounted for 80 per cent of all developing country grape exports (FAO 1992: 141–2).

9. Until 1997, Unifruco held a monopoly position as the marketing board through which South African deciduous fruit exports had to pass. This monopoly position was relaxed in 1997, and fruit exporters could export independently. At the time of writing it was too early to assess the effects of this change of marketing policy.

10. This rough estimate relates to a bunch of grapes retailing in a hypothetical multiple at £0.99, without having passed through the wholesale market, and is not based on any individual multiple chain. The information for this estimate was based on interviews with producers and exporters, combined with weekly prices announced in *The Fresh Produce Journal*. Given that interviewees were reluctant to give price sensitive information, this can only be a guestimate.

11. Just as the production sector within Chile is relatively diverse in comparison to the export sector, because of the nature of global agro-export production, it is also likely that in other countries supplying the global fruit market a variety of diverse forms of production will be found.

CHAPTER 5

1. This chapter draws primarily on three case studies of the *temporeras*: Rodríguez and Venegas 1991, Díaz 1991 and Bee 1996, and additional research carried out separately between 1993 and 1995 by Barrientos (1996) and Vogel (1997).

2. In the normal employment survey, a person can be counted as employed if she or he worked for one hour or more in the previous week (Hojman, 1993: 80), and economically active if she or he worked or sought employment in the previous three months. See Barrientos (1997) for a discussion of the underestimation of female temporary agricultural workers.

3. Gómez and Echeñique (1988: 64) estimate that the total permanent agricultural labour force fell from 208,000 to 120,000 between 1964 and 1987, while the total temporary agricultural labour force increased from 147,000 to 300,000 in the same period.

4. The female participation rate for the country increased from 28.7 per cent in 1980 to 38.5 per cent in 1993 (ILO 1994). See Barrientos (1996) for a discussion of labour flexibility and how the *temporeras* fit into this.

5. Rodríguez and Venegas' (1991) survey included permanent as well as temporary workers, but given the focus of this book, we have extracted their data on temporary workers only, discussed in Table 2, n. 1.

6. Personal communication with Bob Gwynne.

CHAPTER 6

1. The research for this chapter was undertaken by Anna Bee between 1993 and 1994 as part of her PhD. The research was made possible by an ESRC studentship. The two locations selected were the settlements of Chañaral Alto and Tome Alto in the Norte Chico (see Map 6.1). The primary research method of the study was structured interviews based on a standard questionnaire. Through a combination of quota sampling and snowball sampling, the questionnaires were administered to a total of 135 individuals (women and men). On completing the survey 128 questionnaires were coded and analysed using a Quattro Pro Spreadsheet. Extended in-depth interviews were also carried out with selected female respondents. In total 35 women who had participated in the questionnaire survey were interviewed. For further details, see Bee 1996.

2. In 1967 Decree Law 5 of the Agrarian Reform legislation required that the boundaries for each community should be defined and that communal and collective land tenure within the community boundary be clarified. In 1978 Decree Law 108 allowed *comuneros* to sell their land to non-members of their community, provided that land tenure had been regularised (Gwynne and Ortíz, 1997: 30).

CHAPTER 7

1. These case studies are drawn from in-depth interviews with 14 women working in agribusiness in Graneros in the VI Region and Curicó in the VII Region, to the south of the capital, Santiago. These interviews formed part of a wider PhD research project by Isabel Vogel on women in the labour market in Chile, and were carried out in the field during 1993–4. The research was made possible by an ESRC studentship. The interviews were conducted by means of a semi-structured questionnaire, organised around three main subject areas. These were: paid work and the work history of the interviewee; the household and family, covering the women's perceptions of the effect of their employment and income on the dynamics of household and family relations; while a final section on attitudes and opinions dealt with gender relations within the family, the workplace and society as a whole. The extracts in this chapter are the author's own translations of verbatim quotes taken from the interviews. For further information, see Vogel 1997.
2. Some field tasks are also paid by piece rate, for example, the pruning of apple fruit buds are often paid *a trato*, per row of trees, while other tasks, such as the pruning of peach fruit buds, are paid by the day. The difference in remuneration systems seems to depend on the species of fruit and the dexterity required to complete the task. Thus, as the pruning of apples trees apparently requires less delicacy, this task can be carried out relatively quickly, and piecework may help speed up the process. In the peach orchards, the fruit buds are more easily damaged, and care and attention is given more importance than speed, thus daily rates tend to dominate. However, this was a tendency observed specifically in this region, and remuneration may vary again between regions.
3. The exchange rate is calculated at an average of US$1.00 = CH$420 (1994 exchange rate).
4. Information on this is drawn from various interviews.

CHAPTER 8

1. The research for this chapter was based predominantly on qualitative information, obtained through semi-structured interviews with civil servants in SERNAM and INDAP. The fieldwork was undertaken by Ann Matear in two rounds. The first was between October 1992 and March 1993, when SERNAM had only been in existence for 18 months. The second was from October 1993 to March 1994, by which time SERNAM was more fully operational. The second round of research was made possible by an ESRC studentship. The semi-structured interviews were supplemented by quantitative information from internal reports, commissioned research and independent studies. The research on SERNAM and INDAP was conducted at central government level and

in the following five regions: the Metropolitan Region, IV Region, V Region, VI Region and VIII Region.

2. La Demanda de la Mujer Rural, Resoluciones del Primer Encuentro de la Mujer Rural', Punta de Tralca, 17–20 July 1986.
3. This was published as *Tramas para un nuevo destino: propuestas de la Concertacion de Mujeres por la Democracia*, Montecino and Rossetti (eds.), Santiago, 1990.
4. The other issues covered in the document were education, health, family, communications, arts and culture, employment, political participation, low-income women, legislation.
5. By contrast, SERNAM developed a team of experts in housing, employment, justice, health and education issues to plan and coordinate gender-sensitive policies with the respective ministries between 1991 and 1994.
6. Interview with Maria Luisa Rojas, Sectoral Coordinator, SERNAM.
7. S. Venegas, 'El Cuidado Infantil Como Componente del Plan Piloto de Apoyo Para las Jefas de Hogar', in Valenzuela, Venegas and Andrade (eds.), pp. 335–63.
8. This was based on information gained from studies conducted in three municipalities in the V Region which revealed a four-fold increase in accidents among the children of *temporeras* compared with children of women who were not employed. Similarly they had very poor levels of nutrition.
9. The law states that employers must provide crèche facilities in the workplace, or contract the equivalent service in a nearby nursery, if there are more than 20 women working in the company. This law is often flouted and employers generally employ a maximum of 19 women to avoid their responsibilities.
10. The regions are the III, IV, V, VI, VII, VIII and Metropolitan.
11. While members of the Women's Department of the CNC, for example, has been very pro-active on seasonal work, the weakness of unions as a whole is reflected in the fact that less than one per cent of all seasonal workers are union members (Falabella 1993).
12. Local community established centres visited during the course of our research were in Santa María, Los Andes, San Felipe and Talca. However, funding for these centres is precarious, especially as NGO funds have dwindled since the return to democracy.
13. The potential for collaboration was raised in the study by Díaz (1991).
14. This was undertaken by the Information Centres for Women's Rights (CIDEM), a programme which SERNAM operates nationally to empower women by providing them with legal orientation and increasing their awareness of their civil rights.

CHAPTER 9

1. Raven, Lang and Dumonteil (1995) argue that this type of shopping can have important external costs, such as increased pollution through the

use of cars, and reduces the ability of poor households with inadequate incomes or road transport to benefit from it.

2. The Fairtrade Foundation (FTF) was set up as a joint initiative by a number of UK-based NGOS, including Oxfam, Christian Aid, CAFOD, New Consumer, Tradecraft Exchange and the World Development Movement (Fairtrade 1995). Brand-named producers or suppliers are able to apply to the FTF for a product to carry a Fair Trade Mark. FTF inspects the conditions and arrangements for production and sale of the production, and if the requisite standards are met a mark is granted, which FTF continues to monitor.

3. See the Ethical Trading Initiative Information Pack (ETI 1997) for a full list of participating organisations.

4. At the time of writing (December 1997), the Ethical Trading Initiative still was in the process of formation, and precise details of the agreement were yet to be established.

5. For more information on ILO conventions see ILO 1991 and World Bank 1995.

6. Little information was available on US supermarkets at the time of writing.

7. It is believed that the average value of an individual customer to a supermarket over his or her lifetime is £100,000 (personal communication with Liz Orton, Christian Aid), hence the importance of maintaining customer loyalty by supermarkets.

8. This is an important distinction to the consumer boycotts of such goods during the period of dictatorship in Chile and apartheid in South Africa. An important aim of a code of conduct is to positively encourage consumers *to buy* goods covered by them, stimulating other producers to follow suit as a selling point, as opposed to the negative message of consumer boycotts.

9. Raising productivity would reduce the level of employment for any given quantity of output, but in a highly competitive global market it is unlikely Chilean fruit exports will be able to continue growing without raising productivity, and growth could compensate for a fall in employment. Much more research is needed, however, to assess the actual impact a Code is likely to have. All we are attempting here is a general discussion of the possible implications.

10. It is possible that as the international fruit market becomes increasingly competitive, smaller producers will find it increasingly difficult to operate irrelevant of codes of conduct. Anecdotal evidence suggests many smaller producers are already going out of business, and only those who are able to raise productivity and remain competitive are surviving. Hence some restructuring of the sector is already taking place within Chile, leading to increased concentration amongst producers themselves. Producers and exporters with higher productivity are more likely to be able to provide better labour conditions, and thus implement any future code of conduct.

11. There is no common agreement on either the left or right regarding social clauses. The US government is generally supportive of them, whilst the UK government and World Bank oppose them; many trade

unions and NGOs support them, but others are vigorously opposed to them. For a more detailed discussion of social clauses see for example: 'Debate International Labour Standards and Human Rights' in *New Political Economy* (1996) 1: 2 July; Sengenberger and Campbell (1994); World Bank (1995); van Liemt (1989); Longley (1995); LeQuesne (1996); ILO (1995); Sengenberger and Wilkinson (1995).

12.   Venegas (1993) estimated that the *temporeras* were 52 per cent of the temporary fruit labour force. In 1992 the percentage of women in the total population was 51 per cent (INE 1995: 7).

Bibliography

Afshar, H. (ed.) (1998) *Empowering Women: Illustrations from the Third World*, Basingstoke: Macmillan.

Afshar, H. and Barrientos, S. (eds.) (1998) *Women, Globalization and Fragmentation in the Developing World*, Basingstoke: Macmillan.

Afshar, H. and Dennis, C. (eds.) (1992) *Women and Adjustment Policies in the Third World*, Basingstoke: Macmillan.

Anker, R. (1983) 'Female Labour Force Participation in Developing Countries: a Critique of Current Definitions and Data Collection Methods', *International Labour Review*, 122, pp. 709–23.

Apey, A. (1995) *Agricultural Restructuring and Co-ordinated Policies for Rural Development in Chile*. Unpublished PhD thesis, University of Birmingham, Birmingham.

Aranda, X. (1992) *Mujer Rural Vol. I, Diagnósticos para Orientar Políticas en el Agro*, INDAP/Ministerio de Agricultura/FAO/ SERNAM, Santiago.

Arce, A. and Marsden, T.K. (1993) 'The Social Construction of International Food: a New Research Agenda' *Economic Geography*, 3, July, pp. 293–311.

Arizpe, L. and Aranda, J. (1981) 'The "Comparative Advantages" of Women's Disadvantages: Women Workers in the Strawberry Export Agribusiness in Mexico' *Signs* 7:2, pp. 453–73.

Arizpe, L. and Aranda, J. (1986) 'Women Workers in the Strawberry Agribusiness in Mexico', in E. Leacock and H. Safa (eds.) *Women's Work: Development and the Division of Labour by Gender*, New York: Bergin and Garvey.

Arnold, H. (1996) 'Pushing Ethical Boat Out', *Supermarketing*, July.

Asociación de Exportadores (1992) *Estadísticas de Exportaciones Hortofrutícolas*, Temporada 1991/2, Santiago.

Asociación de Exportadores (1994) *Estadísticas de Exportaciones Hortofrutícolas*, Temporada 1993/4, Santiago.

Asociación de Exportadores (1995) *Estadísticas de Exportaciones Hortofrutícolas*, Temporada 1994/5, Santiago.

Barham, B., Clark, M., Katz, E. and Schurman, R. (1992) 'Nontraditional Agricultural Exports in Latin America', *Latin American Research Review*, 11:26, pp. 43–82.

Barratt Brown, M. (1993) *Fair Trade, Reform and Realities in the International Trading System*, London: Zed Press.

Barrett, II., Browne, A., Ilbery, W., Jackson, G., and Binns, T. (1997) *Prospects for Horticultural Exports under Trade Liberalisation in Adjusting African Economies*, Report to ODA No. R6139, London.

Barría, L. et al. (1985) *Participación de la Mujer en la Economía Campesina en Chile*. Instituto de Promoción Agraria e Instituto de Chileno de Educación Cooperativa, Santiago.

Barrientos, A. and Barrientos, S. (1996) *Labour Market and Trade Liberalisation and Women's Employment in Chile*, Employment Studies Unit Paper 9, University of Hertfordshire, Hertford.

213

Barrientos, S. (1996) 'Flexible Work and Female Labour: the Global Integration of Chilean Fruit Production,' in R. Auty and J. Toye (eds.) *Challenging the Orthodoxies*, Basingstoke: Macmillan.

Barrientos, S. (1997) 'The Hidden Ingredient – Female Labour in Chilean Fruit Exports', in *Bulletin of Latin American Research*, 15:4, January pp. 71–82.

Barrientos, S. (1998) 'Fruits of Burden – the Organisation of Women Temporary Workers in Chilean Agribusiness', in H. Afshar (ed.) *Empowering Women: Illustrations from the Third World*, Basingstoke: Macmillan.

Barrientos, S. and Perrons, D. (1996) 'Fruit of the Vine – Linkages between Flexible Women Workers in the Production and Retailing of Winter Fruit'. Paper to The Globalisation of Production Conference, University of Warwick.

Barrientos, S. and Perrons, D. (1998) 'Gender and the Global Food Chain: a Comparative Study of Chile and the UK', in H. Afshar and S. Barrientos (eds.) *Women, Globalization and Fragmentation in the Developing World*, Basingstoke: Macmillan.

Barrón, A. (1994) 'Mexican Rural Women Wage Earners and Macro-economic Policies', in I. Bakker (ed.) *The Strategic Silence*, London: Zed Books.

Bee, A. (1996) *Regional Change and Non-Traditional Exports: Land, Labour and Gender in the Norte-Chico, Chile*, unpublished PhD Thesis, University of Birmingham.

Bee, A. and Vogel, I. (1997) '*Temporeras* and Household Relations: Seasonal Employment in Chile's Agro-export Sector', *Bulletin of Latin American Research* 16:1, pp. 83–96.

Bell, D. and Valentine, G. (1997) *Consuming Geographies: We Are Where We Eat*, London: Routledge.

Benería, L. and Sen, G. (1981) 'Accumulation, Reproduction and Women's Role in Economic Development: Boserup Revisited', *Signs* 7:2, Winter, pp. 279–98.

Benería, L. and Sen, G. (1986) 'Accumulation, Reproduction and Women's Role in Economic Development: Boserup Revisited', in E. Leacock and H. Safa (eds.) *Women's Work: Development and the Division of Labour by Gender*, New York: Bergin and Garvey.

Bernstein, H., Crow, B., Mackintosh, M. and Martin, C. (1990) *The Food Question, Profits versus People?* London: Earthscan Publications.

Bonanno, A., Busch, L., Friedland, W., Gouveia, L. and Mingione, E. (eds.) (1994) *From Columbus to ConAgra, The Globalization of Agriculture and Food*, Kansas: University of Kansas Press.

Boserup, E. (1970) *Women's Role in Economic Development*, New York: St. Martin's Press.

Bourque, S. (1989) 'Gender and the State: Perspectives from Latin America', in S. Charlton, J. Everett, and K. Staudt (eds.) (1989) *Women, the State and Development*, Albany: University of New York Press.

Boyle, C. (1991) 'Touching the Air. the Cultural Force of Women in Chile', in H. Afshar and C. Dennis (eds.) *Women and Adjustment Policies in the Third World*, Basingstoke: Macmillan.

Bradshaw, S. (1990) 'Women in Chilean Rural Society', in D.E. Hojman (ed.), *Neo-liberal Agriculture in Rural Chile*, Basingstoke: Macmillan.

Brant, C. and Too, Y.L. (eds.) (1994) *Rethinking Sexual Harassment*, London: Pluto Press.

Bruce, J. and Dwyer, D. (1988) 'Introduction', in Dwyer D. and Bruce J. (eds.) *A Home Divided: Women and Income in the Third World*, Stanford: Stanford University Press.

Campaña, P. (1985) *Peasant Economy, Women's Labour and Differential Forms of Capitalist Development: a Comparative Study in Three Contrasting Situations in Peru and Chile*, PhD Thesis, Department of Anthropology, University of Durham.

Campaña, P. and Lago, S. (1982) *Y Las Mujeres También Trabajan...*, Research Publication No. 10, Grupo de Investigaciones Agrarias, Santiago.

Carter, M., Barham, B. and Mesbah, D. (1996) 'Agricultural Export Booms and the Rural Poor in Chile, Guatemala and Paraguay', *Latin American Research Review*, 31:1, pp. 33–65.

Castillo, L. and Lehmann, D. (1982) 'Chile's Three Agrarian Reforms: the Inheritors', in *Bulletin of Latin American Research*, 1:2, pp. 21–43.

CEM (1988) *Mundo de Mujer: Continuidad y Cambio*, Santiago: Centro de Estudios de la Mujer.

CEM (1989) *Plagicidas y Pesticidas de la Uva (Temporeras, salud y trabajo)*, Santiago: Centro de Estudios de la Mujer.

CEPAL (1990) *La Cadena de Distribución y la Competitividad de las Exportaciones Latinoamericanas: La Fruta de Chile*, Santiago: CEPAL.

Chant, S. (1997) *Women-headed Households: Diversity and Dynamics in the Developing World*, Basingstoke: Macmillan.

Charlton, S., Everett, J. and Staudt, K. (eds.) (1989) *Women, the State and Development*, Albany: University of New York Press.

Christian Aid (1996) *The Global Supermarket, Britain's Biggest Shops and Food from the Third World*, London: Christian Aid.

Christian Aid (1997) *Change at the Check-out, Supermarkets and Ethical Business*, London: Christian Aid.

Chukryck, P. (1989) 'Feminist Anti-authoritarian Politics: the Role of Women's Organisations in the Chilean Transition to Democracy', in J.S. Jaquette (ed.), *The Women's Movement in Latin America: Feminism and the Transition to Democracy*, Massachusetts: Unwin-Hyman.

Codron, J.M. (1990) *La Fruticultura Chilena. Balance y Perspectivas,* Colloque International de Toulouse, Toulouse, France, December.

Collier, S. and Sater, W. (1996) *A History of Chile, 1808–1994*, Cambridge: Cambridge University Press.

Collins, J. (1993) 'Gender, Contracts and Wage Work: Agricultural Restructuring in Brazil's São Francisco Valley', *Development and Change*, 24, pp. 53–82.

Connell, R.W. (1987) *Gender and Power: Society, the Person and Sexual Politics*, Oxford: Polity Press.

Cook, I. (1994) 'New Fruits and Vanity: Symbolic Production in the Global Economy', in A. Bonanno, L. Busch, W. Friedland, L. Gouveia and E. Mingione, *From Columbus to ConAgra. The Globalization of Agriculture and Food*, Kansas: University Press of Kansas.

Coote, B. (1996) *NAFTA, Poverty and Free Trade in Mexico*, Oxford: Oxfam Publications.

Cruz, M.E. (1992) 'From Inquilino to Temporary Worker; From Hacienda to Rural Settlement', in C. Kay and P. Silva (eds.) *Development and Social Change in the Chilean Countryside*, Amsterdam: CEDLA.

CUT (1992) *Análisis Encuesta: Proyecto Multinacional de Promoción de la Mujer Sindicalista*, Secretaría Técnica de la Mujer, Santiago: Central Unica de Trabajadores, Mimeo.

Deere, C.D. (1986) 'Rural Women and Agrarian Reform in Peru, Chile, and Cuba', in J. Nash and H. Safa (eds.) *Women and Change in Latin America* Massachusetts: Bergin & Garvey.

Deere, C.D. (1987) 'The Latin American Agrarian Reform Experience' in C.D. Deere and M. Leon (eds.) *Rural Women and State Policy, Feminist Perspectives on Latin American Agricultural Development*, Boulder: Westview Press.

Deere, C.D. and Leon, M. (1987) 'Introduction', in Deere, C.D. and Leon, M. (eds.), *Rural Women and State Policy, Feminist Perspectives on Latin American Agricultural Development*, Boulder: Westview.

Délano, B. and Todaro, R. (1993) *Asedio Sexual en el Trabajo*, Santiago, CEM.

Díaz, E. (1991) *Investigación Participativa Acerca de las Trabajadoras Temporeras de la Fruta, San Bernardo,* Santiago: Centro El Canelo de Nos.

Díaz, H. (1990) 'Proletarianization and Marginality: the Modernisation of Chilean Agriculture', in D. Hojman (ed.) *Neo-Liberal Agriculture in Rural Chile*, Basingstoke: Macmillan.

Dixon, R. (1982) 'Women in Agriculture: Counting the Labour Force in Developing Countries', *Population and Development Review,* 8, pp. 539–66.

Echeñique, J. (1990) 'Las Dos Caras de la Agricultura y las Políticas Posibles', *Proposiciones* 18, pp. 145–58.

EIU Retail Business (1991) *Fresh Fruit and Vegetables*, Parts 1 and 2, Market Reports 1 and 2, Nos. 401 and 402, July and August, London.

Elson, D. (ed.) (1991) *Male Bias in the Development Process*, Manchester: Manchester University Press.

Elson, D. and Pearson, R. (1981) 'Nimble Fingers Make Cheap Workers, An Analysis of Women's Employment in Third World Export Manufacturing', *Feminist Review*, Spring, pp. 87–107.

La Epoca (various issues), Santiago.

ETI (1997) *Ethical Trading Initiative Information Pack*, Ethical Trading Initiative, London.

Eurofruit (various issues 1994–7) London.

Fairtrade Foundation (1995) *The Fairtrade Mark, The 'People Friendly' Consumer Label that Guarantees a Better Deal for Third World Producers*, London: The Fairtrade Foundation.

Fairtrade Foundation (1996) *Third World Suppliers Charter, A New Project of the Fairtrade Foundation*, London: The Fairtrade Foundation.

Falabella, G. (1990) 'Trabajo Temporal y Desorganización Social', in *Proposiciones*, 18, pp. 251–68.

Falabella, G. (1993) 'Reestructuración y respuesta sindical. La experiencia en Santa María, madre de la fruta chilena', in *Revista de Economía y Trabajo*, 1:2, Julio–Diciembre, pp. 239–60.

FAO (1992) *Trade Yearbook*, Volume 46, Food and Agricultural Organisation of the UN, Rome.

FAO (1995) *Trade Yearbook*, Volume 49, Food and Agricultural Organisation of the UN, Rome.

Fernandez-Kelly, M.P. (1994) 'Making Sense of Gender in the World Economy: Focus on Latin America', *Organization* 1:2, pp. 249–75.

Fine, B. and Leopold, E. (1993) *The World of Consumption*, London: Routledge.

Fine, B., Heasman, M. and Wright, J. (1996) *Consumption in the Age of Affluence, the World of Food*, London: Routledge.

Folbre, N. (1988) 'The Black Four of Hearts: Towards a new Paradigm of Household Economics', in D. Dwyer, and J. Bruce (eds.) *A Home Divided: Women and Income in the Third World*, Stanford: Stanford University Press.

Foxley, A. (1983) *Latin American Experiments in Neo-Conservative Economics*, Berkeley: University of California Press.

Fresh Produce Journal, various issues, 1994–7.

Friedland, W. (1994a) 'The Global Fresh Fruit and Vegetable System: an Industrial Organisation Analysis', in P. McMichael (ed.) *The Global Restructuring of Agro-Food Systems,* Ithaca: Cornell University Press.

Friedland, W. (1994b) 'The New Globalization, The Case of Fresh Produce', in A. Bonanno, L. Busch, W. Friedland, L. Gouveia and E. Mingione, *From Columbus to ConAgra. The Globalization of Agriculture and Food*, Kansas: University Press of Kansas.

Friedland, W., Busch, L., Buttel, F. and Rudy, A. (1991) *Towards a New Political Economy of Agriculture*, Boulder: Westview Press.

Friedmann, H. (1993) 'The Political Economy of Food: a Global Crisis', *New Left Review*, January–February, pp. 29–57.

Friedmann, H. and McMichael, P. (1989) 'Agriculture and the State System, The Rise and Decline of National Agricultures, 1870 to the Present', *Sociologia Ruralis,* XXIX:2, pp. 93–117.

Frobel, G. Heinrichs, J. and Kreye, O. (1981) *The New International Division of Labour*, Cambridge: Cambridge University Press.

Fundación Chile (1990/1) *Manual del Exportador Hortofrutícola*, Santiago: Departmento Agroindustrial.

Furtado, C. (1976) *Economic Development of Latin America, Historical Background and Contemporary Problems*, Cambridge: Cambridge University Press.

Garrett, P. (1982) 'Women and Agrarian Reform: Chile, 1964–1973', *Sociologia Ruralis*, 22, pp. 17–29.

Garrett , P. (1992) 'Women and the Agrarian Reform', in C. Kay and P. Silva (eds.) *Development and Social Change in the Chilean Countryside*, Amsterdam: CEDLA.

Gereffi, G. (1994) 'Capitalism, Development and Global Commodity Chains', in L. Sklair (ed.) *Capitalism and Development*, London: Routledge.

Gereffi, G. and M. Korzeniewicz (eds.) (1994) *Commodity Chains and Global Capitalism*, Westport: Greenwood Press.

Gissi, B.J. (1976) 'Mythology about Women, with Special Reference to Chile', in J. Nash and H.I. Safa (eds.) *Sex and Class in Latin America,* New York: Praeger.

Goldfrank, W. (1994) 'Fresh Demand and the Consumption of Chilean Produce in the United States', in G. Gereffi and M. Korzeniewicz (eds.) *Commodity Chains and Global Capitalism*, Westport: Greenwood Press.

Goldfrank, W. and Gómez, S. (1991) *World Market and Agrarian Transformation: the Case of Neo-liberal Chile*. Paper to International Congress of Americanists, New Orleans, July.

Gómez, S (1994) *Algunas Características del Modelo de Exportación de Fruta en Chile*, Documento de Trabajo No. 59, Santiago: FLACSO.

Gómez, S. and Echeñique, J. (1988) *La Agricultura Chilena, Las Dos Caras de la Modernización*, Santiago: FLACSO.

Gonzalez, S. and Quezada, G. (1993) *Mujer Trabajadora y Sindicato*, Thesis, Escuela de Trabajo Social, Universidad Católica, Santiago.

Goodman, D. and Redclift, M. (1991) *Refashioning Nature, Food, Ecology and Culture*, London: Routledge.

Goodman, D. and Watts, M. (1994) 'Reconfiguring the Rural or Fording the Divide?: Capitalist Restructuring and the Global Agro-Food System' *The Journal of Peasant Studies*, 22:1 October, pp. 1–49.

Green, D. (1995) *Silent Revolution: the Rise of Market Economies in Latin America*, London: Latin American Bureau.

The Guardian (various issues) London.

Guzmán, V., Lerda, S. and Salazar, R. (1994) *La Dimensión de Género en el Quehacer del Estado*, Santiago: Centro de Estudios de la Mujer.

Gwynne, R.N. (1991). *Chile to 1994? More Growth under Democracy?* Economist Intelligence Unit, Special Report No. 2065, London.

Gwynne, R.N. and Meneses, C. (1994) *Climate Change and Sustainable Development in the Norte Chico: Land, Water and the Commercialisation of Agriculture*, Occasional Publication, School of Geography, University of Birmingham, No. 34.

Gwynne, R.N. and Ortíz, J. (1997) 'Export Growth and Development in Poor Rural Regions: A Meso Scale Analysis of the Upper Limari', *Bulletin of Latin American Research*, 16:1, January, pp. 25–42.

Hamilton, N. (1986) *Modern Mexico: State, Economy and Social Conflict*, Beverly Hills: Sage Publications.

Harris, O. (1981) 'Households as Natural Units', in K. Young, C. Wolkowitz and R. McCullagh (eds.), *Of Marriage and the Market*. London: CSE Books.

Hartmann, H. (1986) 'The Unhappy Marriage of Marxism and Feminism', in L. Sargent (ed.), *The Unhappy Marriage of Marxism and Feminism*, London: Pluto.

Hartsock, N. (1990) 'Foucault on Power: a Theory for Women?', in L. Nicholson (ed.) *Feminism Postmodernism*, London: Routledge.

Henríque Riquelme, H. and Pérez Ardiles, E. (1994) 'La subestimación de la participación femenina en las actividades económicas: encuesta suplementaria a mujeres inactivas', in *Revista Estadística y Economía*, 8, pp. 5–23.

Herrera, S. and Zúñiga, C. (1993) 'Informe Final: Análisis, Evaluación y Sistematización de Programas de Centros de Atención a Hijos de Mujeres Temporeras', Santiago: Grupo de Investigaciones Agrarias/SERNAM.

Hinton, L. (1991) *The European Market for Fruit and Vegetables*, London: Elsevier.

Hojman, D. (ed.) (1990) *Neo-liberal Agriculture in Rural Chile,* Basingstoke: Macmillan.

Hojman, D. (1993a) *Chile, the Political Economy of Development and Democracy in the 1990s,* Basingstoke: Macmillan.

Hojman, D. (ed.) (1993b) *Change in the Chilean Countryside,* Basingstoke: Macmillan.

Hojman, D. (ed.) (1995) *Neo-liberalism with a Human Face? The Politics and Economics of the Chilean Model,* Liverpool, Institute of Latin American Studies Monograph Series, No. 20.

Hoogvelt, A. (1997) *Globalisation and the Postcolonial World, The New Political Economy of Development,* Basingstoke: Macmillan.

ILO (1991) *Summaries of International Labour Standards,* 2nd edition, Geneva: International Labour Office.

ILO (1994) *World Labour Report, Data Supplement,* Geneva: International Labour Office.

ILO (1995) *Governing Body, Working Party on the Social Dimensions of Liberalisation of International Trade,* March–April, Geneva: International Labour Office.

INE (1992) *Encuesta Nacional del Empleo,* Santiago: Instituto Nacional de Estadísticas.

INE (1992–3) *Estadisticas Agropecuarias,* Santiago: Instituto Nacional de Estadísticas.

INE (1995) *Women and Men in Chile,* Santiago: Instituto Nacional de Estadísticas.

Jaffee S. (1993) *Exporting High-Value Food Commodities, Success Stories from Developing Countries,* World Bank Discussion Paper 198, Washington: World Bank.

Jarosz, L. (1996) 'Working in the Global Food System: a Focus for International Comparative Analysis', *Progress in Human Geography,* 20:1 pp. 41–55.

Jarvis, L. (1992) 'The Unravelling of the Agrarian Reform', in C. Kay and P. Silva (eds.) *Development and Change in the Chilean Countryside,* Amsterdam: CEDLA.

Jarvis, L. (1994) 'Changing Private and Public Roles in Technological Development: Lessons from the Chilean Fruit Sector', in J. Anderson (ed.) *Agricultural Technology, Policy Issues for the International Community,* Walingford: CAB International.

Joekes, S. and Weston, A. (1994) *Women and the New Trade Agenda,* New York: UNIFEM.

JUNDEP (1991) *Diagnóstico de la Situación de las Mujeres de las Comunidades Agrícolas de las Provincias de Choapa y Limarí,* Unpublished paper, Ovalle.

Kabeer, N. (1994) *Reversed Realities, Gender Hierarchies in Development Thought,* London: Verso.

Kabeer, N. and Humphrey, J. (1993) 'Neo-Liberalism, Gender and the Limits of the Market', in C. Colcough and J. Manor (eds.), *States or Markets? Neo-liberalism and the Development Policy Debate.* Oxford: Clarendon Press.

Kandiyoti, D. (1988) 'Bargaining with Patriarchy', *Gender and Society,* 2:3, pp. 271–90.

Kardam, N. (1995) 'Conditions of Accountability for Gender Policy: the Organisational, Political and Cognitive Contexts', *Institute of Development Studies Bulletin*, 26:3, pp. 11–22.

Kay, C. (1989) *Latin American Theories of Development and Underdevelopment*, London: Routledge.

Kay, C. (1993) 'The Agrarian Policy of the Aylwin Government: Continuity or Change?', in D. Hojman (ed.) *Change in the Chilean Countryside*, Basingstoke: Macmillan.

Kay, C. (1997) 'Globalisation, Peasant Agriculture and Reconversion', *Bulletin of Latin American Research*, 16:1, January, pp. 11–24.

Kay, C. and Silva, P. (eds.) (1992) *Development and Change in the Chilean Countryside*, Amsterdam: CEDLA.

Korovkin, T. (1992) 'Peasants, Grapes and Corporations: the Growth of Contract Farming in a Chilean Community', *Journal of Peasant Studies* 19:2, pp. 228–54.

Kritzinger A. and Vorster, J. (1996) 'Women Farm Workers on South African Deciduous Fruit Farms: Gender Relations and the Structuring of Work', *Journal of Rural Studies*, 12:4 pp. 339–51.

Lago, M.S. (1987) 'Rural Women and the Neo-Liberal Model in Chile', in C.D. Deere and M. Leon (eds.) *Rural Women and State Policy: Feminist Perspectives on Latin American Agricultural Development*. Boulder: Westview Press.

Lago, M.S. (1992) 'Rural Women and Neo-Liberal Model', in C. Kay and P. Silva (eds.), *Development and Social Change in the Chilean Countryside*, Amsterdam: CEDLA.

Lawson, V. (1995) 'Beyond the Firm: Restructuring Gender Divisions of Labor in Quito's Garment Industry under Austerity', *Environment and Planning D: Society and Space,* 13, pp. 415–44.

Le Heron, R. (1993) *Globalized Agriculture, Political Choice,* Oxford: Pergamon Press.

Leiva, F. and Agacino, R. (1994) *Mercado de Trabajo Flexible, Pobreza y Desintegración en Chile, 1990–94*, Oxford: Oxfam, Mimeo.

LeQuesne, C. (1996) *Reforming World Trade, The Social and Environmental Priorities*, Oxford: Oxfam Publications.

Longley, S. (1995) 'Fair Trade: Can it Help the Plantation Sector?', *Labour Education, Special Issue on Rural Workers*, Geneva: International Labour Office.

Macintosh, M. (1989) *Gender, Class and Rural Transition, Agribusiness and the Food Crisis in Senegal,* London: Zed Books.

Marcus, T. (1989) *Modernising Super-Exploitation, Restructuring South African Agriculture*, London: Zed Books.

Marquez, G. (ed.) (1995) *Reforming the Labour Market in a Liberalized Economy*, Washington D.C: Inter-American Development Bank.

Marshall, B.L. (1994) *Engendering Modernity: Feminism, Social Theory and Social Change*, Cambridge: Polity Press.

Matear, A. (1995) 'The Servicio Nacional de la Mujer (SERNAM): Women and the Process of Democratic Transition in Chile 1990–93' in D. Hojman (ed.) *Neo-Liberalism with a Human Face? The Politics and Economics of the*

Chilean Model, Monograph Series, No. 20, Liverpool, Institute of Latin American Studies.

Matear, A. (1996) '*Desde la Protesta a la Propuesta:* Gender Politics in Transition in Chile', in *Democratization*, 3:3, pp. 246–63.

Matear, A. (1997) 'Gender and the State in Rural Chile', *Bulletin of Latin American Research*, 16:1, pp. 97–106.

Mattelart, M. (1976) 'Chile: The Feminine Version of the Coup d'Etat', in J. Nash and H.I. Safa (eds.) *Sex and Class in Latin America*, New York: Praeger.

Mattelart, M. (1977) *La Cultura de la Opresión Femenina*, Mexico: Era.

McBride, G.M. (1936) *Chile: Land and Society*. New York: Octagon Books.

McBride Stetson, D. and Mazur, A. (eds.) (1995) *Comparative State Feminism*, London: Sage Publications.

McGee Deutsch, S. (1991) 'Gender and Socio-political Change in 20th-century Latin America', in *Hispano-American Historical Review*, 71:2, pp. 259–306.

McMichael, P. (ed.) (1994) *The Global Restructuring of Agro-food Systems*, New York: Cornell University Press.

McMichael, P. (1996) *Development and Social Change, a Global Perspective*, California: Pine Forge Press.

Medel, J.R., Olivos, S. and Riquelme, V. (1989) *Las Temperadoras y su Vision del Trabajo*, Santiago: Centro de Estudios de la Mujer.

Medel, J. and Riqueleme, V. (1994) *La Salud Ignorada: Temporeras de la Fruticultura*, Santiago: Centro de Estudios de la Mujer.

Meller, P. (1991) *Adjustment and Equity in Chile*, Paris: OECD.

Meller, P. (1992) 'Review of the Chilean Trade Liberalization and Export Expansion Process (1974–90)', in *The Bangladesh Development Studies*, XX: 2&3, pp. 155–184.

El Mercurio (various issues) Santiago.

Michie, J. and Grieve-Smith, J. (eds.) (1995) *Managing the Global Economy*, Oxford: Oxford University Press.

MIDEPLAN (1993) Ministerio de Planificación y Cooperación, *La Impresión de las Cifras. Niños, Mujeres, Jovenes y Adultos Mayores*, Santiago: MIDE-PLAN/ UNICEF.

Mintel Market Intelligence (1994) *Fruit and Vegetables*, April, London.

Mitter, S. (1986) *Common Fate, Common Bond, Women in the Global Economy*, London: Pluto Press.

Mohanty, C.T. (1991) 'Cartographies of Struggle: Third World Women and Politics of Feminism', in C.T. Mohanty, A. Russo, and L. Torres (eds.) *Third World Women and the Politics of Feminism*, Bloomington: Indiana University Press.

Molina, N. (1989) 'Propuestas Políticas y Orientaciones de Cambio en la Situación de la Mujer', in M.A. Garretón (ed.) *Propuestas Políticas y Demandas Sociales,* vol. 3, Santiago: FLACSO.

Momsen, J. and Townsend, J. (1987) *Geography of Gender in the Third World*. London: Hutchinson.

Montecino, S. (1990) 'Símbolo Mariano e Identidad Femenina', *Estudios Publicos*, Santiago: no. 39, Winter 1990, pp. 283–90.

Montecino, S. (1991) *Madres y huachos: alegorías del mestizaje chileno*, Editorial Cuarto Propio, Santiago: CEDEM.

Montecino, S. Dussuel, M. and Wilson, A. (1988) 'Identidad Femenina y Modelo Mariano en Chile', in *Mundo de Mujer: Continuidad y Cambio*, Santiago: CEM.

Montecino, S. and Rossetti, J. (eds.) (1990) *Tramas Para un Nuevo Destino: Propuestas de la Concertación de Mujeres por la Democracia*, Santiago.

Morris, I.D. (1991) 'Locality Studies and the Household', *Environment and Planning A*, 23, pp. 165–77.

Moser, C. (1993) *Gender Planning and Development: Theory, Practice and Training*, London: Routledge.

Muñizaga, G. and Letelier, L. (1988) 'Mujer y Regimen Militer', in *Mundo de Mujer: Continuidad y Cambio*, Santiago: CEM.

Muñoz, A. (1988) 'Fuerza de Trabajo Femenina: Evolución y Tendencias', in *Mundo de Mujer: Continuidad y Cambio*, Santiago: Centro de Estudios de la Mujer.

Murray, W. (1996) *Neo-liberalism, Restructuring and Non-traditional Fruit Exports in Chile: Implications of Export-Orientation for Small-Scale Farmers*, PhD Thesis, University of Birmingham.

Murray, W. (1997) 'Competitive Global Fruit Export Markets: Marketing Intermediaries and Impacts on Small-Scale Growers in Chile', *Bulletin of Latin American Research*, 16:1, January pp. 43–56.

Nash, J. and Fernández-Kelly, M.P. (1985) *Women, Men and the International Division of Labour*, Albany: State of New York University Press.

Nash, J. and Safa, H. (eds.) (1986) *Women and Change in Latin America*, Massachusetts: Bergin and Garvey.

NEF and CIIR (1997) *Open Trading, Options for Effective Monitoring of Corporate Codes of Conduct*, London: New Economics Foundation and Catholic Institute for International Relations.

Nelson, N. and Wright, S. (1995) *Power and Participatory Development*, London: Intermediate Technology Publications.

New Political Economy (1996) 'Debate: International Labour Standards and Human Rights', 1:2 July.

ODEPA (1970) *Plan de Desarrollo Agropecuario 1965–80*, Ministerio de Agricultura, Oficina de Planificación Agricola, Resumen 2nd Edición, Santiago.

Ong, A. (1987) *Spirits of Resistance and Capitalist Discipline: Factory Women in Malaysia*, Albany: SUNY Press.

Ortíz, J. (1989) 'Organización Espacial de dos Valles Modernizados del Norte Chico: Un Análisis Comparativo', *Primer Congreso Nacional de Planificación*, Santiago: July.

Ortíz, J. (1990) 'Impacto Sociogeográfico de la Modernización Agrícola en Dos Valles del Semiárido Chileno', *Revista Geográfica de Chile Terra Australis*, No. 33, pp. 61–78.

Pearson, R. (1994) 'Gender Relations, Capitalism and Third World Industrialization', in L. Sklair (ed.) *Capitalism and Development*, London: Routledge.

Petras, J. and Leiva, F. with Veltmeyer, H. (1994) *Democracy and Poverty in Chile, the Limits to Electoral Politics*, Boulder: Westview Press.

Phillips, A. and Taylor, B. (1980) 'Sex and Skill: Notes towards a Feminist Economics', *Feminist Review* 6, pp. 151–63.

Pontificia Universidad Católica de Chile (1993) *Oportunidades y Desafíos Competitivos de la Fruticultura de Exportación de Chile,* Departamento Economía Agraria, Serie de Investigación No. 65, Santiago.

PREALC (1990) *Ciclos Ocupacionales y Disponibilidad de Mano de Obra Temporal en Dos Communas de Valle de Aconcagua,* Programa Regional del Empleo para America Latina y el Caribe, No. 344, Santiago.

Rabobank (1993) *The World Fresh Fruit Market,* The Netherlands: Rabobank Nederland.

Raven, H. and Lang, T. with Dumonteil, C. (1995) *Off Our Trolleys? Food Retailing and the Hypermarket Economy,* London: Institute for Public Policy Research.

Raynolds, L. (1991) 'Women and Agriculture in the Third World', in W. Friedland, L. Busch, F. Buttel and A. Rudy (eds.) *Towards a New Political Economy of Agriculture,* Boulder: Westview Press.

Redclift, N. (1985) 'The Contested Domain: Gender, Accumulation and the Labour Process', in N. Redclift and E. Mingione, *Beyond Employment: Household Gender and Subsistence.* Oxford: Basil Blackwell.

Redclift, N. and Mingione, E. (1985) *Beyond Employment: Household Gender and Subsistence.* Oxford: Basil Blackwell.

Remmer, K. (1989) 'State Change in Chile, 1973–88', in *Studies in Comparative International Development,* 24:3, pp. 5–29.

Rivera, R. (1993) 'Informe de Consultoría. Informe Final. Trabajadoras Temporeras de la Agricultura: Análisis de su Inserción en el Mercado Laboral y Fuentes de Generación de Ingresos', Santiago: Grupo de Investigaciones Agrarias/SERNAM.

Rodríguez, D. and Venegas, S. (1991) *Los Trabajadores de la Fruta en Cifras,* Santiago: GEA.

Rodríguez, D and Venegas, S. (1989) *De Praderas a Parronales: un Estudio sobre Estructura Agraria y Mercado Laboral en el Valle de Aconcagua,* Santiago: GEA.

Romaguera, P., Echevarría, C. and González, P. (1995) 'Chile', in G. Márquez (ed.) *Reforming the Labor Market in a Liberalized Economy,* Washington D.C.: Inter-American Development Bank.

Rowbotham, S. and Mitter, S. (1994) *Dignity and Daily Bread, New Forms of Economic Organising among Poor Women in the Third World and First,* London: Routledge.

Rowlands, J. (1997) *Questioning Empowerment, Working with Women in Honduras,* Oxford: Oxfam Publications.

Roxborough, I., O'Brien, P. and Roddick, J. (1977) *Chile: the State and Revolution,* Basingstoke: Macmillan.

Ruiz-Tagle, J. (1991) *Trabajo y Economía – en el retorno a la democracia,* Santiago: PET.

Sachs, C. (1996) *Gendered Fields, Rural Women, Agriculture and Environment,* Boulder: Westview Press.

Scott, C.D. and Litchfield, P. (1993) *Common Property and Economic Development: an Analysis of Latin American Experience in the Light of*

Contemporary Theory. Unpublished mongraph, London School of Economics and Political Science, University of London.

SERNAM (1993) *Informe evaluativo. Programa Centros de Atención a Hijos de Mujeres Temporeras, 1992–93,* Santiago: SERNAM, mimeo.

SERNAM (1994) *Atención a sus Hijos Mientras Trabajan. Temporada 1993–94,* Informative Leaflet, Santiago: SERNAM.

Sengenberger, W. and Campbell, D. (eds.) (1994) *International Labour Standards and Economic Interdependence,* Geneva: International Labour Organisation.

Sengenberger, W. and Wilkinson, F. (1995) 'Globalisation and Labour Standards', in J. Michie and J. Grieve Smith (eds.) *Managing the Global Economy,* Oxford: Oxford University Press.

Serrano, C. (1987) *Economic Crisis and Women of the Urban Popular Sectors in Santiago de Chile.* Paper presented at DAWN and CLACSO's Research Group on Women at XIV CLACSO's General Assembly, Recife, Brazil, November.

Shaw, L. (1996) *Social Clauses,* Catholic Institute for International Relations Briefing, London.

Sigmund, P. (1977) *The Overthrow of Allende and the Politics of Chile, 1964–76,* Pittsburgh: University of Pittsburgh Press.

Silva, P. (1991) 'Technocrats and Politics in Chile from the Chicago Boys to the CIEPLAN Monks', *Journal of Latin American Studies,* 23:2, May, pp. 385–410.

Sokoloff, N.J. (1981) *Between Money and Love: the Dialectics of Women's Home and Market Work* New York: Praeger.

Standing, G. (1989) 'Global Feminization Through Flexible Labour', *World Development* 17:7, pp. 1077–95.

Staudt, K. (ed.) (1990) *Women, International Development and Politics: the Bureaucratic Mire,* Philadelphia: Temple University Press.

Stichter, S. (1990) 'Women, Employment and the Family: Current Debates', in J. Parpart and S. Stichter (eds.), *Women, Employment and the Family in the International Division of Labour,* Basingstoke: Macmillan.

Swift, R. (1997) 'The NI Interview: Angelica Alvarez Cerda', *New Internationalist* December, p. 31.

Teubal, M. (1987) 'Internationalization of Capital and Agroindustrial Complexes, their Impact on Latin American Agriculture' *Latin American Perspectives,* 14:3, Summer, pp. 316–64.

Thrupp, L. (1995) *Bittersweet Harvests for Global Supermarkets, Challenges in Latin America's Agricultural Export Boom.* Washington D.C.: World Resources Institute.

Tusscher, T. (1986) 'Patriarchy, Capitalism and the New Right' in J. Evens, J. Hills, K. Hunt, E. Meehan, T. Tusscher, U. Vogel and G. Waylen, *Feminism and Political Theory,* London: Sage Publications.

Valdés, T. and Weinstein, M. (1993) *Mujeres que sueñan: las organizaciones de las pobladoras en Chile 1973–89,* Santiago: FLACSO.

Valdés, X, (1988) 'Feminización del mercado del trabajo agricola: Las temporeras', in *Mundo de Mujer-Continuidad y cambio,* Santiago: Centro de Estudios de Mujer.

Valdés, X. (1992) 'Al son de la modernidad. Cambios en los bordes del campo y la ciudad: las *temporeras*', *Proposiciones 21: Género, Mujer y Sociedad,* Santiago: Chile.

Valdés, X. (1993) 'Del prestigio a la gestión: poder y liderazgo en las mujeres del campo' in *Proposiciones* 22, Actores sociales y democracia, Sur Ediciones, Santiago: pp. 241–8.

Valdés, X., L. Rebolledo and R. Willson (1995) *Masculino y Femenino en la Hacienda del Siglo XX,* Santiago: CEDEM.

Valenzuela, E. (1993) 'Sistema político y actores sociales en Chile', in *Proposiciones* 22, Santiago.

Valenzuela, M.E. (1991) 'The Evolving Roles of Women under Military Rule', in P.W. Drake and I. Jaksic (eds.) *The Struggle for Democracy in Chile,* Lincoln: University of Nebraska Press.

Valenzuela, M.E. Venegas, S. Andrade, C. (eds.) (1994) *De Mujer Sola a Jefa de Hogar: Género, Pobreza y Políticas Públicas,* Santiago: SERNAM.

van Liemt, G. (1989) 'Minimum Labour Standards and International Trade: Would a Social Clause Work?', *International Labour Review* 128:4 pp. 433–48.

Venegas, S. (1992a) *Una gota al día, un chorro al año, El Impacto Social de la Expansión Frutícola,* Santiago: GEA.

Venegas, S. (1992b) *Mujer rural: Campesinas y Temporeras.* Ministerio de Agricultura, Santiago, INDAP.

Venegas, S. (1993) 'Programas de apoyo a temporeros y temporeras en Chile', in S. Gómez and E. Klein (eds.) *Los pobres del campo, El Trabajador Eventual,* Santiago: FLACSO/PREALC/OIT.

Venegas, S. (1994) 'El Cuidado Infantil Como Componente del Plan Piloto de Apoyo Para las Jefas de Hoger', in M.E. Valenzuela, S. Venegas, C. Andrade (eds.) *De Mujer Sola a Mujer Jefa de Hogar. Género, Pobreza y Políticas Públicas,* Santiago.

Venegas, S. (1995) Las *Temporeras* de la fruta en Chile", in *Mujer, Relaciones de Género en la Agricultura,* Santiago: Centro de estudios para el Desarollo de la Mujer.

Vogel, I. (1995) 'Gender and the Labour Market: Women's Experiences of Labour Force Participation in Chile', in D. Hojman (ed.) *Neo-Liberalism with a Human Face? The Politics and Economics of the Chilean Model,* University of Liverpool, Institute of Latin American Studies, Monograph Series, No. 20.

Vogel, I. (1997) *The Labour Market, Gender and Rapid Social Change in Chile: Working Women's Experiences,* PhD thesis, University of Liverpool.

Ward, N. and Almas, R. (1997) 'Explaining Change in the International Agro-food System', *Review of International Political Economy,* 4:4, pp. 611–29.

Waylen, G. (1986) 'Women and Neo-liberalism' in J. Evens, J. Hills et al. *Feminism and Political Theory,* London: Sage.

Waylen, G. (1992) 'Women, Authoritarianism and Market Liberalisation in Chile, 1973–89' in H. Afshar and C. Dennis (eds.) *Women and Adjustment Policies in the Third World,* Basingstoke: Macmillan.

Waylen, G. (1995) *Women's Movements, the State and Democratisation in Chile,* IDS Bulletin, Vol. 26 No. 3, pp. 85–93.

Whatmore, S. (1995) 'From Farming to Agribusiness: the Global Agro-food System', in R.J. Johnston, P.J. Taylor and M. Watts (eds.) *Geographies of Global Change, Remapping the World in the Late Twentieth Century*, Oxford: Blackwell Publishers.

Wilson, F. (1985) 'Women and Agricultural Change in Latin America: Some Concepts Guiding Research' *World Development*, 13 (9).

Women Working Worldwide (1996) *World Trade is a Women's Issue, Promoting the Rights of Women Workers in a Changing World Economy*, Briefing Paper, Manchester.

World Bank (1995) *Workers in an Integrating World*, World Development Report, New York: Oxford University Press.

Yotopoulous, P. (1989) 'The (Rip)tide of Privatisations: Lessons from Chile', in *World Development*, 17:5, pp. 683–702.

Young, K. (1991) 'Reflexiones Sobre Cómo Enfrentar las Necesiadades de la Mujeres', in V. Guzmán and P. Portocarrero (eds.) *Una Nueva Lectura: Género en el Desarrollo*, Lima: Centro Flora Tristán.

Young, K., Wolkowitz, C. and McCullagh, R. (1981) *Of Marriage and the Market,* London: CSE Books.

Index

agrarian counter-reform 51–3, 58, 59–60, 167, 198
Agrarian Plan 206n
agrarian reform 2, 16, 41–9; exclusion of women 44–5
Agrarian Reform Council 44
Agrarian Reform legislation 44, 208n
agribusiness and women 13ff
agribusiness, expansion of 18
agribusiness, female integration in 34–5, 36
agribusiness, global 1
agribusiness, postwar growth 18
agriculture, commercialised 17, 25
agriculture and gender 14–18
agriculture, Latin America 14–18
agriculture, peasant-based 5
agriculture, small-scale 116, 119
agriculture, state policy 16
agro-chemicals 5, 22, 100–2, 199; see also health problems
Allende, Salvador 43, 47
Alliance for Progress 42
Area Mujer 169, 172
asentamientos 44, 46
atomisation 6, 86, 107

birth defects 101
blue months 93, 157, 171
Brazil, female employment in 25
business ethics 189

campesinas 116–19
campesinos 37–8
capitalisation 44
casetas 113, 124
Cattle Plan 44
CEMA-Chile centres 55, 56
CEMAs 46, 206n
Central America, female employment in 25
Centros de Madres see CEMAs
Centros de Reforma Agraria 47

Chañaral Alto 112–13, 118, 127–9
child nutrition 175
childcare 145–6, 172, 174–7, 183, 195
childcare, company provision 123, 172, 179
childcare, informal 122, 148, 165
childcare, state/statutory 145, 174, 202
childcare centres 104, 146, 176, 178
Childcare Programme for the Children of *Temporeras* 173, 176–7, 180
codes of conduct 189–97, 203, 211n
collective activity 33
collective bargaining 28, 60, 163, 181, 203
collectivisation 43
Colombia, female employment in 25
Comisión Nacional Campesina 89
commodity-chain, consumer-led 79
communal land 111–12
communications 21, 186
community organisations 181
comparative advantage 3, 5, 21, 22, 58
competition, Southern Hemisphere 76–7
competitive advantage 188, 196
competitiveness 26
comuneros 112
Concertación de Mujeres por la Democracia 57, 168–9, 170
Concertación Nacional de Mujeres por la Democracia 57
confidence, women's 32–3
consumer boycotts 211n
consumer campaigns 189, 190
consumer confidence 192
consumer goods 124, 147, 164
consumption patterns 1, 5, 22, 73, 78, 79, 192
contract farming 19

228   *Index*

contract workers   104, 153
contracts   143; temporary   171
'cool chain' supply system   5, 22, 69
co-operatives   44
COPEFRUT   68
Coqimbo   65
CORFO   49
cruzando los brazos   163–4
cultural norms   16, 31
Curicó   136, 152–9

debt, personal   125
debt crisis, Chile   21
del Curto, David   58,   68
Demanda de la Mujer Rural   168
democracy   168; demand for   57;
   transition to   90, 167ff, 202
desmochadura   143, 144
Development Corporation   44
development theory   32
Dirección de Trabajo   171
distribution   22–3
Dole-Chile   68
domestic role, women's   6, 31
domestic work   119–22, 148
double day/burden   120–2, 148, 149,
   165, 201
drip irrigation, computerised   3, 5,
   22, 69

economic crisis   56
economic liberalisation   21, 22, 24
Ecuador, female employment in   25
employment, concentration of   99
employment, female   1–2; growth in
   55–6
employment rights   60, 170, 182
empowerment   2, 32–4, 159, 165,
   170, 180, 200
enfranchisement of women   40
environmental standards   192
equality, legal   168
equity with growth   167, 202
ethical sourcing   192
ethical trading   190
Ethical Trading Initiative   191, 193,
   194, 211n
exchange rate, peso/US$ 58, 59, 63,
   78

export boom   62–5
export capital   199
export companies   68–70
export funnel   79, 186
export industry   26–7
export production, structure   65–73
export promotion   24
export specialisation   3, 198
export-led growth   3, 21, 51
exports, non-traditional   18–24

Fairtrade Foundation   190, 192, 211n
family, supremacy of   53
family farming   14–15
family labour, unpaid   15, 40
family/household structure and
   responsibilities   119–20
fatherland   54
FEDEFRUT   207n
female labour, demand for   60, 154,
   200
female employment participation
   rate   13, 25, 56, 86–7, 174, 208n,
   212n
feminisation of labour   25, 60
fieldwork/tasks   96–7, 137, 144
first food regime   205n
flexible employment   6, 88–9, 200
Fordism/post-Fordism   19
forestry sector   95
fragmentation   26, 29, 86, 105–8,
   186
free market economy   3, 16–17
freedom of association   194, 203
Frei, Eduardo   2, 41, 43–4
fruit exports, Chile   2–3, 64–5;
   competitors   76–7; expansion
   58–9; principal markets   74–5;
   volume   74
fruit farms, size of   65
'Fruit Plan'   2, 36, 49–50, 83, 199
Fundación Chile   59

gender and agriculture   14–18
gender consciousness   56
gender equality   168
gender ideology   54
gender inequality   169
gender and neo-liberalism   53–8

gender and NTAEs   24–9
gender relations   2, 6, 29, 30–2, 137;
   in the *hacienda* system   37–41
gender role, domestic   46
gender segregation   2, 88, 94–100
gender stereotypes   94–5
gendered division of labour   38–9
global economic order   18
global food supply chain   18, 185–8
globalisation   26, 73, 18, 185
grape boycotts   102
grape economy   63, 98, 112–15
grape farm work   110–11
grapes, price of   111
grassroots activity   56, 181
growth with equity   167, 188
Guatulame Valley   109, 111–33

hacienda system   37–41
head of household, female   56, 93,
   179–80, 206n
head of household, male   16, 31, 45,
   54
health and safety at work legislation
   171
health problems   101
high-value food commodities   20
home, hierarchy of   54
hours of work   6, 102
household relations   30, 121
huerto   39

identity, feminine   16
identity, masculine   15
ideology, right-wing and gender
   relations   53
ILO conventions   191, 196, 203
import-substitution industrialisation
   16, 39
INDAP   44, 87, 169, 172, 173
industrial accumulation   19, 24, 105
industrial action   163, 201
infrastructure, Chile   3, 5
inquilinos   37–8, 40
Institute of Agrarian Development
   see INDAP
*Instituto Nacional de Desarrollo
   Agropecuario*   169
Instituto Nacional de Estadistícas   87

integration   186
international division of labour   26
International Monetary Fund   21

job insecurity   6, 28–9
Junta Nacional de Jardins Infantiles
   122–3, 174
juvenile crime   176

kinship ties   111
kiwi fruit market   207n

Labour Code   90, 104,   171
labour conditions   193–4, 195
labour costs   28, 81; *see also* pay
   rates
labour demand   28, 60, 91, 106
labour force, atomisation   105–8
labour force, availability of   29
labour force, feminisation   25; *see
   also* female labour, demand for
labour force, gender specificity
   113–15
labour force, heterogeneity   86, 89,
   109
labour force, male   87
labour market deregulation/reform
   59–60, 88
labour relations   160
labour rights   195
labour standards   188–9
labour, unpaid   15, 40
land dispossession   17
land expropriation   48
land redistribution   42
land reform   16
land, repossessed   53
land tenure system   112, 116
landholdings   37, 44; communal
   111
landowners, power of   40
landownership concentration   68
Las Mercedes   135, 140–52
Limari Valley   97–8
living standards   39
low wage employment   28

machismo   15–16, 42, 45
machista ideology   199, 200

March of the Empty Pots 54
marginalisation of women 15–16, 186
marianismo 16, 54
mechanisation 38–40
Mexico 206n; female employment in 25
migrant workers 15, 38, 56, 91, 171
minifundia 37–8
minimum wage 40
mobilisation of women 54, 56–7, 168
monocultivation 3, 6, 24, 25, 28, 106
moral values 54
mozo 96
Mujer y Trabajo 101

natural hazards 69, 83, 105, 199
Neighbourhood Associations 46
neo-liberalism 3, 51
new political economy 18
New Right 51, 53
NGOs 181, 189, 190, 191
non-traditional agriculture 19–20, 21, 26–7, 205n
non-traditional agricultural exports 20, 21
Norte Chico 106, 111
North American Free Trade Area 196

onion harvest 143
Organizaciones Económicas Populares 56
outsourcing 19, 26, 186
oversupply 18, 77

packaging 27, 187
packing plants 70, 71; female employment in 96, 102, 114–15, 150, 152–3
parcelas/parcelisation 51–3, 58, 198
parronales 111, 118; female work on 122
patriarchal relations/patriarchy 15, 29, 37, 47, 54, 55
pay rates 102–4, 141, 150, 153
peasant protest/revolt 42

peasant unions, female membership 46
peasants, landless 15, 38, 40, 52–3, 59, 60, 95
peones 38
perishability 22, 71
permanent workers, female 88
piece rates 28, 115, 137, 209n
Pinochet, General Augusto 2
Plan Laboral 59, 88
Poder Femenino 54
poverty 40, 55, 60–1, 137, 170
power relationships 32, 33
pre-school education 174–5
price structures 81–2
prices, volatility 81
producers/exporters relationship 70
production, dispersal of 26
production and marketing 22
production and packing 5
production relations 14
production-consumption cycle 23–4
production/reproduction, women's role 14, 17, 29, 31, 40
profitability 69, 70, 199
Programa de Economía del Trabajo 87
proletarianisation 17
protectionism 50, 196

quality 22, 77, 202

raleo 142
remuneration system 137
repetitive strain injury 101
Revolution in Liberty 46, 47
right-wing ideology 53
risk minimisation 73, 83
rural labour, displaced 17

salas cunas 174
San Antonio 65
Santiago 3, 65, 91
seasonal temporary workers *see temporeros/temporeras*
seasonality 113–15
second food regime 18, 19

SERNAM   146, 169, 170–1, 172, 173, 176, 180, 182; regional officials   182
Servicio Nacional de la Mujer see SERNAM
sex discrimination/harassment   160–2, 182, 203
sexual division of labour   14
skilling   27
skills, 'feminine'   27, 38–9, 95, 106, 137
skills, 'masculine'   97–8
social agenda   189
social clauses   195–7,   203
social interaction   201
social relations   32–3, 45
specialisation   62–5; flexible   19; regional   44, 65
standard-setting   187, 192
standardisation   23
state policies   47–9, 53, 167ff
state, role of   7, 42
strike action   163
structural adjustment programmes   21, 24, 189
subcontracting   26; *see also* outsourcing
subordination of women   2, 15, 30, 32, 47, 186
subsistence production   15, 18, 24, 37
supermarkets   187–8, 202; own brands   193; quality specifications   79; sourcing policies   192
supply chain   80–1; global   62ff; internal   71–3

table grape production   111
technical support   70
technological innovation   2, 21, 22
technological expertise   3, 50, 84
temporary contracts   171

temporeras/temporeros   1, 5–7, 86ff; classification   89–90; emergence of   60–1; marital status and age   91–3; *see also* case studies, chapters 6 and 7
tomato cultivation   118, 124, 125
Tome Alto   111, 112, 113, 116
tradition agriculture   15, 36, 205n
transnationals   5, 68, 186, 192; domination   18; growth of   26
transportation/storage   5, 71

UK multiples   79
unemployment, male   52, 55
unfair advantage   196
Unidad Popular   47–8, 206n
Unifruco   207n
UNIFRUTTI   68
unionisation   46, 59–60, 104, 163, 181
Upper Limari valley   109
UTC   68

Valparaiso   3, 65
VI Region   135
VII Region   3, 65, 135

wage labour   2, 5, 17, 25–6, 40; dependence on   137; use of   126
wage negotiations   163–4
wage, average weekly   141
wealth redistribution   43
wholesale markets   79
wholesale prices   70
women's movement   57, 169
work stoppages   163
working conditions   100–5, 143
World Bank   21
World Trade Organisation   195–6

ZEUS   68